THE INSIDE TRACK
Getting Hired To Teach in a Canadian School
Second Edition

What others say about *The Inside Track*

√ "[*The Inside Track*] is more than a rich resource of the basic nitty-gritty of applying successfully for a teaching job and entry into the teaching profession. Patton appropriately raises the status of the profession of teaching to one requiring the most-skilled and best-suited people. The Inside Track should be read by administrators and teacher candidates alike. Our schools and our students deserve the best people as their staff."
— *Margaret Dempsey, Principal, and College Council Member, Ontario College of Teachers (in* "Professionally Speaking," *magazine of the Ontario College of Teachers)*

√ "The Inside Track is a great resource both for prospective teachers looking for employment (or re-location) and for principals, vice-principals, and superintendents directly involved in hiring. The extensive section on 'typical interview questions' is extremely useful, as are the lists of addresses and telephone/fax numbers and web sites. The book is worth every penny."
— *Byron Grant, former Principal, Toronto Board of Education*

√ "Prospective teachers in today's market are facing challenging and competitive hiring conditions. The successful candidates are those who are not only the most qualified for the position to which they applied, but also they are the candidates who are the most prepared to enter a hiring competition."
— *Robert Sampson, Executive Director, Northern Centre for Instructional Leadership (former Superintendent of Personnel)*

√ "Here, in one package that is specifically targeted to aspiring teachers are the keys to getting an interview and winning a position — the book was a gem. When I went for the interview I really was prepared — in my case, the book really did provide an 'inside track'."
— *Dr. George Sheppard, Teaching Master, History Department, Upper Canada College*

√ "The book reads more as a conversation rather than a dry resource — interview section is amazingly accurate. The possible questions you listed [include] the exact questions that were asked at my substitute teaching interview."
— *Nancy Butler, Teacher, Dryden Board of Education*

√ "Good solid information — incredibly comprehensive and particularly helpful — especially good for new teachers."
— *Torry Hansson, Principal, Carleton Board of Education*

√ "Advice is excellent. He helped me get a teaching job and now I use his advice with my Adult Education students and they're doing well from it."
— *Michelle Goulet, Commission Scolarie Lac-Temiscamingue*

√ "Very readable — humourous — made the résumé writing not so daunting a task — answered questions about the infinite details." — *Heather Atkins, Occasional Teacher (graduate of Faculty of Education, University of Western Sydney, New South Wales)*

√ "On the cutting edge with regard to helping people get that all-important first job — there's a plethora of information, more variety, and better than any other resource I know — it answers questions before you ask them."
— *Jack Jones, Professor, Faculty of Education, Nipissing University*

√ "It contains a lot of 'inside information' on a very complex process — very practical — could be useful to principals as well, both those new to interviewing and those with experience."
— *Fred Mandryk, Principal, Northumberland and Newcastle Board of Education*

√ "Up until now, my experiences with information regarding the writing of a curriculum vitae have been somewhat dry. Thank you for changing that!"
— *Elaine Bailey, Author, Special Education Policy Writer, Department of Education, Northwest Territories*

THE INSIDE TRACK

Getting Hired To Teach in a Canadian School

SECOND EDITION

Barlow S. Patten, B.A., B.Ed., M.A.
Principal

THOMPSON EDUCATIONAL PUBLISHING, INC.
Toronto

Requests for permission to make copies of any part of the work should be directed to the publisher:
   E-mail: publisher@thompsonbooks.com
   Web site: www.thompsonbooks.com

Copies of this book may be ordered from our distributor:

General Distribution Services Limited
325 Humber College Boulevard
Toronto, Ontario M9W 7C3
1-800-387-0141 (ON/QC)
1-800-387-0172 (Rest of Canada)
Fax: (416) 213-1917
E-mail orders: customer.service@ccmailgw.genpub.com

Canadian Cataloguing in Publication Data

Patten, Barlow S.
 The inside track: getting hired to teach in a Canadian school
2nd ed.
Includes bibliographical references and index.
ISBN 1-55077-114-0

1. Teaching — Vocational guidance — Canada. I. Title.

LB1780.P37 2000   371.1'0023'71 C00-930156-9

Cover design: Elan Designs
We acknowledge the financial support of the Government of Canada through the Book Publishing Industry Development Program (BPIDP) for our publishing activities.
Printed in Canada.

1 2 3 4 5 05 04 03 02 01 00

TABLE OF CONTENTS

HOW THIS BOOK CAME TO BE

When I graduated from a Faculty of Education in Northern Ontario in the early 70s, we were constantly barraged with the unsolicited revelation and most disheartening bit of rumoured wisdom that we would never get a job in teaching and should proceed forthwith to seek employment selling either shoes or hamburgers, or perhaps even soap, door-to-door. It was common knowledge that there were just no jobs to be had in teaching. It was a bad time to be graduating. Everything was wrong, wrong, wrong, including, probably, the positions of the stars. But a very compassionate and pragmatic and just plain down-to-earth professor, Fred Bell, pointed out to me that I could ignore "common knowledge" and didn't need to worry about the relative availability of teaching positions across the whole country: I only needed one job! And I got one. So, take heart. You, too, need only one job. You can get the one you want!

When I graduated, the faculties offered essentially no training in the process of getting a job. For decades it had been relatively simple, and they had not yet adjusted to the fact that it had suddenly become very difficult. Thus, I knew very little about presenting myself to those who were hiring. I had good training as a teacher and excellent background experience, but how could I communicate this to potential employers? I managed, but not as well as I should have. What is really intimidating, now, is to realize that expectations regarding format, clarity and overall professionalism of the application package have increased exponentially in the intervening years. Were I to handle the application and interview process now as I did then, I would probably be laughed out of the building.

A couple of years later, again heeding the advice to ignore "common knowledge" and "go for it," I got a job as a principal based upon my experience both in and out of education. (This was with the kind support of Doreen Wright, a school office manager, who prepared for me what was really my first conventional résumé. Never underestimate the power of a secretary in the field of education!) At age 24, I was one of the youngest principals in Ontario at the time and have worked in that position for over twenty years now in two Boards of Education: one southern and one northern. During my M.A. studies, I was involved in investigating the totality of the staff selection process and how its stages and methods can be modified to increase the degree of its predictability of excellence in performance. That whole topic continues to be, for me, an area of keen interest. I have also enjoyed lecturing rather widely on the topic of securing employment and ran for several years, as part of a consulting company, a supplementary-income business (otherwise known as moon-lighting) professionally preparing résumés and offering job-search counselling. I have enjoyed working with selected management groups helping them to develop strategies to recognize excellent employment candidates.

Calling upon the rich meaning of the word παρακλητος (parakletos) this book is designed to be a paraclete: an advocate and companion who travels at your side interceding for you and helping you along every step of the journey. When I phased down my workload preparing C.V.'s and

"I wanted to help people become the instrument of their own destiny ... bring out the greatness in people."

—*Ralph Stayer*

providing job-search counselling, so that I could spend more time with my family and on other fun stuff, I found myself trying to write down the things I had learned in my training and experience as a principal and in my experience helping others get the jobs they wanted. This was so I could just hand it all in a neat package to those who asked for help. When a colleague, Dr. Anne Jordan, suggested I include the information on all provinces and territories so it would be more useful to those wanting to expand their horizons, the package expanded. As more and more people read it and suggested areas that should be covered and, more importantly, asked questions I had not answered in the document, it grew into this!

I sincerely trust that my experience, together with that of my colleagues, new teachers, experienced teachers, principals, vice-principals and other administrators, will help you get the job you want in our very important and exciting field.

Remember: you only need one job. And you can get the one you want!

"No-one is born under a bad star. There are just those who mis-read the skies."
—*The Dalai Lama*

ACKNOWLEDGEMENTS

My sincere thanks to those over the years who entrusted me with the preparation of their C.V. Thank you for your vote of confidence and satisfaction which you signalled by not taking advantage of my money-back guarantee.

My thanks also to my wife, Meg, and son and daughter, Jonathan and Sarah, for their tolerance of the many hours I have sat interviewing and counselling clients, then more hours in front of a word processor, both writing résumés and now writing about writing them. My wife deserves special mention for her careful combination of criticism of the work and support of me.

My thanks to the teachers who asked for anonymity when they shared their less-than-wonderful experiences with me. Your candour and trust have helped to make this book a reflection of the many and various realities of our profession.

My thanks to all the unnamed and unsung employees of the various government and professional teachers' union offices who were so helpful in getting me the information I needed.

Also my thanks to those who critiqued this project in its various stages, including: Keith Thompson of Thompson Educational Publishing, Merri King, Linda Ouderkirk, Louise Green, Darren Jackson, Tammi Harnett (Faculty of Education students), Carol Miller (Executive Assistant to the Director: Nipissing Board of Education), Dr. George Sheppard (Upper Canada College), Torry Hansson (Principal: Carleton Board of Education), Peter Hill (Principal: Nipissing Board of Education), Fred Mandrych, (Principal: Northumberland / Newcastle Board of Education), John Stephens (Vice-principal: Nipissing), Elaine Bailey (Consultant: Norman Wells: N.W.T.), Michelle Goulet (*L'Envol* Adult Education Program: Commission Scolaire Lac-Témiscamingue, Québec), Dr. Anne Jordan (Chair: Department of Special Education: Ontario Institute for Studies in Education), Dr. Sandra Reid, Jack Jones, Cher Evans-Harvey (Professors: Faculty of Education, Nipissing University), Paul Moffat (Private School Principal, Trinidad), Robert Sampson (Executive Director: Northern Center for Instructional Leadership, former Superintendent of Human Resources), Reg Ferland (Past-President: Ontario Public School Teachers' Federation). My thanks also to Catharine Rankin (Tembec Inc., P.Q.) and Barry Foreman, (Boart-Longyear Canada Inc.) for their "business" perspective to supplement the "education" one, and to Damien McLaughlin for his assiduous attention in proofing this document. (Errors that remain are mine!)

My thanks to all of them for their time and expert advice. All the nice things they said about this effort were appreciated. (And the not-so-nice things they said, and the spirit in which they said them, helped a lot, too.)

Teachers, good and bad, have played a significant role in my life. I would be truly remiss if I didn't thank an incredible personal and professional role model, and my former high school teacher, Jim Moodie.

"We are not primarily put on this earth to see through one another, but to see one another through."
—*Peter de Vries*

After my ten horrible years in other schools, by showing the care he felt for his students he turned me around so I didn't drop out as soon as I turned 16. I am also indebted to him for encouraging me to write, and thus opening to me what has been a financially and professionally rewarding pursuit over the years.

I want to thank a fellow-teacher, Michael Pannabecker, for inciting and inspiring me, several years ago, to develop an understanding of Information Technology, its future in education, and what it can offer both pupils and teachers today. The accuracy of his foresight and his truly exceptional expertise—both conceptual and technical—have been a godsend to me.

I owe a great debt of thanks to the late Al Johnson, whose wisdom, command of grammar and joyful pursuit of *le mot juste*, continues to inspire and challenge me. Thank you all.

Names of agencies, companies and persons in this book are entirely fictitious. Any references to actual persons or corporations are accidental. Actual names of some School Boards and Boards of Education are used for a touch of verisimilitude, but most names of individual schools are fictitious.

A few of the examples and ideas in this book are derived from applications I have received and candidates I have interviewed over the years. The vast majority of examples are from clients for whom I have prepared a résumé; so if you think you may recognize yourself, you will readily see that enough has been changed so that no-one else will. My promise of confidentiality was, and is, sincere.

INTRODUCTION

This book is designed for you, if you are now in the same position I was in many years ago: looking for a job in teaching, and rather selective in your approch. It provides access to the "inside track" on teaching jobs across Canada, whether you are: (a) newly graduated or almost ready to graduate and are looking to take the next step; (b) an experienced teacher looking for a move to a better position within your same board or school; or, (c) looking to move anywhere across Canada. This book will help you make it easy for them to give the job to you.

We are finally getting over the teacher-abundance crisis in Canada, and teaching jobs have become available and, in some areas, plentiful. But if you want to teach calculus in Vancouver, the offer of a grade two class in Port Aux Basques might not really hold much appeal. Similarly, if you enjoy the fresh air of Churchill, you may not be too tempted by a job in Windsor, in the shadow of the Detroit smog. You want to be selective. You have specific and valuable experience and talents to offer. You have the right to be discriminating. Contemporaneously, however, those who are hiring are much more selective than in the past. They are increasingly looking for teachers with non-traditional aspects to their background. What sets you apart? Why are you a better "match" for the position you want than any other candidate? If your résumé does not tell them, how will they know?

This book will help you to do that. It will also help you prepare to present yourself at an interview. You have something very special to give: this book will help you clarify what it is and how to promote it. You can potentially save yourself a consultant's fee of several hundred dollars, while still getting the excellent quality of personalized résumé you would expect from a professional with extensive experience in the field of employment-search consulting.

As an added bonus, the data here is exclusively teacher-related. It is aimed directly at the teaching profession, with its unique culture, and addresses the wide range of information necessary for "Getting Hired to Teach in a Canadian School."

Specifically from the perspective of a career in education, this book addresses:

- step-by-step résumé preparation: what is important in a teacher's résumé, what to put in, what to leave out!
- how to pique their interest: presenting each element in its most compelling form
- avoiding the pitfalls
- modifying your résumé to match specific job postings
- using the Internet to your best advantage
- featuring your Information Technology capabilities: "getting into the 21st century!"

"Prospective teachers in today's market are facing challenging and competitive hiring conditions. The successful candidates are those who are not only the most qualified for the position to which they applied, but also they are the candidates who are the most prepared to enter a hiring competition."
—*Robert Sampson*

- electronic-application "how to"
- relating your past job experience to working in the field of education
- over 125 detailed examples of C.V. entries for specific situations
- choosing your references: anticipating what they will be asked
- avoiding boredom: writing an effective cover letter, together with annotated samples
- getting it all into the right hands
- fax protocol in the application process
- surviving the interview and more: what to expect and how to cope
- be ready: over 195 sample interview questions divided into 22 job-related categories, together with selected suggestions on how you might respond to such questions
- effectively and professionally responding to improper or illegal questions in the interview
- relating to five distinct "types" of committee chairpersons: what does each "type" want?
- contract technicalities: avoid being in breach of contract; turn them to your advantage!
- occasional teaching: how to parlay it into full-time teaching
- the value of volunteering: its benefits and limitations
- photocopy-ready checklists for the occasional/replacement teacher: always be your best!
- how your teachers' union/federation/society/association can help, including address, phone and fax numbers for each by province and territory
- addresses, phone and fax numbers for each provincial and territorial department and ministry responsible for education in Canada
- working effectively with a Teacher's Assistant—building and maintaining the relationship
- certification requirements by province and territory, and cross-certification: getting your teaching license accreditation transferred to other provinces and territories
- contract types, details, dates and deadlines for termination and duration of contracts by province and territory
- provincial and territorial teachers' union regulations and policies re: volunteerism
- profiles of effective teachers: the image you want to convey—personal and professional
- alternative and related careers: there are many other places to teach
- annotated list of related resources

You can prepare yourself to get the job you want!

"Shared vision is not an idea,
but a force."
—Peter Senge

PART I

THE BASICS OF THE PROCESS

A Curriculum Vitae (Résumé) does not get you a job; a good one does, however, get you an interview. Without getting to the interview you don't get the job, so developing your résumé is a very necessary part of the process.

The Curriculum Vitae (Latin: "course of life")—or C.V., or Vitae, or Résumé, as it is variously called—is a brief account of your career and qualifications, designed to convince the employer that you should be considered very seriously for the position. It is your first introduction to the interviewer. As long-time administrator Jack Jones describes it, it's "you, on paper." This is your opportunity to turn them on, turn them off or bore them, before they even meet you. Obviously, if it is one of the latter two you won't meet them. A well-prepared résumé will, however, help make it easier for them to include you on the short-list, on the "inside track," and that increases the likelihood that they will eventually hire you.

The Screening Process

If you can convince the person(s) responsible for each level of screening that you are the best candidate (or among the very top candidates), you will make it through to the interview. That is where you get the chance to sell yourself: to convince them that they can't get along without you, or at least they are passing up a great opportunity if you don't join their team.

In smaller boards or in boards committed to principal autonomy, you may be interviewed by the same person or persons who screen and "short-list" the résumés—usually the principal, vice-principal, department head, etc. Expect to find both genders represented on the interview committee. Expect, too, that there will be a committee since many boards require by policy that interviews be conducted by an interview committee or a selection committee rather than by just one person. On a selection committee each member has relatively equal authority and weight in the decision: all of them together make the selection. On an interview committee some members hold advisory power only. This distinction, however, has very little significance to you as a candidate.

In boards with extensive Human Resources departments (usually the larger ones, at least until funding cutbacks hit them too), that department's staff will usually screen the résumés and eliminate those lacking the specified qualifications (education, experience, traits, etc.— whatever has been stipulated) and then either develop a short-list of candidates for the interviews or perhaps pass on to the committee for short-listing all the applications which have passed the first screening.

Calling the board and asking to whom general applications should be sent will tell you if they are sent to a central committee or a specific superintendent or to each individual principal. If you are applying for a specific position, rather than a general "if an opening comes up in your school" application (both types are addressed herein), the advertisement

"No great thing is created suddenly."
—*Epictetus*

LONG-SHOTS

Don't be afraid to apply just because you lack related experience. Lacking basic qualifications is different and usually insurmountable, though, if no qualified person applies you may be considered if you customize your résumé appropriately. Surprisingly often, innovative principals interview and then end up hiring someone they added to the list as a "long-shot." A calculated risk is taken to inject new life, instead of a "recycled" person, into the school.

will tell you to whom you apply. Then, apply to that person, regardless of who you may know in that board. If you do know someone there, however, let them know you are applying.

Usually the number of candidates has been pre-established, so it is especially important, as we will discuss later, to show that you have everything needed and a lot more. You have to measure-up to the competition. This is especially the case when you want to win a specific assignment. The résumé is your only chance at this point! You do not want to miss the short-list because you failed to tell the personnel department that you do indeed have related experience which could form a perfect match for what the position requires. Equally regrettable is failure to mention experience or qualifications that would be a match for another position they could consider you for. But don't despair: we are already working on getting you set with both feet firmly planted on the "inside track!"

In many boards "pool hiring" is done. With this method of selection, a group of administrators including principals and others in positions of added responsibility are conscripted into forming the interview committee. They are given hundreds of C.V.'s, which have been pre-screened by the Human Resources Department staff, and it is their job to narrow the list down to a short-list which may include anywhere from five to fifty candidates. From these they will then hire a "pool" of employees who are deemed to be the best of those available and who will be slotted into whatever positions arise within the board. In this case it is not the intention to make a "perfect match" as no one knows in whose school they will be working anyway.

In these boards, you will still be subjected to a rigorous interview, but it may be somewhat more perfunctory. On the other hand, if the Board has gone to "pool hiring" because of a past concern with the quality of staff hired by some principals, you may find the committee is selected from among those very capable in personnel matters, in which case the interview will be very intensive and your references will be pressingly interrogated. Your best course of action is: *be prepared.*

Remember, though, especially in a board where the principals hire their own school's staff, the principal assisted by the interview team is looking for a perfect match to his/her school, specifically. There is a lot more to a perfect match than having the basic qualifications and directly related experience. Responsible principals are looking for the perfect fit, not just an acceptable one. They don't want to take the risk of hiring someone they will later have to go to the effort of dismissing. Also, some principals find their security threatened when they hire someone who doesn't make them look good. You see, it can be argued that the most important decision a principal makes is the personnel she or he selects as this literally controls the quality of a school, by determining the people who work in it.

You can let your personality work for you during the interview and hope for opportunities to mention the extras, but your résumé is all you can count on to get you to the interview. If it doesn't, you don't. It's as simple as that.

Organization of Data

Careful organization of the data is vital—in fact, it is the key. It ensures that the most important data is presented first; it ensures that emphasis is placed on the desired areas; it prevents confusion or misunderstandings; it facilitates reading, thus encouraging more lengthy and intensive examination of the résumé and consideration of you as a candidate. This keeps you safely on the "inside track." It takes a lot of careful effort to control the data and not allow the data to over-run the document. One question which sometimes calls out to be answered when a confusing C.V. is being read is: "If given essentially unlimited time and opportunity for revision he cannot organize his own career story, why should a hiring principal expect him to be able to organize a curriculum, a classroom, or extra-curricular activities?" By following the format and direction of this book, you will prevent that question from even arising in their suspicious minds!

If a principal or vice-principal gets to the end of your résumé without either conscious or (even more important) subconscious uneasiness or concerns (those nagging little doubts), they are more inclined to feel positively about your candidacy. Many C.V.'s are set aside, not because of major gaps but because they just caused a general nebulous discomfort; not something readily identifiable, just uneasiness. Many "constants" are suddenly changing in education, and to make it worse the plethora of management fads and fixes—to which many educators seem to have become addicted—are with increasing rapidity being replaced by a whole group of new ones, none of which seem to last or hold the attention of the fad promoters any longer than the most recent "solution" they have now suddenly replaced. As are teachers, many administrators are feeling rather insecure and tending to be even more cautious than usual. You can, however, turn this situation to your advantage by showing that you will be good for the children, will make their school function better and make them look better, and you won't "rock the boat."

No administrators who fancy themselves already overloaded are eager to hire and work with someone with whom or about whom they are uncomfortable. First of all, they may suspect (or rationalize) that the children may be at risk. Secondly, they do not want to jeopardise their reputation with their peers by hiring someone who is not excellent. Thirdly, they do not want to have to deal with the inconvenience and effort required in dealing with the dismissal which results from an ill-advised decision in staff selection. So, give them all the information they need to feel comfortable about you and about their decision to interview you. Get on and stay on the "inside track." *Make it easy for them to give you the job!*

Errors

Another part of organization of data is the avoidance of errors. If you intentionally give false information on a résumé, you are subject to dismissal without further cause, and your appeal in courts of law will, with very few exceptions, be unsuccessful. It is as simple as that. Of course, we will look at ways to emphasize some items and ways we can de-emphasize others. That ability, too, is a part of being on the "inside track."

Point form is acceptable in the C.V., of course, but there are a few things which seem to jump off the page at most administrators. One thing that tends to detract significantly from a C.V. is errors in the simple things like spelling, typing and grammar (such as noun/verb agreement and split infinitives). You could consider avoiding the use of contractions in a formal document like a C.V., because some administrators still look for such precision in form. Another very noticeable thing is inconsistent format: if you indent a sub-title five spaces on one page it really is important to do exactly the same throughout the document. Fair or not, care in these little things, too, is often seen as a predictor of your later behaviour.

MAKE IT EASY

If the short-listing committee or the principal can readily get well-organized answers to all their questions, they are more likely to be impressed enough to eliminate other candidates in favour of you. They hold the key to the position. Make it as easy as possible for them to give it to you—easier than it is to give it to anyone else!

Presenting them with the information they need in order to see that you are an excellent candidate is a part of this simple, straightforward strategy; letting them see this easily, clearly and quickly is another important part.

SPEED KILLS

Take the time to make your package error free. "Speed kills" applies to job applications, too. Although there is a possibility she was referring to something other than preparation of a formal Curriculum Vitae, the comment by Mae West does apply: "Anything worth doing is worth doing slowly."

HIDDEN BENEFIT

Preparing and having a well-organized C.V. also has a hidden benefit: it makes you more immediately aware of, and more confident in, details of your qualifications and experience.

Again, enquiring minds want to know. If you are not sufficiently careful to attend to correctness on a C.V., when you really want a job and have essentially unlimited time to prepare, what will you be like—in a worst-case scenario—when you think things don't matter because you have a permanent contract? Absence of errors does not contribute much to your overall candidacy, but presence of them detracts significantly.

Copy Quality

Quality of the photocopy is also important. Eyestrain causes headaches and you probably don't want anyone, un-consciously or consciously, to associate your résumé with a headache! This, too, can be seen as a predictor: principals may wonder if that is the quality of copy you will send home to parents on newsletters from your classroom. Don't let their suspicions even start to be aroused—that could knock you off the "inside track."

Thanks to the technology that has accompanied the Information Age, it is no longer necessary to get your résumé typeset. A good laser printer, especially one printing at 1200 dots per inch (dpi), will now produce high quality results and 600 or even 300 dpi is almost as good on text. (The extra 600 dpi on high-end laser printers is usually only used for graphics-rich documents.) I have, for years, recommended a certificate stock paper since it feels nice without being ostentatious. Use of parchment and other really expensive paper sometimes seems, perhaps, a bit overdone to some, from my experience on committees. Some administrators—those, apparently, who are more sensitive to the colours in the world around them—seem to like coloured paper for a résumé, feeling that it helps that particular one to stand out. (You can usually spot these administrators by the impeccable colour co-ordination of their offices.) In the opinion of many others, however, white paper is best or, if you really feel that you want to be a little different, paper that is just slightly off-white.

Please avoid the temptation to use paper with pictures or scenery or clouds on it; it's just too cluttered and, like paper of a very intense colour, can detract from the content and clarity. While canary yellow may be fine when applying for a job in advertising, and dark green print on pale green paper looks very nice, you may want to look more traditional, especially in your first few years in the profession. Without their even knowing it, many administrators are influenced by the social tendency identified by the late Dr. Marc Gold in his "Competence-Deviance Hypothesis:" you have not yet developed as much credibility (perceived competence) as you will, so very little deviation in your behaviour will be tolerated for a while. And, you sure don't want to get bumped off the "inside track" by something so incidental as that.

Length

How long should it be? Many people seem to become almost preoccupied with the issue of length. An arbitrary point is often suggested: three pages maximum, two pages maximum, one page maximum, depending on who you listen to. A better guide is: *keep it as short as you can while still giving all useful information.*

In an effective C.V. most people find that organization is paramount: present necessary information first (the need-to-know) and present the extra "enrichment" data (the nice-to-know) later in a manner that clearly delineates the two. That way the package does not appear so dauntingly endless, the reader has a chance to skim, only reading carefully the parts

"It's not the size that matters."
—*Dr. Ruth*

that intrigue her or him and they don't tend to set yours down because of sheer boredom! It also allows you, however, enough space to tell the principal who is interested in starting an Outdoors Club the following September that you worked as a canoe builder and backpacking guide for seven years! That could possibly have been the thing that tipped the balance (but not the canoe) in your favour.

On this issue, over the years I have frequently asked principals from various areas how long they like a résumé to be. Their usual response is something in the area of one or two pages. Then I have asked them to think of the last three teachers they hired and, after allowing a few moments for the images to clarify, I asked how long those particular teachers' résumés were. Invariably, they have looked surprised. You see, they think they want and will claim they want a short "bare bones" C.V., one which is "really to the point," but the candidates they short-list and hire are the ones who provide a bit more detail, who show what they have to offer, who "hook" their interest and impress them!

In Summary

Your résumé says a lot about you, so be certain it says exactly what you want it to say. As human rights and labour legislation and privacy and freedom-of-information laws make it increasingly difficult for those in hiring positions to acquire possibly predictive information about a candidate, and it becomes increasingly more difficult to dismiss an employee without due and often lengthy process, principals and boards are becoming more careful about whom they interview and hire.

Though rarely admitted aloud, it is generally recognized among persons working in the personnel field that interviews, unless very skillfully structured and controlled, are exceptionally poor predictors of post-hiring behaviours. Interviewers are severely limited in the types of questions they can ask. In Ontario, for example, under the *Freedom of Information Act* (1990) and resulting case law, there are stringent limits on who can be contacted for a reference check, and references, to avoid litigation, are often at best vague in what they say. One study reported in 1985 by Robert Half showed that managers, even when giving references to their friends, tend to be candid only 67% of the time. (Non-acquaintances and others can probably expect even less!) Personnel officers had a candour rating of 43%. So the résumé gets close scrutiny indeed. It is considered by many to be one of only a few possible predictors left.

Your résumé is an investment. It can put you onto the "inside track" to the position you want! The cost of the time and the out-of-pocket expenses are a small part of what you will recoup in a single year if you land the job you want. And, axiomatically, if you don't get an interview, you won't get the job! So, first we'll look at developing a great C.V., then a cover letter that grabs their attention and arouses their interest in you. Then we'll get you really primed and ready for the interview. We'll also take a look at how you can further improve your position on the "inside track" by strategic volunteering and occasional teaching, and the appendices will provide a lot of contingency information that you may find helpful along the way.

Now it's time to get down to developing your C.V.—so, let's do it!

HOW LONG?

It is not the length that is the concern, but the organization and control of the data. In résumés, as in books, it is content and organization (in other words writing style) that determine which ones get set aside. The keys are: brevity, clarity and detail.

Put in all the required data, but in the fewest words possible. Choose each word carefully. Remember the comment by former U.S. Vice-present Dan Quayle: "Verbosity leads to unclear, inarticulate things."

"Only the curious will learn and only the resolute overcome the obstacles to learning. The quest quotient has always excited me more than the intelligence quotient."
—*Eugene S. Wilson*

LET YOUR LIGHT SHINE

Our deepest fear is not that we are inadequate.
Our deepest fear is that we are powerful beyond measure.
It is our light, not our darkness, that most frightens us.
We ask ourselves, "Who am I to be brilliant, gorgeous, talented and
   fabulous?"
Actually, who are you not to be?
You are a child of God.
Your playing small doesn't serve the world.
There's nothing enlightened about shrinking so that other people won't
   feel insecure around you.
We were born to make manifest the Glory of God that is within us.
It's not just in some of us; it's in everyone.
And as we let our own light shine, we unconsciously give other people
   permission to do the same.
As we are liberated from our fear, our presence automatically
   liberates others.

   — *Marianne Williamson* (quoted by *Nelson Mandela,* Inaugural
   Speech, 1994)

PART II

A STEP-BY-STEP GUIDE TO THE BEST RÉSUMÉ IN THE PILE

This section combines brief examples of finished format together with extensive explanatory notes to guide and direct you as you proceed. See PART V for a sample of a completed application package and how it all fits together.

This outline may include headings that your own C.V. may not require or that are not appropriate. You can leave them out, substitute or combine to meet your needs. As Bertrand Russell once said, "Every system should have loop holes and exceptions, for if it does not, it will in the end crush all that is best in mankind." What follows, therefore, is not a prescription, but a guide which gives a lot of alternatives to help you decide what your personal C.V. needs. Use this section, along with the additional examples in PART III, to tailor your résumé to your own specifications and needs.

Forsan et haec olim meminisse juvabit—"Perhaps one day this, too, will be a pleasure to look back upon."

So, here we go!

CURRICULUM VITAE

About seven or eight lines from the very top of the page, start with: **"CURRICULUM VITAE"**. This should be centred and in all capital letters. You may even want to go with an outline or shadow script, but nothing too flamboyant. This just titles the document. More important is what follows! Then, a couple lines down, centred, goes:

YOUR NAME

This should be in **bold** print if possible, but Script, Old English, neon colours or whatever can be a distraction. Don't become overly concerned yet about format; as indicated above, there is an example in PART V of how it should look on the page. Right now we are just getting the data down. As we go further through the book, we can re-organize and revise.

You really should give your full name on a résumé unless you have a specific reason for not doing so: you wish your parents had never heard of that obscure saint you are named after, for example. If you are called by a second or third name (e.g., your name is "Mary Susan" and you go by "Susan"), an easy way to show this is just to underline the name by which you are known. Nicknames should be avoided, unless they are relatively common and generally accepted in mainstream society: "Elizabeth (Betty) Sarah Jones" carries with it a little more dignity on a C.V. than "Gerald Henry (Shorty) Smith."

GET FREE E-MAIL

If you don't already have a "normal" e-mail account, you can get a free account from a number of web-site sources (such as: www.hotmail.com or www.yahoo.com). Once you have set up an account (easy to do), you can then send, receive and store e-mail—and you can do so from anywhere in the world that you can log on to the internet (your local library, for example, or a library in Hawaii while you are on vacation). It is very easy to set up such an account and it is easy to access it from practically anywhere. Interested employers can then contact you quickly and easily—and you too can contact them! Indeed, it's the millennium thing to do.

"The closest a person ever comes to perfection is when they fill out a job application form."
—*Stanley J. Randall*

YOUR OWN WEB ADDRESS

In addition to free e-mail (see previous page), you can also establish your own world wide web address (currently at about US$75 per year and probably even less). You can even do this now by yourself online to avoid service charges.

Moreover, increasingly, companies are "giving away" free web space.

With free e-mail, free web space, and fairly cheap www address (URLs), you can have your own personal, permanent presence on the web—but, in selecting your web address, be sure you choose a name that you are willing to live with forever!

PERSONAL DETAILS

One good reason not to include personal details is that some boards reject outright applications containing any data they believe goes beyond the most minimalist interpretation of "freedom of information." Some boards, using a black pen, stroke out such proscribed information.

Check with the human resources department of the board you are applying to in order to find out their policy on such "optional" data. (If you know a principal in the board, she or he could give you an honest description of the board's policy, formal or informal. If in doubt, leave it off!)

PERSONAL DATA

About three more lines down, you will start the **PERSONAL DATA** section. Just follow the format below. This section is comprised of several key items: **Address**, **Date of Birth**, **Telephone**, **Family**, **School Support**, and **Languages**.

Address

When you list your **Address**, be certain to give the full street address and postal code. Even though they probably won't be contacting you by snail-mail, it is considered "proper." If you know you will be moving, list your current address and state "until June 30" or whatever, and then give your new address, if you know it, and say "after July 1," or give a friend's address "for messages." If you have an e-mail address and you check your mail regularly, give that; it fulfills a double purpose: it makes it easy to maintain contact and, as there is a recognized shortage of I.T.-competent people in education right now, it sets you apart! If you are one of the very few teaching candidates (so far) who have their own web page (and this self-promotion technique is only going to increase), be sure to give your "home page" address on your printed C.V.! This will speak volumes!

Note, please, that the **Personal Data** items listed at the bottom of this section followed by a question mark are bits of information which, in most Canadian provinces and territories, may not legally be required nor demanded of you, some until after you have been offered a position (e.g. Social Insurance Number) and some even after you are hired, such as family status or citizenship. You may, however, be asked if you are legally able to work in Canada. There is a systemic difference between the two questions: "citizenship" and "work status." Of course, as you will see going through this book, there are exceptions to almost everything; the exception to avoiding the topic of citizenship would be when applying to provinces or territories with citizenship or residency requirements for those applying from areas outside those provinces/territories. (See APPENDIX 6 for specifics on that.) If you want details on the areas or subjects which may and may not be addressed in an interview, consult The Human Rights Code of your province and, in Ontario, the Freedom of Information Act or the comparable Act in your province or territory. You can get a copy, or a summary, from your provincial or territorial department or ministry responsible for labour.

Having said this, please consider providing at least some of this data unless there are specific reasons not to do so. It provides a feeling of openness and friendliness, a three-dimensional person rather than a flat, sterile view. It's the "Here is someone I could be comfortable working with" sort of thing that we are trying to project. It also prevents a feeling of "What are they hiding? They haven't told me anything about themselves." This may be a more common reaction farther away from cosmopolitan centres or among older executives. It does, however, exist. You must decide whether the risk is worth it. Above all, include only that with which you are comfortable. To do otherwise will make you uneasy and this discomfort may very well come out in the interview.

While on the topic of personal information, gender sometimes is seen as a difficult issue. Some names like Dale and Terry are common to both genders. Similarly, a lot of people have trouble remembering whether Frances or Francis is the female form. (It's Frances.) As well, sometimes, "new Canadian" names are not easily recognized and if your name is unusual, like mine, you may want to specify gender. This is just to make it easier for them to know whether to address a letter to Mr. or Ms. It is one more way of giving them information before they have to wonder and worry: just one more little way of making them comfortable and making it easier to give the job to you. One simple way to accomplish this is just putting your title (Ms., Mrs., Miss, Mr., Fr. or Sr.) after your name under your signature on the cover letter. Of course, you cannot be asked your gender or title (Mr./Ms etc.) when applying, but offering this information makes things a little easier, I have found. Legitimate or not, gender may be considered more relevant by some when you are applying for a position such as a high school gym teacher.

Many people object to listing anything that is not required, even when the board does not discriminate against those who do so, because they feel it is an invasion of privacy. That could really work in your favour! Their reluctance increases your chances of appearing more personable and getting the interview instead of them. Besides, what is the advantage of having everyone wonder whether the next person scheduled to be interviewed is male or female and then half of them feeling silly because they were wrong in their guess. You want them to feel good about working with you, not embarrassed. In most cases, after a forty-five minute interview they can guess anyway, so what has anyone concealed?

Date of Birth

Date of Birth (D.O.B.) is another similar area of sensitivity. But what is the use trying to surprise them or "keep them guessing"? An interview is not an advertisement for "anti-ageing snake oil." Unless you have been out of the recognized workforce for a long while, most interviewers can guess your approximate age by the number of things you have done in your life and for how long.

If you do decide to put in your date of birth, it is best to list it using words to prevent any confusion (e.g., 01-07-59 could be January 7, 1959 or July 1, 1959). With the advent of computers, the old day/month/year format is increasingly being replaced by the scientific format of recording time: year:month:day:hour:minute:second, with each number separated by a full colon. (Of course the hour and second are not necessary in a d.o.b.!) Probably best of all, though, is simply to name the month and avoid all the confusion!

Telephone

Under **Telephone** you may want to list a "current" and a "permanent" one, or "until June 30" one, if you will be moving in the near future, and then your new number, if you know it. If you will be in *limbo*, get permission to give a friend's or relative's number and specify on the C.V. that it is "for messages." You still want them to be able to get in touch with you **easily**! You may find an answering machine worth the investment if you will be out of the house a lot. If you have one, you might seriously consider having a message on it that sounds professional and business-like; this probably is not really the time for gag lines or rap music. A lot of administrators are still very traditional, and we don't want to upset them until after we get the job!

Family

Under **Family** (assuming you decide to include this information), unless legally married, divorced or widowed, just put "single." You may also want to decide whether the area or board to which you are applying will consciously or unconsciously discriminate against divorced people or

PHOTOGRAPHS

It is usually not advantageous to attach a photo to your application. It will usually detract more than it adds. If you don't include one, and for some unusual reason they require a photograph of you, they will ask for one or for permission to take one.

A problem with photographs is that they have been found to contribute to discrimination and allegation of discrimination. It's a nuisance to have to deal with the accusation: "He knew I was a member of a visible minority (or variously "a member of an over-represented majority") and that is why I was not interviewed." While this is a "long shot," again we do not want to arouse either suspicions or unease. That does not make it easier for them to feel good about you. That would not make it easier for them to give the job to you.

"Do not regret growing older. It is a privilledge denied to many."
—Anon.

21

JUST THE FACTS

Remember, too, anything on the résumé may be questioned in the interview whether or not it is a "politically incorrect" topic. Thus, you may decide, for example, that you want to leave off the "HEALTH" part unless yours is "excellent." You don't want to exclude yourself from competition unless your health concern would genuinely prevent you from fulfilling a "bona fide occupational requirement" (BOR).

SCHOOL FUNDING

The Ontario government has centralized school funding. Residents no longer direct taxation to either the Roman Catholic or Public system. It may, though, be impossible for Ontario to follow Newfoundland, at least in the near future. Because of the British North America Act (BNA) of 1867, funding of Catholic schools may prove to be a "constitutional right" in Ontario. Quebec, however, the other province addressed in the BNA, and whose "Protestant" schools used to be funded, has moved to dividing schools by language, rather than religion.

people who are in non-married relationships. If it will raise more questions than it answers, leave it off. This is an area that can sometimes help you to get on the "inside track" though. Having children of your own can be the basis of a common bond with others, and some administrators prefer teachers who have had "experience" with their own children. (Also, some "sweatshop" types prefer the opposite, thinking that your own children will distract you from your career between the hours of midnight and five a.m., but that is rare.) If you are married, that can be another "shared experience" with others—most adult Canadians are married. Like it or not, it is one of the ways we relate to other people in society: "what they do for a living" and "are they married and, do they have any kids?"

If you have children, and you want to state that, this is where to put: "Married, three children: 11, 9, 7." Even if you are not currently married, you may still want to list the ages of your children: "Two girls, aged 9 and 7." You decide, taking into account the area to which you are applying.

School Support

School Support can be sticky. In most provinces of Canada, Roman Catholicism is the only religion that receives government funding and Roman Catholic school boards tend to view tax support of Roman Catholic education as being very important in their staff. Similarly, in areas where other churches have had an historic right to tax funding, those church-controlled school systems consider adherence to their beliefs to be very important in the teachers in their schools. In the same way, many public boards of education are coming to value in their staff a belief in the merit of public education and the tolerance of religious variety and multi-culturalism that public school education develops in children. One very visible indicator of support of the philosophy and values of either a public or a separate education system is the direction of tax dollars.

Newfoundland had a unique tradition of denominational schools. Until the early 1990s, there were 27 denominational school boards in Newfoundland. A small community could have four or five religious schools, each with only a handful of pupils. In 1997 the people of Newfoundland voted to remove church control of schools and to establish a system where all religions were equally respected. Of course, religious leaders are objecting to this loss of control.

On the other hand, Quebec, Manitoba, Saskatchewan, Alberta and British Columbia now offer some public funding to private schools, many of which are religion-based. Ontario seems rapidly headed that way, with the possible introduction of "charter" schools. How this will influence Ontario teachers, however, is open to debate. Still another issue is the extent to which teachers across Canada are required to *observe* specific religious traditions, as contrasted with the requirement only to *respect* these traditions. For further details on private schools and certification requirements to teach in them for these and other provinces, see APPENDIX 5. There are specific advantages to teaching in such schools.

Public boards of education do not discriminate on the basis of religion. For example, many Roman Catholics are public school supporters. If, however, you want to teach for a Roman Catholic separate school board, except under very unusual circumstances, you must be both a practising Roman Catholic and a separate school supporter. (You will usually have to provide a Pastoral Letter from your priest or clergy attesting to the fact that you practice the applicable faith. This is because some non-Roman

Catholics are separate school supporters; i.e., their spouse may be Roman Catholic.) In cases where a qualified Roman Catholic is not available, and they are forced to hire a non-Roman Catholic, there is usually a requirement that the applicant: (a) be approved by a priest and (b) sign a statement that, as a condition of employment, they will not seek advancement. As a result of the issue of state funding, this whole question of the religious requirement of staff in tax-funded schools is being examined through the courts, so there may be changes in the near future.

If you are a Roman Catholic separate school supporter and are applying to Roman Catholic separate school boards, or are a member of another religion and are applying to private church schools or schools operated by the church to which you adhere, you should bring this to their attention by stating it in the section **School Support**. If special training is required to teach in those schools, where you list your certification, indicate clearly that you are so qualified. In Ontario, for example, under your B.Ed. in the **Education** section, be certain to specify that you took the option: "Religious Education in Roman Catholic Schools" (see example 2 under **Education** in PART III) or otherwise indicate clearly that you are so qualified. If you are a public school supporter and applying to the public boards of education, point that out by stating it under the **School Support** heading. If you are a combination of the two, best leave it off as it won't help you. As indicated above, these guidelines apply similarly (*mutatis mutandis* is the legal term) to parochial schools of other faiths.

NOTE: It is not your religion that is important (unless, for example, you are a non-Roman Catholic applying to a Roman Catholic separate school board); it is your tax support (which school system you pay taxes to) that is important.

Languages

An area which may not apply to everyone is **Languages**. If you speak, read, or write—or all of the above—more than one language, why not indicate so? If you have varying proficiencies, specify: "Fluent in French, can read and have working knowledge of Spanish, Russian and Polish," for example. (If you are fluent in only one language, however, leave this section out: it would only draw attention from your other abilities.)

If you are skilled in computer programming language, you might want to state that here, too. With the dearth of people competent in information technology (I.T.) in education, this could draw attention to your skills in the field and do more to make you "desirable" than almost anything else! Computer literacy is a really, really big advantage now; use it if you can. In this case you might say "Fluent in German and Spanish, also comfortable in html and visual basic programming languages." You should also mention in your cover letter your knowledge and abilities in I.T. As we will discuss later, this is a real "selling point."

PHRASE CAREFULLY

You probably want to choose the description of your linguistic ability more carefully than the author of this one: "Exposed to Spanish for two years, but many of the words are not appropriate for school."

***

Now, fill in the blanks below (the ones you have decided to include), and on we go to the next section of your C.V. (Note all the "optional" ones followed by question marks.)

E-MAIL ADDRESS

Not only does an e-mail address help show that you are comfortable with information technology, but it is already a common tool in employment communications. Make it easy for them to get in touch with you!

See page 19-20 on how to get a free and very convenient web-based e-mail address if you don't already have one.

ADDRESS	TELEPHONE
E-MAIL	
S.I. NUMBER: (?)	LANGUAGES: (?)
D.O.B.: (?)	FAMILY: (?)
HEALTH: (?)	SCHOOL SUPPORT: (?)

INVERSE ORDER

Please note that they should all be listed in *inverse* chronological order. Start with those still in process; indicate "19__ to present" on them.

EDUCATION

In a teacher's C.V., **EDUCATION** is usually the next section. (One exception to this rule is discussed later.) A good format is: date of completion followed by name of degree, certificate (or whatever), followed by institution, city, province, territory or state, followed by options or specifics, viz.:

1998 to present: Studies toward degree: Doctor of Philosophy: School of Graduate Studies: University of Western Ontario: London, Ontario.
- thesis: "Evaluation of Post-Secondary School Curricula for Native Students: An Evolutionary Model."
- coursework completed; dissertation in process.
- anticipated graduation: 2001.

1991   Course: Computers in the Classroom I: Faculty of Education: York University: Toronto, Ontario.

1990   Certificate: First Aid Standard I: St John's Ambulance: Toronto, Ontario.

1990   Additional Qualification: Teaching in the Intermediate Division (Geography and Math): Faculty of Education: Queen's University: Kingston, Ontario.

1989   Degree: Bachelor of Education: Faculty of Education: Nipissing University College: North Bay, Ontario.

- certification in Primary and Junior Divisions
- option: Education of Native Canadians

1987   Degree: Master of Science (Anthropology): Faculty of Science: University of Western Ontario.

- thesis: "The Influence of Potential for Self-Determination on Community Support for Higher Education in Traditional Cultures"

1986   Degree: Bachelor of Arts (Honours): University of Manitoba: Winnipeg, Manitoba.

- majors: Anthropology and Sociology

1982   Honours Secondary School Graduation Diploma: Kenner Collegiate and Vocational School: Peterborough, Ontario.

It is usually not advisable to leave out any items. For example, if there are a lot that are not directly related to teaching and also a lot that are, and you are afraid the list will seem interminable, you may wish to divide them into: **Teaching-Related Education** and **Other Education**, or **Instruction-Related Education** and **Engineering-Related Education**. Just do whatever it takes to present the information in an organized fashion which presents the **most relevant** information first—the really teaching-related items. This prevents the readers from having to go through a lot of information that they may deem to be irrelevant, while yet succinctly providing the additional information in case they are intrigued and want details on a specific part. Again, you are making it easy for them to get what they need. This will help them give you what you need. Oh, the benefits of juggling!

To make the relevant data really stand out, you can even **"bold"** format the specific degrees or required courses. When you have several courses or degrees from the same university, you don't have to repeat the university's address; just give its name. This helps prevent unnecessary verbiage. It is usually a good idea to list the concentration or "major" area of studies in a degree, or the thesis title, especially if it is related to teaching or is interesting enough that it will intrigue the reader and thus help your application.

It is considered acceptable to go back as far as your secondary school, but usually no further. (This is related to systemic discrimination issues related to religious schools. It is mostly an issue in Ontario from before RCSS schools were totally funded by taxes, and in other areas of Canada it is still not usually considered relevant.) An exception might be if you attended the elementary school you are applying to. Then it could qualify as "intriguing." By the way, if you don't have the exact qualifications required, it may be insurmountable; but, if you have a **lot** of related experience try submitting a C.V. anyway. A stamp doesn't cost much. The technique here would be to put **Related Experience** first and **Education** second, to draw attention to your strength: the experience. This is the exception to the rule we mentioned earlier. I know of cases where this method has been successful!

TEACHING EXPERIENCE

You might want to expand this to include the categories of **Teaching-Related Experience** or **Child-Related Experience** if much of your background is not specifically "teaching." You may also want to use this alternate section title if your teaching was done before your certification; some administrators are quite sensitive to the fact that in education law a teacher is defined very specifically as a person who is qualified to teach in a school, that is, holds a teaching permit valid for the province or territory involved. Some may take exception to your including this pre-certification work, or out-of-school instructing, in the **Teaching** category. The wider title **Teaching-Related** will accommodate the range without upsetting them.

Volunteer work, both pre- and post-certification, certainly could fit the category of **Teaching-Related Experience**, even though it would not be called teaching in strict Ministry or Department of Education contractual language. (See PART IX re: volunteering in schools.)

List **Teaching Experience** before **Teaching-Related Experience**, and that before **Other Employment Experience** if you include those other categories. The idea is to hit readers with the most recent and/or most directly related experience first, thus to show them right away that you belong on the "inside track." Then, follow with progressively less related categories. (All entries within each sub-category are listed in inverse chronological order.) If there are gaps in your C.V. (or periods of time not addressed for one reason or another, regardless of how legitimate) the use of several sub-categories may also help to deflect attention from this by breaking up the straight chronology.

Especially if you are just entering the profession and your experience is somewhat limited, why not be really careful to include such things as teaching swimming lessons, camp craft, Sunday School, Catechism, Scouts and Guides, coaching children's teams, etc. It is all **Teaching-Related Experience**. See PART III for more examples.

HOW SPECIFIC?

It is not usually necessary to specify separate courses in a degree or diploma unless you have a very definite reason for listing that one or ones individually (i.e., it is a specific requirement of the position).

If, however, you have a very relevant selection of courses, especially in advanced degrees, you may want to list the most directly related ones: "Coursework included: The Maladjusted Young Child, Family Dynamics in One-Parent Homes and Sound Patterning in the A.D.H.D. Child."

IMPROVE YOUR ODDS

You can dramatically improve your application by keeping the reader's needs in mind. If you have a lot of teaching experience, how about having your first category called *Related Teaching Experience*, and then put in it only the experience which relates directly to the advertised position? That will certainly keep their interest long enough to get them thoroughly hooked! Then list your *Other Teaching Experience* as the next category.

"We are the sum of our
experiences."
—*Anon.*

It is really important always to give a "**Reason for leaving**." No matter how unusual your reason, it is still much better than a suspicious administrator's imagination running wild! It answers their questions and puts them at ease. Besides, it can almost always be related to a family move or a positive career move. If, however, you really do not want to state the **Reason for leaving**, about all you can do is hope for the best and don't list the reason for any other positions, so the pattern is consistent.

OTHER EMPLOYMENT EXPERIENCE

Now here's your chance to include all the other things that make you a better or more interesting person. Remember to include committees you worked on or T.V. appearances, if frequent or really remarkable, and other interesting jobs that set you apart from the crowd: "Astronaut Trainee" is a good one! Wow them with your potential!

Unless you have had three different jobs every month, I encourage you to include all or most of them, but **keep the details short** and try to relate the skills or duties to teaching. This, too, is part of getting onto, and staying on, the "Inside Track." See PART III for help in this. The following is a good format:

1987–89   **Dispatcher**: CDF Transport: Windsor, ON.

Duties:

– responsible for coordinating fleet of twenty-seven trucks travelling both Ontario and Michigan.

– conflict resolution part of daily duties.

– also responsible for dealing with any dissatisfied customers; this was especially good experience.

Reason for leaving: return to university.

1985–87   **Waitress**: Angelo's Home of Fine Italian Foods: Kenora, ON.

Duties:

– waiting on tables, also short-order cooking when sous-chef absent.

– excellent opportunity to hone inter-personal skills.

Reason for leaving: move with family to Thunder Bay.

1984   **Assistant Groundskeeper**: Troy Golf and Country Club: Red Deer, AB. (Summer)

Duties:

– cutting grass, moving sprinklers, applying nutrients, replacing turf.

– also assisted with crowd control during Alberta Championship competition.

– helped Pro, on volunteer basis, with **mixed children's classes** after my regular work hours.

Reason for leaving: return to university.

KEEP IT SIMPLE

By using this format, an administrator can skim— reading all the job titles, and then reading in detail only the ones that interest or intrigue her or him. Remember, it's a good idea to **bold** the job title or description, and especially relevant phrases to further facilitate skimming.

If you are listing positions or experiences which were in many ways similar, do not repeat yourself: instead say, "similar to above; also ..." and list the "additional" or "extra" stuff you did that was related to teaching. This is important: if the readers find repetition they will quickly stop reading!

Again, remember to consider using multiple-categories to help to deflect attention away from any disruptions in chronology which you may wish to de-emphasize.

SELECTED WORKSHOPS AND SEMINARS PRESENTED

Note that this is seminars *presented*, not ones you attended. Those you attended would go under **EDUCATION**. All should be listed in inverse chronological order, with dates, locations, titles and, if appropriate but not self-evident, brief descriptions of clientele. These don't have to be directly related to teaching; it also helps to show you are a recognized authority in another field, be it pure science, architecture, arts, literature, plumbing, horticulture or whatever.

If you did a lot on a regular basis, it may go under **Teaching-Related**, but the **Seminars Presented** category may be "more impressive," especially if you already have quite a bit under **Teaching-Related**. If you are new in your career and have only presented one or two, put them under **Teaching Related** so they don't look "lonely." Effective juggling among categories like this, to achieve maximum impact, is a very important part of your C.V. preparation!

If you are not having a separate section for **Publications**, you could include books and journal articles published in this category. In that case, remember to call the category **Publications and Seminars**. If you are including this section, a sample entry could be:

1993   "Streetproofing the Pre-School Child": a 20 hour series of train-the-trainer seminars for staff at YMCA: Schomberg: Prince Edward Island.

PUBLICATIONS

This is where you list books, articles in magazines, journals, newspapers, etc., you have had published (or co-authored). If extensive, you may wish to sub-divide by category or topic, including the by-now-familiar: "**Teaching-Related**" and "**Other.**"

Cater to their ego—if you can! Most principals like to have published persons on staff (if all other factors are equal), especially if topics relate to the profession. (It may be best, however, to omit this section if you were published only in "underground" publications or in those magazines which occupy the very, very top shelf of the magazine rack.) They also like people who could write newspaper articles, etc., or at least know what a reporter is looking for when he/she comes to the school. Effective control of the press is a skill. As well, there is—justified or not—an assumption that if you can write for publication, you can write a good progress report or newsletter. A reasonable format parallels that in a bibliography; books could be entered thus:

> *The Kindergarten Child at Play: An Observational Guide for Teachers.* Toronto: York University Press, 1991.

Or, if you edited and wrote an introduction and study notes for a collection by several authors:

PUBLICATIONS AND SEMINARS

Don't feel left out if you can't include a section like this in your C.V. Let's face it, very few will have anything here, but if you have, it helps set you apart!

PERSONAL WEB PAGE

Even if you have published it only on your own web-page, this reinforces your I.T. awareness. If you thus get them to read it, and it is well written and well reasoned, it could add significantly to your profile.

The Early Works of Piaget and Related Criticism. [ed., intro., notes] 2 vols. Toronto: Doubledog, 1989.

Or, you could use the A.P.A. format, like this, if it is in the field of sciences rather than the humanities:

1993 *The Consistency Deprived Child: Relevance to Predictability of Incarceration* (Toronto: Torrie-Hall).

If you are published on the internet, give the authors' names—you can omit this if you are the single author—the title, date and the URL. Using the MLA format, you could list it thus:

The Role of the Grade One Teacher in Determining Future Commitment to Self-directed Learning, 1996.
<http://www.ubc .edu.bc.ca/grstd/gr1-sdl> (August 9, 1996).

By typing the URL within angle brackets, you prevent its exact characters from becoming mixed with surrounding text, especially punctuation. Note, please, that in URL entries the date at the end, in parenthesis, indicates the most recent date of revision of the web site.

See PART III for specific examples of books in foreign languages, parts of books, journals, etc.

AWARDS

This can include academic awards, athletic awards, humanitarian awards, sales awards, etc., even prizes won at a dog show (although it is probably the dog which is most deserving in that case). That would show you have varied interests!

All should be listed in inverse chronological order. Consider dividing them into categories: "academic," "athletic," etc. or "teaching-related," and "other," etc. If you have several awards that are directly related to your training or experience as a teacher, and even more so if they are particularly related to the position being sought, why not put this entire section right under your **EDUCATION** section? That will make sure they are noticed (because they are listed early in the C.V.) and will draw the reader's attention to their specific relevance to your proficiency in teaching.

Wherever the section goes in your particular C.V., format should be: date, followed by name or description:

1987   Dean's Award for Consistent Kindness to Fellow Students: Ryerson Polytechnical Institute: Toronto, Ontario.

1985   Archibald MacPherson Award for Scholarship in History: Trent University: Peterborough, Ontario.

1984   Most Valuable Defensive Back: Holy Cross School: Moose Jaw, Saskatchewan.

1983   Grade 12 Honours List: Regional Secondary School: Edmunston, New Brunswick.

This section could also be called **AWARDS AND HONOURS** to include such things as:

1984   Named to All-Star Team: Ohio University Invitational Triple-A Hockey Tournament: Athens, Ohio.

See PART III for many more examples to stimulate your memory!

"Dignity does not consist in possessing honours, but in deserving them."
—*Aristotle*

SPECIAL INTEREST AND ABILITY AREAS

This can be called **PERSONAL INTERESTS**. I would suggest avoiding the title "Hobbies;" to me, it sounds too trite. Give a short title and description of your expertise, if appropriate, and, if not self-evident, how it relates to the position sought. Try not to make the list endless so you don't appear to be "stretching." It can be sub-divided into: Sports, Interpersonal and Counselling Activities, Community Work, etc.—whatever will make the list more organized.

A good format might be:

Sports: Cross-country Skiing, Swimming, Volleyball.
    – would be willing to coach or assist with teams.
Music: Play piano, trombone, sing in community choir.
Games: Bridge, chess.
    – average but enthusiastic player.
    – would be willing to help with extra-curricular activities.

This might be the best place to list your capabilities in **Information Technology** if you are self-taught (and thus your **EDUCATION** section would not list courses, etc., in this field). Then you could specify something like: "comfortable in both Macintosh and Windows environments, including Windows 98," and/or state that you have "worked with information technology for six years" or "am very comfortable with internet research procedures" or "enjoy troubleshooting I.T. systems."

Now that will put you on the "inside track," but don't be surprised if you are asked to fix something on somebody's computer the first time you set foot in the school, even just to drop off your C.V.!

PROFESSIONAL AFFILIATIONS

This area is more related to pathologists, engineers, photographers, etc., where a professional affiliation is deemed to be a sign of license. In the teaching profession it is the Teacher's Certificate (the exact name of this licence varies by province) which is the official indicator of qualification (the *sine qua non*, we could say). Other affiliations or certifications could, however, add a depth to your profile.

Press accreditation, as mentioned above, is a selling point as it is often seen to have public relations implications. "P.Eng" on a C.V. seems to impress almost everybody in this technological age. Have you kept up your membership privileges and affiliation in a former career or field: nursing, for example? (Don't claim you are a lawyer if you aren't, however. That's been tried already!)

I suggest listing professional affiliations only if there are a lot of them or if some of them directly apply, e.g., professional teachers' associations (other than the federations, unions, etc.), curriculum councils, research councils or such. You may wish to list some that are not related to education, to make the category seem less "sparse," if you have one or two which should be mentioned and you don't want them to look lonely on the page.

If there are just not enough for a section on their own, instead of leaving them out why not try to work them into an **Interests** category? This will add depth to your C.V.

"The larger the island of knowledge, the longer the shore line of wonder."
—*Ralph W. Sockman*

CHURCH GROUPS AND ACTIVITIES

If you have included a list of affiliations, this could be the place to list church groups and activities (although, unless you are clergy, it may not be a strictly professional affiliation). It is probably not the place to mention that you are still a member in good standing of an outlaw motorcycle club, no matter how proud you are of that!

REFERENCES

This is perhaps the most important and the most difficult section of the whole résumé. Please, please, please do **NOT** say "References available upon request." Remember, make it easy! Let's pretend, for a moment, that the decision has already been made to interview five people and you are tied for fifth spot. Now imagine that the references are listed for the other person who is tied with you for the last place on the interview schedule. Their references can be easily contacted, but you happen to be out and not answering your phone that night so the principal or vice-principal can't even find out whom to call. You can see who will make it onto the short list and who won't!

Besides, when you want to customize your application by sending different lists of references to different potential employers, you can do so by sending a different last page (which includes the **REFERENCES** section) with the rest of your résumé when you apply. There is absolutely no advantage to sending it later. When you are serious enough to send anything, send your list of references, too.

List their name, position, relationship to your career (if not self-evident), full mailing address (please **make sure it is current**), phone number including area code and the extension number of their work phone, their fax number, and e-mail address. While time restraints make the idea of contacting references by snail-mail ridiculous, it is usually considered proper form to give the full address, including postal code, as well as the other data.

If you can, get permission to list home phone numbers. Many busy administrators like to check references in the evening when they are not being constantly interrupted. Providing the home numbers will mean they don't have to wait until next morning to call yours. **Remember: we are trying to make it easier for them to interview you than anyone else.** We are trying to get on, and stay on, the "inside track." If only one or two allow their home number to be listed, my advice is: "better one than none."

Remember, too, the Belgian Proverb: "Don't make use of another's mouth unless it has been lent to you." It is really important always to get their permission to use them as a reference and tell them **every** time you apply for a position. Then they don't sound surprised when they get a call. They will then know your new name if it has changed due to marriage, divorce, etc. Also, a call by you helps just to make sure they are still alive— it has happened when I was calling to check references and makes for an uncomfortable moment!

There is also another reason for calling to ask for permission to list someone as a reference. I have worked with a lot of people who, I am certain, have forgotten me (and maybe one or two who wish they could). Ego-deflating as it is for all of us, you, too, may temporarily slip from someone's mind. A call will, however, often trigger the memory of an administrator who meets or works with a large number of people. They can talk with you and remind themselves of when you were with them, for how long, some of the things you did especially well, and so on. As a principal, over the years I have had many calls to check references (usually on teachers who did practice teaching or volunteer work in my school) when, for the life of me, I could not remember ever having met them, much less the quality of their work. Had they called me, I could have renewed the acquaintance and then probably have given a reasonably positive reference. Given time, though, I am afraid that even the best of us can blend into a crowd.

HOW MANY REFERENCES?

You will find it useful to list four people as references. Three is easy but it's the fourth, if you are asked for it and you have not thought it out, that will be the "loose cannon." It does not hurt to list even five or six, but that should probably be the maximum.

Also, please be aware that some boards are demanding, as a condition of application, permission to contact any and all of your former employers. This is important and is further addressed in PART IV. Increasingly, boards across Canada are requiring a copy of a recent Criminal Reference Check (CRC) or permission to conduct such a check on applicants for positions where the employee will come into direct contact with children, and that certainly includes teaching! (PART IV also addresses the issue of a CRC.) In the Yukon, a part of the contract demands the right to have the R.C.M.P. do a background check on you and the Northwest Territories require such a background check before you are allowed to sign a contract!

If you are new to the profession, you could name one of your university professors who is familiar with you and your work. You may wish to vary the type of references: one personal and three professional, for example. For your "personal" reference, pick someone who knows you well but who also has a solid reputation or a credible position in the community: a police officer, post-master, bank manager, etc. (the type of person who signs passport applications or someone who is bonded). They might well have more credibility than your dear old uncle who just loves everything you do!

Select, for a reference, persons who are well-spoken. If their conversation tends to be heavily punctuated with pauses it may cause the caller to wonder if they are having a hard time thinking of positive things to say! They need to sound sharp and professional. (It may also be worth noting: you can avoid conflict of interest if you are careful to see that those you choose to provide references have not also applied for the position.)

What Will They Be Asked?

When selecting persons who will give a good reference, it may help to know just what most administrators are looking for when they call. Your people need to be prepared for a barrage of questions, some of them quite pressing! Questions could include:

- do they know you well, for how long, and in a variety of circumstances—through a selection of good and bad times?
- how did you handle the bad times?
- what is your general attitude: are you a winner or a whiner?
- are you upbeat, or a downer who also drags everyone else down with you?
- are you helpful?
- are you flexible?
- can you see when something needs to be done? Do you then go ahead and do it without having to be told every little thing?
- can you deal with the unexpected?
- are you co-operative? Do you get along with other staff?
- are you respected and liked by the community?
- are you a skillful teacher?
- are you interested in research?
- do you keep current?
- are you interested in innovation?
- do you have good classroom management skills?
- are you honest?

SECONDARY REFERENCE CHECKS

If you don't want an administrator to check with your current employer, in Ontario (and in most other provinces there are similar restrictions) current *Freedom of Information* legislation—for what it is worth—forbids checking "secondary references" (names suggested by a listed reference) or any references not listed (or permitted) on the résumé.

I said, "for what it is worth." Unless there is a really big problem, pick some person where you currently work who has nothing against you, let him or her know you are applying, and get their permission to use them as a reference. It will help to preclude a lot of suspicion. Loyalty is also an issue. Most people do not want to hire someone who is going behind their present supervisor's back. Then they wonder if you would do the same to them in a couple of months or years?

SOME REFERENCES ARE BETTER THAN OTHERS

Plutarch is credited with saying: "A word or a nod from the good has more weight than the eloquent speeches of others." Just so, many principals tend to give more credibility to a superintendent's or another principal's reference than that of a teacher.

There is an unspoken factor just slightly in evidence here: an administrator usually realizes that his/her own professional reputation is at stake and recognizes that they will be judged against the person they recommend, so their references tend to be more careful and, therefore, more credible.

- if you say you are going to do something, do you do it?
- can you work without supervision?
- are you respectful of the chain of command?
- can you be involved without having to dominate?
- what is your level of competence in _____ (whatever you have indicated as your area of expertise, or is, in fact, the skills set required)?
- one very important question often asked is: "Would you hire them?" If they have had opportunity and did not, they may be asked why they did not. Then, if there is no readily evident reason, their reference loses credibility.
- were there any "little disappointments" about you while you worked with them?
- they may also check to confirm dates you specified on your C.V.

Your references may be subjected to quite a grilling. If your referrer seems hesitant, or in any way less than forthcoming, this will arouse suspicions. A good format for listing those willing to provide references is:

Mr. John Smith, Principal
Middlebury Senior Elementary School
795 Northwoods Lane
Bennington, Alberta
T0Z 5R7

Office: (613) 347-9812
Home: (613) 429-6734
Fax: (613) 347-9935
e-mail: smithj@mses.sd9.edu.ab.ca

Ms. Sheila Thompson, Manager (long-time friend)
Dolby Funeral Home
459 Justin Street
Thunder Bay, Ontario
R5G 8J1

Office: (807) 360-9912
Home: (807) 361-5206
Fax: (807) 360-8362

If a reference has moved, to explain the relationship to your work that they formerly had, you can insert that information in parenthesis to the right of their name thus:

Sr. Mary Hobbes, Principal   (former principal: St. Mary's School)
Holy Rosary School
123 Church Street
etc., etc.

"No, I don't understand my husband's theory of relativity, but I know my husband and I know he can be trusted."

—Elsa Einstein

Letters of Reference

What about letters of reference? Should you attach copies of them? That depends (of course). Do they refer to skills directly related to teaching and are they from a credible source: preferably someone in a position of responsibility in the community or, much better, a teacher, principal or superintendent? If so, you might want to include a copy of one or two of them. If they fail either test, don't bother.

You see, letters of reference don't carry much weight because they are not subject to cross-examination the way a reference who can be phoned is. Also, how many reference letters did you get that weren't good before you got a couple that you were comfortable attaching? You see how a suspicious administrator's mind works? All in all, they probably won't detract, but they probably won't add much either, so it is probably best to include only one or three at the most, and only ones which fit the criteria above. If they seem irrelevant, it may suggest deficiencies in the application package.

A PERSONAL WWW SITE

While it is unusual for a Canadian principal to be forced to do a web-search to find a teacher to fill a position, it can be of use if you have really specific or unusual qualities or qualifications that they might be looking for. It can also be helpful in locating a position off-shore (see also APPENDIX 12). An administrator who is looking for North American teachers can easily find you if you are on the internet.

Another advantage of having a web site is that it can be a back-up to your résumé. It can be much longer than a C.V. and still be kept interesting with colour, graphics, fonts, music, sound bites, video files, active files and so on. While your C.V. would not likely be twenty-five pages deep, your web site can be. If you are published, or an artist, you can even link to excerpts, or full versions, of some of your work. You could include scanned letters of glowing praise or letters of appreciation from parents of children you have worked with. (Please don't forget to get their permission—they are serving as a reference now—and definitely remove their address from the letter; believe me, they don't want the whole world to have access to that!)

This can be how you show them all the "supporting information." It's also a good way to provide high-interest details. If you are accomplished in sports, for example, you could feature photos and descriptors of your trophies, or place finishes, or photos of you in action. If you want to make it easy for them to contact you, you could include a "return e-mail" link.

If you have limited experience in layout and graphic design, you might want to consult some books on professional web site creation. There are several on the market, readily available in the "computer" section of bookstores. Surfing can also really help you to get ideas of what looks good, what works, and what doesn't. If a feature has impact, and is unobtrusive, go for it. If the style overpowers the message, however, you might want to think again about what you are trying to convey.

Remember that such additions as drop shadow on the titles, feathered edges on pictures, and sound overlay can all add significantly. You want your site to look professional, to reflect your competence and characteristics as a caring and careful expert.

DETAILED EXAMPLES

In PART III are examples of how to handle variations in you C.V. that are a little more complex. In PART V there are two different samples of complete cover letters together with C.V. to show how it looks when they are all fitted together. The first sample (Mr. Lavoie) represents a relatively new teacher, while Sample 2 (Mrs. Jeffereson) demonstrates the case of a very highly trained and extensively experienced candidate.

INFORMATION TECHNOLOGY EXPERTISE

Having a well-constructed site does add very considerable depth to your profile. It also shows both your awareness of the importance of I.T. and your capabilities in it. Why not list your URL on your C.V.?

BLANKET COVERAGE

If you are just "covering" an area, drop in at all the schools, with a personalized cover-letter to each principal (a word-processor is so handy), and a poster, if you have one. Ask if you can do replacement teaching. (See PART VIII.) You might even offer to volunteer. (See PART IX.)

Get your résumé **and you** into schools! Show them, by doing a good job, that they just can't get along without you!

GETTING YOUR APPLICATION, AND YOU, INTO SCHOOLS

Now, for getting it out there where it will do some good. The best way is to deliver it in person to those in decision-making positions, so that if they invite you to, you can chat about it with them as they quickly go through it. It also "personalizes" you. You may even phone and ask for a few minutes to do so, but be careful not to be too insistent or your hard-won few minutes may be a Pyrrhic victory! (Don't ask for more than a quarter of an hour; if you can't "make your pitch" in less than that, you won't be able to in an interview either!) If you do ask for a few minutes, specify the amount of time you need; that way the secretary knows you don't expect to take half a day of the administrator's time.

A neat way to do it, one that is just a bit refreshing—and, if quirky, harmlessly so—is to ask for a slightly off-beat amount of time: seven minutes, or eleven minutes. Then, if they ask a lot of questions and you begin to run over the requested time, you can very tactfully point out that you would be delighted to stay and talk to them, but you promised the receptionist that you would take only eleven minutes and you see that that time is now up. If they say goodbye, they were very busy and/or uninterested anyway, and they will appreciate your respect for their time, and may remember you for that. At least they won't remember you as the one who "wasted" their time. If they say they have a few more minutes, you have made a good point, so feel free to carry on. Either way, it may intrigue them enough to help them remember you, and it reassures them that you are time-conscious; someone who asks for "ten minutes" often wants, and tries to take, forty!

The Mini-Poster

If you are the confident type, and are perhaps just a little flamboyant, how about a mini-poster on the staff room bulletin board. It doesn't have to be any bigger than 8½ by 11 paper—in fact, if it is too big it may look overpowering or may get taken down to make room for other stuff. If it is in colour, though small, it can still have a great impact.

I know one young replacement teacher who made up an effective advertisement poster using a high-quality colour printer and, with permission of the principals, posted it in the schools where he wanted to work. He started getting a lot more replacement work, this increased his "exposure" and he soon got a permanent job. His poster had in bold letters across the top and just inside a bright border: **Occasional Teacher Available Anytime,**" and a sub-title "**No Class Too Challenging.**" He's an accomplished Mountain Bike racer and in the centre is a scanned colour photo of him with his bike after winning a race. Down one side is a bulleted list of his "Special Interests": "the environment, computers, visual arts and crafts, conflict mediation, extra-curricular activities, mountain bike racing, alpine and X-C skiing, canoe/kayak tripping and rock climbing." His education was listed down the other side of his photo. Below that were two high-impact statements, "I enjoy teaching students of all ages (Junior Kindergarten through OAC)"—in Ontario, OAC is Grade 13—and "I am prepared to bring my own curriculum resources, if required!" Below this he listed "Three Great Ways to Contact Me!" and gave his primary home phone, alternate home phone number and cell phone number. An ill teacher did not have to try to locate the list of Occasional Teachers. He made it easy for them to think of, and ask for, him. He also says that giving his cell phone number allowed him to receive calls no matter where he was, and no matter the time of day; as soon as they thought of him, they could get him! (Yes, he turned on the answering machine when he was teaching.)

"A ship in a harbour is safe, but that is not what ships are built for."
—C. Swindoll

PART III

SELECTED EXAMPLES FOR SPECIFIC CASES

You may be able to pick ideas or bits and pieces of wording from these examples, selected to try to cover a broad range of contingencies. They are selected from real C.V.'s I have prepared over the years, with details changed to "protect the innocent." Browse with pleasure. Borrow and adapt what you can. Perhaps some of these will stimulate your memory of some experience you have had. In my work preparing résumés, rarely, if ever, did clients remember all their relevant experiences without prompting. In absence of being able to be examined with probing questions, perhaps this will guide and jog your thinking. Go back and fill in, re-organize and change spots in your draft. Now you are at the revision stage!

These examples are arranged by category as they would normally appear in the C.V., starting with **EDUCATION**. (Most of the "options" within the **PERSONAL DATA** section were addressed in PART II.) Please note that, as repeated often in this book, your particular background will determine how you will combine and/or separate various categories and sub-categories.

Examples of combination and differentiation are presented here, with a few suggestions as to why each would be used.

EDUCATION

1. If the course requires some definition or explanation, you can add something in parenthesis:

    | 1987 | Word-Processing Operator Training: Featherstone Business College: Toronto, Ontario. (120-hour course) |

2. If you are wanting to teach in a religious school, remember to specify that you have the required qualification such as:

    1989   Degree: Bachelor of Education: Faculty of Education: Queens University: Kingston, Ontario.
    – Certification: Junior and Intermediate Divisions.
    – Option: Religious Education in Roman Catholic Schools.

    and/or, you may have other specific training in religion which will strengthen your application, such as:

    1986   Eucharistic Minister Certificate: Steinbach Catholic Renewal Centre, Steinbach, Manitoba.

YOU REALLY MUST BE CONSISTENT!

In the following examples, an extensive variety of reasonably minor format details are illustrated: number of spaces following a job title, skipped lines, double hyphens, bullets, em-hyphens, indentations, capitalizations, punctuation, date configurations, etc. Pick one you like, or that works for you, and then stick with it exactly.

"What we're after is a person of vision; a person with drive, determination, fire; a person who never quits; a person who can inspire others; a person who can pull the company's bowling team out of last place!"

—*Herbert V. Prochnow*

"When we escaped from Cuba, all we could carry was our education."
—Alicia Coro

3. If you have not completed a degree, after listing certification levels, concentrations, major(s), if appropriate you can state: "—anticipated graduation:" and give the date, viz:

> 1993 to present. Studies toward degree: Bachelor of Education: School of Education: Lakehead University: Thunder Bay, Ontario.
>> – Certification: Junior and Intermediate divisions.
>> – Option: Education of Native Canadians.
>> – Anticipated graduation: April 1994.

4. If you have not completed a degree, but moved on to other studies, or passed the time limit on graduate studies, and do not plan to complete it, you can show it this way:

> 1981-83 Completed two years of study toward honours degree in journalism: Carleton University, Ottawa, Ontario.
>> – Interesting experience, and one which will help me in "marketing" education and in teaching language arts.
>> – Left to pursue teaching certification: I want to work directly with children.

or, a format variation:

> 1986-87 Master of Science Program: Faculty of Science: Department of Neurobiology: University of Regina: Regina, Saskatchewan,
>> – First year completed.

or, yet another way:

> 1973-75 Studies toward degree: Doctor of Philosophy: Stanford University: Stanford, California.
>> – Final dissertation not completed.

5. If you have taken several un-related courses, not working toward any specific degree or accreditation, you may wish to lump them together:

> 1987-90 A variety of personal interest courses: Sir Wilfred Laurier University: Waterloo, Ontario.
>> – One first-year History, one first-year Philosophy, one second-year French, one third-year Sociology, and one third-year Psychology.

Or, another similar example, stressing the higher level study:

> 1986-88 Selected Graduate courses in Experimental Psychology: University of Calgary, Calgary, Alberta.
>> – Philosophy of Psychology, Uni-variate Statistics, Advanced Neuro-physiology, Psychology of Pica Deviance.

6. List your "updating" courses:

   1981   Montessori Refresher Course: Dallas Montessori School: Dallas, Texas.

7. Workshops attended, if of significant nature or **directly** related to the position sought, can be listed like this:

   1987-89   High Scope Workshops in Primary Curriculum Development. Total of eight days training in Buffalo, Syracuse and Albany, New York.

   or, a slightly different format:

   1978-83   Series of Workshops (totalling 28 days) in "Communication," "Counselling" and "Transactional Analysis" from Dickson Training Associates: Whitehorse, Yukon Territory.

8. If you do not have the specialized additional qualification needed for the position, but will be able to become qualified before commencing employment, you can easily show this. Let's assume, for example, that you are applying specifically to teach intellectually handicapped pupils in Ontario, where the position demands the additional qualification: "Teaching Trainable Retarded Children." This is an A.Q. option which can be taken with either Core I or Core II Special Education Additional Qualification in Ontario. So, if you are just completing the prerequisite (i.e., Core II), after listing the prerequisite, say "plan to take" (or better yet, if you can enrol early, say "enrolled to take") the Teaching Trainable Retarded Children option, thus:

   1991 to present.   Additional Qualification: Special Education: Core II: York University, Toronto, Ontario.
   - Option: Measurement and Evaluation
   - Registered to take additional option: Teaching Trainable Retarded Children: Summer 1992

   This shows that you have been working on the Special Ed. II over the winter of 1991-92, and in the summer of '92 you will be doing the T.R. option.

9. If there has been a significant delay between the pre-requisite course and this one (using the example above, if you did your Special Ed. several years ago), you could list your plans to take the T.R. option in your cover letter for emphasis, and you could also put it on your C.V., as above, despite the chronological gap. Or you could list it as

BE SELECTIVE

If you have been teaching for a while, you probably don't want to list every P.D. event you attended. If you did, the more important ones would be hidden among the less related!

a separate education item above all the others (remember to keep inverse chronological order), and then you could state "anticipated completion," something like this:

1992   Enrolled to take Teaching Trainable Children option: Lakehead University, Thunder Bay, Ontario.
     – Anticipated completion: summer 1992.

10.   Be creative! You may have not received any specific awards, but have a particular talent that was evident in much of your university work. You can address that by listing it as a specialty; the example below would show that you worked in many different media but were more accomplished in some:

1985   Degree: Bachelor of Arts: University of Prince Edward Island, Charlottetown, Prince Edward Island.
     – Major: Fine Arts
     – Specialty: sculpture and print-making

11.   A separate section on **AWARDS AND HONOURS** is discussed later, but if you don't have a long list of them you may want to list them with the degree so they don't look lonely off on their own; e.g.:

1987   Degree: Bachelor of Arts: University of Manitoba, Winnipeg, Manitoba.
     – Dean's Honour List, 1985, 1986, 1987.

12.   If you have several certificates but not quite enough awards to make a separate category called **AWARDS**, you can include them all quite nicely by breaking your **EDUCATION** into two sections, and including the awards with the certificates, viz:

Degrees
1990 etc., etc., list them here as demonstrated above.

Certificates and Awards
1988 etc., etc.

In such a category could be everything except degrees: all Community College work, C.P.R. or First Aid, Fitness Instructor certification, etc., as well as academic and citizenship or other awards; e.g.:

1988   Boardsailing Instructor, Level II: Canadian Yachting Association: Ottawa, Ontario.
1987   Leonard P. Whaling Award for Most Valuable Team Member: Canadian Boardsailing Championship: Royal Britannia Yacht Club: Ottawa, Ontario.
1986   National Certified Coaching Program: Level I Theory (general) and Level I Technical (tennis): Sport Canada: Toronto, Ontario.

"My advice is to consult the lives of other men, as one would a looking-glass, and from thence fetch examples for imitation."
—*Publius Terence*

Note that except for the "Whaling" award, the examples above could go under either the general title **EDUCATION** or a sub-heading **Certificates**. If you have a lot of certifications (especially sports-orientated) you may want to go for the separate category (even one called "**Sports Certificates**" might be appropriate), unless you are combining them to avoid having a single non-sports award excluded.

Please note that you may have to explain some awards; for example, the fictitious "Newberry Legion Award" may benefit from the explanation: "The Female Swimmer Deemed to Have Most Competitive Potential While Maintaining First-Class Honours Grades in a Minimum of Three Advanced Math Courses," or whatever. If it is not clear, answer their question before they think of it. That helps to prevent unease and helps to keep you on the "inside track."

JUGGLING

As you can see, it is very much a juggling act. What looks best? What flows most naturally? How can we best present the most relevant information, without leaving out anything we want included? In summary, the key is not just inclusion of all relevant data, but the *effective control of the data.*

13. An exception to this "sports-oriented certificates" suggestion might be a martial-arts certification at the black belt level which could be considered a degree and could reasonably be listed with other degrees; e.g.:

1987   Degree: Master of Arts in Education Administration: Central Michigan University: Mount Pleasant, Michigan.
  – Concentration: Community-School Relations.
  – Thesis: The Post-Vietnam Resurgence of Adult-Oriented Education in Inner City Schools.
1986   Third Degree Black Belt: Karate: Butoku-Kai of Hamilton: Hamilton, Ontario.
1983   Degree: Bachelor of Education: University of New Brunswick: Fredericton, New Brunswick.

If you took your martial-arts training in some areas of Japan rather than a western country, you may not have received any coloured belt under black. (In some dojos there, they remain white until they qualify for black; here in North America, we seem to require more instant gratification, so are granted intermediate steps in the form of deepening shades of belts toward black.) Then you could show it as:

1987 to present.   Studies toward Black Belt: Karate: etc. [and then give either the name of the dojo or sensi, then city and province.]

Unless you are already close to Black level, however, you probably would be best to list it in the non-degree category if you have a separate one. It may seem to more traditional martial artists somewhat presumptuous to voice anticipation of the honour of a black belt.

If you have certification in several branches of martial arts, at a level below sensi level, you might want to list them under a category other than degrees, unless you have Black level in at least one of them. Then list the Black, with date awarded, and list the others as: "Also Orange Belt in Jujitsu and Senior Brown Belt in Aikido."

INDENTATION

Notice in this example that the data is not indented. This method can be used to de-emphasize dates (for example, if you wish to minimize attention to a break in chronology).

14. How about qualifications from non-English-language universities? Here you can give the exact name of the degree or qualification and the name of the university or school exactly as it appears on the official transcript (sometimes another third language such as Latin is used on the actual diploma), and put the translation in square brackets right after, like this:

> 1987 Filosofian maisperi: Helsingin Yliopisto [Master of Philosophy, Helsinki University]: Helsinki, Finland.

15. What if you have "a million" extra qualifications? Let's say you live near a university, and over the past twenty years you have taken an additional qualification course almost every year, all from the same university. Then you might want to prevent a lot of repetitive listing of a university's name, something like this:

> Additional Qualifications and Courses from Faculty of Education: York University: Toronto, Ontario:
> - Adult Education, 1990
> - Behaviour, 1989
> - Psychological Disorders in Children, 1988
> - Specific Learning Disabilities ,1987
> - Specialist: Primary Education, 1986

and so on. Instead of leaving any courses out just to make the list shorter, why not use a more condensed recording method like the above? Remember to keep them in inverse chronological order, unless you use sub-categories so you can give special emphasis to one by putting it at the top of a list, for example, "**Related Additional Qualifications**" and "**Other Additional Qualifications.**" Then you would maintain inverse chronology within each sub-category.

EXPERIENCE RELATED TO BOARD'S GOALS

This is another category which might help you. If there is mention made in the posting that the successful candidate will have experience relating to, or familiarity with, the board's or school's goals, that means they take them seriously. Why not put this category even before your category of **TEACHING EXPERIENCE** (or **OTHER TEACHING EXPERIENCE** if most of this category is teaching) to grab their attention and let them know you are on the same wavelength as they?

In this category could be included non-teaching work; for example, if one of the board's goals has to do with Social Issues, then work in a shelter, or as a social worker, or on community committees could well fit. This could position you ahead of the other candidates, and on the "inside track," so **don't wait for the reader to wade through and make the connections; point them out!**

"It is essential that the student acquire an understanding of and a lively feeling for values. He must acquire a vivid sense of the beautiful and the morally good. Otherwise he, with his specialized knowledge, more closely resembles a well-trained dog than a harmoniously developed person."
—Albert Einstein

TEACHING EXPERIENCE

1. If you are now newly certified, it is not necessary to list all your practice teaching sessions; you will be attaching copies of all the reports, both those from associate or mentoring teachers and the evaluations by faculty members. Instead you can simply state: "All Practice Teaching reports received to date are attached. Others will be forwarded as they become available."

   This is brief and clear; it also indicates openness. You are really putting yourself at a disadvantage if you don't send them all—even the bad ones. Otherwise the principal's mind runs amok trying to imagine how bad it was for you to hide it, and that's worse than any report.

   It also lets the readers know more are coming; more important, it gives you an opening to forward more information, a bit at a time, thus keeping your file near the top of the pile and your name familiar. Just attach a little note when you send the next bit asking if they would, please, attach it to your application. If they don't, there was not much lost by trying and, in most cases, they will!

STAY FRESH!

This is one way to keep your name familiar, especially when applying directly to a school rather than a central office.

2. If all your practice teaching has been done in the area where you are applying, you may wish to specify so. Most administrators prefer to talk to, or read an evaluation from, someone they know professionally. Then you could say in your cover letter as well as your résumé:

   > All School Assistance and Practice Teaching placements have been in Public Schools in the LaRonde and St. Boniface School Districts. Practice Teaching has included all Elementary and Junior High grades, together with two weeks of half-days with a Special Education Resource Teacher.

   or whatever is appropriate to your case. This gives a quick overview and stresses your school experience and support. If you are a supporter of religious schools, you will probably have done your practice teaching in those parochial schools; it will usually help to indicate that right up front. That will also help to hook their specific interest and get you more securely onto the "inside track!"

3. Private-school experience you can list like any other teaching experience, but you may want to draw attention to things that were different: how many schools teach the ancient and honourable sport of fencing?

   > 1963-66   Teaching Master: Albert College: Belleville, Ontario. Duties: Taught grade nine to eleven Latin, also fencing, and swimming. Coached rugby team to two Canada-Wide Boys' Private-School Championships: The Roynan Cup.

DO IT!

Just do whatever you believe will make your experience most relevant, interesting, varied and *easy to check*.

4. If you do not have much regular classroom teaching, but you have done a lot of "Occasional" or "Replacement" or "Supply" teaching (as it is variously known), you should definitely list that:

1979-81   Occasional Teacher: 57 days total, Grades 1, 2, 3, 5, 7, and Kindergarten, in schools of the Red Deer School District # 7: Alberta.

If you worked for two boards, you could specify: "27 days in Peel Board of Education schools and 32 days in Dufferin Board of Education schools, Grades 2 to 6, also Section 27 Behavioural Class," for example.

If you like, you can even list the schools in which you taught so they can check with the principals about how you did. If it is a very small school system where everybody knows everybody else, and **with permission of the teachers,** you can even list their names: "in Mrs. Smith's, Mr. Jones', and Ms. Harping's classrooms: West Side School," etc.

TEACHING-RELATED EXPERIENCE

Alternatively, if the title seems to fit better, you could call this section: **CHILD-RELATED EXPERIENCE** or **INSTRUCTION-RELATED EXPERIENCE** or **EDUCATION-RELATED EXPERIENCE**. Use whichever title encompasses exactly and specifically the types of experience being presented.

Sometimes we think that many our experiences aren't related to teaching, but is there a way in which they are?

1. Working as a Lunchroom or Study-Hall Supervisor could be included here: it is not "teaching" but it is "related" to what is done in schools, viz:

Sep 1988-Jun 1989. Lunchroom Supervisor: Our Lady of Seven Sorrows School: St. Leonard, New Brunswick.
Duties: Supervising the pupils in the lunchroom and outside on the playground after they finished eating.
Reason for leaving: end of school year.

If you have handled a lunchroom, you probably have a better-than-usual chance in a classroom!

2. Teaching done in some private schools and in institutions other than elementary or secondary schools might be classed as teaching or teaching-related, as teachers in these institutions are not always required to be provincially certified. (See APPENDIX 5.) Especially if this teaching was done before you were certified, I would urge caution and include it in **RELATED EXPERIENCE**, like this:

1978-81   Part-time Instructor: Loyalist College of Applied Arts and Technology: Belleville, Ontario.

Duties: Three consecutive years (evenings) taught Behaviour Modification Course (part of Developmental Services Worker Certificate program), while attending university during the day.

Reason for leaving: graduated: moved to Kingston, Ontario, to study for Bachelor of Education degree.

Your **Reason for leaving** could be simply that the course ended or that you moved away for some good reason or that you were too busy with your own studies or something similar.

REASON FOR LEAVING?

Do try always to give a *Reason for leaving:* as mentioned earlier, it limits their imagination!

3. If you worked as an Education Assistant you should list that as **TEACHING-RELATED** or **SCHOOL-RELATED** experience to avoid disputes between unions. Below is a good format:

1984-85 **Instructional Assistant**: Early Pioneers Memorial Secondary School: Portage-la-Prairie, Manitoba.
Duties:

- under direction of a teacher, developed a co-operative education work experience program for adolescents, Grades 9-12, who had learning disabilities and behavioural exceptionalities.
- also assisted in development of individual educational and behavioural programs.
- assisted with preparation of pupil documentation for program conferencing.

Different boards identify these positions by a variety of titles: Education Assistants, Educational Assistants, School Assistants, Teacher Assistants, and so on. As people in these positions fill a relatively new role in education, and as in most provinces there is no Ministry or Department of Education certification process, there is not yet any standardized title. Whatever term your board used, that is the one you should use on your C.V. If there is a possibility of misunderstanding, you can put in brackets what the board you are applying to calls it, like this:

1984-87 Classroom Support (**Instruction Assistant**): Holy Names of Jesus, Mary and Joseph Catholic School: St. Ignace, Nova Scotia.

Another similar example, but with more specific emphasis on behaviour development, could be worded as:

"To be prepared is half the victory."
—*Le Cervantes*

Oct 1987- Jun 1989 **Social Adjustment Aide**: MacDonald Memorial Public School: Charlottetown, Prince Edward Island.
Duties:
— Provided crisis intervention assistance: removed, calmed and returned to class students whose loss of control was disruptive to class.

- In co-operation with principal and teacher, developed and implemented a behavioural program to increase the students' self-control.
- Also provided tutoring for these students in math and reading. Met with them a minimum of twice per week.

Reason for leaving: enrolled in Faculty of Education.

4.   Volunteer work is good to include; often it can be teaching-related:

1986-87   **Volunteer Early Childhood Helper**: Southside Nursery School and Day Care: Hamilton, Ontario.
Duties: included assisting program manager, helping with daily needs of children, implementing some programs including circle time, supervising outside activities and directing children's play.

Sep 1984-Apr 85   **Volunteer Coach** (weekends) Boys' and Girls' Mixed Basketball: Cornwall YMCA: Cornwall, Ontario.

Especially relevant is volunteer work in a school:

1986-87   **School Volunteer**: St. Joseph the Traveller School: Come By Chance, Newfoundland.
Duties:
etc., etc.

5.   Tutoring counts!

1986   **Private Tutor**: Calculus. North Battleford, Saskatchewan.

Duties:
Worked with two students to help them pass Grade 10 math. They did.

(You might find the "They did." a bit flippant, or it may fit your sense of humour and hope it fits theirs. You decide.)

A slightly different format could be:

1985   **Mathematics Tutor**: Campbellford, British Columbia. Worked with learning disabled Grade 3 pupil for one term. She was then able to be promoted to Grade 4.

6.   Don't forget Sunday School.

1983-87 Sunday School Teacher: First Baptist Church: Fogo, Newfoundland.
Duties: Singing, activities and weekly lessons to children aged 4 to 6. This confirmed my desire to teach in the primary grades.

USING BLANK SPACE

The line of blank space here between the job title and the duties description draws attention to the "Duties". White space can be a very effective tool for emphasis.

USING INDENTS

An alternative format using no indentation.

44

or

1980-84   Catechist (Grade 1) (Canadian Catechism Program):
            St. Joseph's Parish: Bracebridge, Ontario.

It is not necessary to specify the church (there could be concerns about systemic discrimination) unless it would help because it was in a church related to the school system applied to—for example, if your work was in a Roman Catholic church and you are applying to a Roman Catholic separate school board (or, similarly, your work was in a parochial school of another religion, and that is the system to which you are applying). Then it will help.

7. Instructional work outside any school system can be "**TEACHING-RELATED**." If necessary, in parenthesis, explain briefly what you did:

1974-78   **Life Skills Instructor**: La Crèche Workshop: Mississauga, Ontario. (This workshop is part of the L'Arche International network founded by Jean Vanier. La Crèche includes two residences and a sheltered workshop for 15 intellectually handicapped adults.)

Duties:
— Responsible for the development and implementation of programs for skill-building in food preparation, janitorial maintenance, personal hygiene, physical fitness/awareness, crafts and hobbies.
— Also, in conjunction with the Social Education Instructor, I assisted in organizing outings to restaurants, shopping malls, and cultural events.
— I assisted the Vocational Instructor, as needed. Involved both **1:1 and small-group** work.**Teamwork** with the instructors and residence workers is an essential aspect of La Crèche and L'Arche philosophy.
— Participated actively in **Program Planning meetings, sign language classes, case conferences** with psychiatrists and social workers, **meetings with parents** and other family and community gatherings.
— Excellent experience. Gave me an appreciation of the difficulty some people have in learning, and the importance of carefully considered instructional techniques. Also deepened my appreciation of all people: exceptional and otherwise.
    Reason for leaving: accepted position more closely related to career goal of teaching.

NOTE: This is a very good *"Reason for leaving"* to use if you later became, for example, an Education Assistant on your way to becoming a teacher.

In a long one, such as above, it can be a good idea to **bold** format the key words such as "1:1 and small groups," "teamwork," "sign language," "meetings with parents," etc., to make them "jump out."

CONSISTENCY

Please remember: the different formats illustrated in this section may offer some variety from which you can select one you like. Whatever you choose, however, it is vitally important that you remain precisely consistent throughout.

Because it is not a school, many administrators, especially those with no special education background, will have little or no idea what it is or what you would have done: hence the extensive detail. As indicated in PART I, even if they are not interested, because your C.V. is well organized they will be able just to skip this section by reading the title "**Life Skills Instructor**" and then move on to the next section, so no harm is done. If they are interested, the detail will help them understand how clearly related to teaching it is, so it may very well help to put it all in (in its most abbreviated form). It is important to let them know what you actually did, rather than just giving the title because, as Jean Racine put it, "What they have done is of more interest than what they have been."

In a similar vein, but showing a different type of experience and how it relates:

1986-89 **Counsellor: Adult Resource Centre**: Rockyford, Alberta.

Duties:
– Planned, wrote and supervised local implementation of Substance Abuse Program now used as treatment model by fifty-three similar centres across Alberta.
– Individual and group therapy with families of drug-dependent children.
– Individual and group therapy with approximately 575 youth aged 9 to 18, mostly young offenders.
– Therapy with total of about 500 adults aged 19 to 29.
– Therapy with families of suicide victims, including the development of a twelve-step program of support.
– Still do part-time work there on weekends.

Reason for leaving: to obtain Bachelor of Education degree.

1984-86 **Assistant Vocational Instructor**: Sunburst Enterprises: Cambridge, Ontario.

Duties:
– Taught Mentally Handicapped adults in a sheltered workshop.
– Was involved in all aspects of the programming process: assessment, interpretation of the assessment, diagnosis of learner needs, setting priorities for instruction, program design, program implementation, learners' progress evaluation, program revision and the setting of new individual objectives.
– Of particular benefit to me was the training I received while there re: the instructional process technology of Dr. Cynthia Labelle.

The above examples help illustrate how working with developmentally and emotionally challenged persons can relate to the steps of a career in education.

8. Why not show your human, caring side; for example, in describing a job teaching a group of top ESL students in an international university exchange program, you could say under "Duties":

– Another component of the position was providing a range of support; these students were far from home, and in a strange environment: geographically, financially and culturally.

– Although these were probably the most highly motivated students it is possible to find, it was a very stimulating challenge to be constantly aware of their human and emotional needs.

– It gave me an understanding of the difficulty some learners can have with what we may assume are very simple skills or concepts.

FOR EMPHASIS

This is an example of how you can emphasize the number and variety of duties which were a part of an experience—by moving the first line of each separate point out to the margin and indenting the following lines within each point, you prevent them from all flowing together.

9. Teaching or Coaching fits under **TEACHING-RELATED**!

1981-82 **Assistant Coach**: McGill University Ski Team: McGill University, Montreal, Quebec.

Duties: – After skiing with the team 1978-80, skied and was assistant-coach for 1981-82.

– Responsible for **analyzing strategic weaknesses** in performance of team members, and **prescribing corrective measures**.

– Coordinated dry-land training for all team members.

– Also involved in **team fund-raising**, and **wrote Ski Column** in university newspaper.

You could also consider coaching back in high school as being "teaching-related":

1978-80 **President: Power-Lifting Club**: Thomas A. Stewart Secondary School: Peterborough, Ontario.

Duties: – Weight training instruction to members and guests; also coordinated seminars by weight training and fitness specialists.

– Good experience in development of coaching skills.

Reason for leaving: graduation.

FOR DETAIL

As in example 10, if the classes were combined adults and children you could say "to children and adults, aged 4 to 65." (Mention children first, unless you are applying for an adult education position.) If the classes were separate—children one night, and adults another night—you can say: "to children and to adults" to separate the groups, as in the example at the left.

10. Teaching for Parks Departments is certainly **Teaching-Related**:

Jan 1990 to present: **Aerobics Instructor**: Vaughn Township Recreation Department: Concord, Ontario.
Duties: teaching evening classes to adults and to children.

Such details are important as they answer potential questions before they arise. And, remember, all questions stimulate mild anxiety in the mind of the reader. Even if they are addressed later in the C.V., the nebulous feeling of doubt can linger!

ALTERNATE FORMAT

This example illustrates a reversal of the hanging indent usually found on resumes. Here the date is indented. This is a good style if you want to especially emphasize the experience and de-emphasize the dates, either because it was of a relatively short duration or you do not want to bring attention to a break in chronology.

Remember, though, if you choose this style, all entries on you C.V. must use the same format!

Another example of running sports training programs being related to teaching:

Summers 1980-88 **Canoeing and Kayaking Program Instructor**: YMCA: Kamloops, British Columbia.

Duties:
- **Developed skill and safety curriculum** for YMCA Camp small craft program, and **trained the Junior Leadership Assistants** to help with the program.
- **Taught** 175 children ages 6 through 16 using a variety of instructional techniques and strategies, on the water, on the beach, and in the classroom.

Reason for leaving: seasonal employment.

As above, teaching in sports camps, or in summer camps, is **TEACHING-RELATED**:

Jul-Aug 1984 Assistant Director of Hockey Opportunity Camp: Golden Valley, Saskatchewan.

Duties:
- Design, implement and evaluate outdoor activities for a different group of one hundred boys (aged 10 to 17) each week, for eight weeks. Instruction was given to groups of 15 at a time.
- This provided me with a very valuable opportunity to gain experience working with a large variety of active young people.

Reason for leaving: end of season and return to university.

When giving a "**Reason for leaving**," it helps if you try to relate it to: (a) your ultimate goal of teaching (e.g., "commence university studies," or to "accept position more closely related to teaching children," or "accept a helping-role position") or (b) directly to next job taken (e.g., "promoted," or "to accept position with more responsibility") or (c) a "family" reason (e.g., "moved closer to home," or "moved with family to Saskatoon"). Whatever the case, try to give a reason if at all possible without detracting from your application; don't let the paranoid principal's imagination get started. **Remember: we don't want even subconsciously to arouse any questions or indefinable anxieties, so do not give them cause to wonder. Make it easy for them to feel comfortable giving the interview, and the job, to you!**

11. It doesn't hurt to show that you see the relationship to teaching but also recognize the differences. You don't want to upset a pompous or self-important snob who over-values his "professional training" and certification:

Summers: 1985, 86 **Camp Counsellor**: YMCA Summer Camp: Thunder Bay, Ontario.

Duties: **Teaching** and supervising **swimming**, ball games, nature walks, etc.

This experience made me recognize the need for specific teacher training.

Reason for leaving: to enrol in university.

12. Work with Brownies, Guides, Cubs and Scouts is excellent:

> 1987-89   Assistant Tawny Owl: First Moncton Brownie
> Pack: Moncton, New Brunswick.
>
> Duties: Helped organize, assist with and supervise outings and activities for girls aged 6-8: skating, craft work, knotwork, weekend camp, and annual summer and winter camp-outs.
>
> Reason for leaving: move to St. John's so my two oldest children could attend Memorial University.

13. Did you work in the summer with exceptional kids?

> 1989 Summer. **Special Needs Leader**: Department of Leisure Services: Corporation of the Town of Climax, Saskatchewan.
>
> Duties: Worked with four children, aged 7 to 11, all severely intellectually and physically challenged. Adapted the summer playground program to meet their needs, both giving them a fun summer and ensuring that gains were not eroded over the holiday.
>
> Reason for leaving – return to school.

14. Some teaching-related activities may be more related to extra-curricular teaching, but you can sometimes help yourself by putting it in. It may show that you have organizational abilities:

> 1978-88 President's Designate: Racing Committee: Royal Halifax Waterski Club: Halifax, Nova Scotia.
>
> Duties: assisted in **organizing** and hosting the Nova Scotia Under-25 Waterski Championship.

Could this also be where you list your own extra-curricular experiences while you were in school? Could you pass along enthusiasm and skills to your students? You decide.

15. So you had a summer job working in a park. Here is an example that makes that experience come alive for a principal. Perhaps this describes your work:

> 1985-89 (May-Sep) **Interpretive Guide**: Lower Fort Garry National Historic Park: Selkirk, Manitoba.
>
> Duties included:
> - conducting, while dressed in period costume, guided tours for all age levels: children to senior citizens, especially "Discovery Tours" for **pre-school and elementary school children**.
> - oganizing and directing special events for the "Rendez-vous," including historic **games** for "voyageurs": the visiting **children**, to help nurture understanding of the early 1800's.
> - planning, **organizing and directing the Summer Volunteer Program** for young people aged 13 to 16, including evaluation of both the program and participants,

USING INDENTATION EFFECTIVELY

This specialized format of indenting the description of the duties but not the "Duties" title helps make the "Duties" heading stand out and draws attention to what you actually did.

You might want to use this format when what you did is more relevant than the title of the job.

Remember, though, if you use this format once, you have to use it all through the C.V. If it won't work for the other entries as well, then probably you should avoid it altogether.

WATCH THE TENSE

If you use the present tense for any experiences or events that are "past," use it in all entries. Otherwise, use the infinitive or past tense, consistently.

STYLE GUIDE

Even though the statement under "Duties" in number 17 is not a complete sentence, you can use the capital letter on the first word and a period at the end, as long as you are consistent throughout. Below, by contrast, lower-case letters are used at the beginning of each point.

Also notice the past and present tense difference between numbers 16 and 17.

Pick a style and stay with it.

researching and writing paper on "The History of Leisure," a **resource document to help pupils** understand the period.

– this experience confirmed my desire to pursue a career in teaching.

16. What school team would not like someone willing both to help organize the graduation and get in some good public relations at the same time?

Mar 1987 Graduation Representative and Chairperson of Recreation: Students' Organization: University of Manitoba: Winnipeg, Manitoba.

Duties:

Included co-ordination of all aspects of graduation ceremonies: planning program, dinner, dance, and the fundraising for The Children's Hospital of Manitoba as part of the graduation week celebrations.

17. A good mixer is important on staff, both for other staff and helping pupils through transitions:

Sep 1986 Coordinator: First Week Orientation for First-Year Students: University of British Columbia: Vancouver, British Columbia.
Duties: Organizing and preparing orientation workshops, social events and information to **facilitate transition of new students** into university life.

18. If you have a lot of experience which, again, is not really teaching but is related to the vast multitude of duties and responsibilities of an excellent teacher, you may want to list them under **TEACHING-RELATED EXPERIENCE** or **SCHOOL-RELATED EXPERIENCE**. You could, for example, as in a C.V. I once prepared for a client with extensive social work as a former member of a religious order, state:

Organizational Duties have included:
– production of musical and dramatic productions at high school, parish and community levels.
– co-ordination of workshop: "Role of the Laity in Light of Vatican II" for students and seminarians at Christ The King College: Lunenberg, Nova Scotia.
– executive member of Students' Council.
– founding member of Knights of Columbus Council 9615: Lunenberg, Nova Scotia.

Community Conscience Work has included:
– active member of St. Lawrence O'Brien Parish in Bancroft, Nova Scotia, serving as lector, usher, and choir member. Also **coordinate children's events** in the parish.

- work with Bancroft and Lunenberg Right to Life.
- involvement with Bancroft Third-World Development and Peace Organization.
- work with St. Francis Xavier Social Justice Group. Was chosen in May 1984 to participate in Latin America Exposure Tour to the Centres for International Dialogue and Development in Mexico, Nicaragua, and Honduras.

Community Service Work has included:

- volunteer work at Downtown Hospitality Centre (soup kitchen) in Calgary, Alberta.
- volunteering in the Palliative Care Unit, Eastside Hospital, Calgary, Alberta.
- fundraising: Canadian Cancer Society, Canadian Heart and Stroke Foundation, Canadian Liver Foundation, St. John Bosco Parish, Cornwall, Ontario.

GOOD CITIZEN

It is usually expected of applicants for a principal's position that their package will include a section on "Community Involvement." This can really add to your package, too! Could it demonstrate that you are a good corporate citizen with a broad range of abilities and interests?

19. Under a title such as **CHILD-RELATED EXPERIENCE** you could list being a foster parent, or even adoptive parent:

> May 1964 to present: Adoptive Parent: Ottawa Valley
>   Children's Aid Society: Eaganville, Ontario.
>
> Duties:
>
> This experience has developed in me an understanding of the special needs of adopted children and their parents.
>
> It has also helped me to recognize the value for children of a strong, organized and secure home; also the need for a teacher to be ready to give that extra for children without such.

20. Being a parent can help, especially in a very short résumé:

> 1983-84   Full-time mother caring for my son during his second and third year.
>
> Duties:
>
> - all the usual nurturing, disciplining, motivating, guiding responsibilities of a mother.
> - while not paid work, this has, I believe, made me much more receptive and understanding of children and their needs. I am grateful that I took this opportunity. In addition to the obvious family bonding, I have learned a great deal from it.

MORE ON STYLE

Here we have no capital letter beginning the individual points but we end each point with a period.

21. Work in a Social Service Agency could be child-related, whether with C.A.S., youth employment agencies, juvenile court, closed-custody group homes, drop-in centres, re-habilitation centres, etc. With these it has more impact if you try to specify how each relates to children or your desire to teach.

22. Involvement with Big Brothers or Big Sisters could be beneficial:

    > 1978-85   Big Sister: Soda Creek, British Columbia.
    > Duties: Volunteer work with one "Little Sister" for five years: socialized, took her to movies, on short trips, she had meals with my family, went for walks, skated, and so on. Basically tried to set positive role model and give this highly disturbed young girl from a difficult home a friend she could count on. Was also involved in a number of fundraising activities with the Big Sisters organization.
    >
    > Working with her, as well as my contacts and involvement with the other Little Sisters at group activities, confirmed my desire to be a teacher.
    >
    > –   Reason for leaving: Little Sister turned 16, and the demands of my job and family precluded my starting to work with another.

23. Under **SCHOOL-RELATED EXPERIENCE** you could list things like:

    > Sep 1984-Apr 86   School-related duties and involvement included:
    > Member of the Sociology Organization Committee of Guelph University.
    > Member of Sociology/Anthropology Department Committee: this committee oversees all academic issues in the Department.
    > Student representative to the Academic Planning Committee: this committee was responsible for planning future direction of the faculty of Sociology at Guelph University.
    > Student representative to the Undergraduate Appeals Committee: this committee evaluates the grade appeals made by undergraduate students at Guelph University.

    Let's face it: this is not really experience which will make you indispensable, but why not use whatever you have! Besides, perhaps your experience on the department academic committee and the appeals committee, for example, will help you be more understanding, or better at negotiations, resolving disputes, etc.

LEADERSHIP EXPERIENCE

This can be a real asset in a teacher's C.V. Under this title you could list self-help groups you coordinated, sports groups you trained or coached, special community events which you coordinated, committees you served on, or better yet, chaired. Boards of Directors on which you served and any executive positions, etc., etc., also fit here, anything which allowed you to practice skills which will help you with classroom management, or pupil motivation, or offering extra-curricular activities, or working with parent or community groups—the possibilities are almost endless! An example could be:

ABBREVIATIONS

Currently accepted format includes listing month names by a three-letter code (Jan, Feb, Mar, etc.) with no period after the short form. Note, however, that this means that June is Jun and July is Jul. For this reason, some purists go to four letters for June, July and Sept, but that leaves April as Apri and March as Marc! There is no reason not just to be straightforward and blend the formats: three letters where reasonable and four where three look like a spelling mistake!

1992-94 Vice-president and President: Essex County Red
Cross Society: Windsor, Ontario.
- Established agendas and chaired monthly and
annual meetings
- Appointed members to committees and sub-
committees
- Chair of Fund-Raising Committee
- Ex officio member of all other committees

That indicates you could quite capably organize school committees,
etc., etc.

OTHER EMPLOYMENT EXPERIENCE

1. Here you should list all other jobs you held. Be especially certain
not to leave out interesting ones, and make them seem related to
teaching if at all possible; e.g.:

Feb-May 1976   Cook and Deck Hand: "The Princess Diana"
(West Coast Herring boat): Kamloops, British Columbia.
Duties:
- Meal preparations and whatever else needed to be
done on board at the time.
- An enriching experience: a rare opportunity to
experience the West Coast's geographic beauty,
together with the cultural values of the native people.
- Truly memorable.
Reason for leaving: end of herring season.

Isn't that intriguing? Think what experiences you could share with
your classes! Would your lessons on coastal geography and the
relationship of aboriginal peoples to the land ever be the same again?

2. Here is one job that shows an organizational relationship:

1984-86   Yardman/Trainman: Canadian Pacific Railways:
Brandon, Manitoba.
Duties:
- Responsible for safe and efficient movement of rail
traffic.
- Helped me to develop an appreciation of
well-organized and planned activity and efficient
operation.
Reason for leaving: commence studies toward Manitoba
Teacher Certification.

3. This shows good inter-personal and group management skills:

1984-86 (summers) Tour bus operator: Downtown Sightseeing
Tours: Niagara- on-the-Lake, Ontario.
Duties:
- Drove bus, and provided live commentary on tours of
the historic and architecturally unique parts of the town.

A REMINDER

Note that in these examples,
like the ones before, some
descriptions under the "Duties"
subheading begin with double
hyphens, some start with
capital letters, some drop down
one or two lines and some do
not. This is done to illustrate
various styles.

Be *certain* on your C.V. that
you choose one style and
remain consistent!

MIND YOUR WORDS

Your "reason for leaving" can
significantly help to prevent,
and even preclude, any
misunderstandings or questions
in the reader's mind. You might,
however, do better in the
wording than the following
example taken from an
enlightening collection of really,
really bad C.V. comments:
"NOTE: Please don't
misconstrue my 14 jobs as 'job-
hopping.' I have never quit a
job."
—*Fortune Magazine,* 1997

- Responsible to make the trip safe, enjoyable and informative.
- Group management and inter-personal skills a requirement.

4. Working as a Nurse's Aid may not be related to teaching directly, but the "extra" activities might be:

Mar 1981-Aug 82 Nurse's Aid: Northern Lights Nursing Home: Flin Flon, Manitoba.

Duties:

- Assisted nurses with their duties.
- Also assisted Activities Coordinator with organizing and running crafts, art, exercises, games, dances, teas, etc., for the residents.
- This work has helped develop my ability to remain calm even in very stressful situations.

5. How about this relationship:

Mar 1986-Jul 86   Tourism Marketing Assistant: Peterborough, Ontario.

Duties:

- Contract work designing, issuing and analyzing research for Tourism Marketing Plan: Sociology Department of Trent University, with Kawartha Lakes Tourist Association.
- This was good preparation for evaluating pupil progress and designing and evaluating individual programs for exceptional pupils placed in out-of-school work experience programs.
- Later, when volunteering with the pupils from the Modified Basic class in Adam Scott Collegiate, I found this experience to have been helpful.

Note:—this is a very specific situation which allows such a co-relationship to be extrapolated, but it may illustrate that truly, almost all things in life are related and we are the sum total of our experiences. The extra effort at establishing the link is often worth it. This could, with this explanation, even possibly be moved into the **TEACHING-RELATED** category! With the careful thought which your C.V. deserves, many things are found to be relevant, but it is your responsibility to point out the connection, rather than wait for the administrator to guess at what it is. This was a large part of my duties when preparing C.V.'s professionally and was usually drawn out of a client by questioning during the first and second meetings.

A STRETCH

Don't say you were in charge of NASA if you really just worked in the cafeteria! If you go so far that you have to "haul back" when asked to elaborate, you run the risk of losing all credibility. I have seen this happen in an interview when, under questioning, the candidate was forced to admit that their description of their responsibilities had misled the committee. The damage was palpable; so don't understate, but be careful not to overstate too much either!

6. How is working in a beer store can be related to the teaching career?

1986-89 Clerk (Casual Part-time): Brewers' Retail: Niagara Falls, Ontario.

Duties:

Stock control, general maintenance and customer service.

> I enjoyed this work as I had opportunity to meet a lot of very different people.
>
> Also enjoyed the challenge of having customers (usually American tourists) who were angry about the Canadian prices, leave the store smiling.

or in a similar vein:

> 1984-86   Part-time Waitress: The Curiosity Shoppe: Kelowna, British Columbia.
>
> Duties: Assisted with meal preparation and serving, greeting guests, and responsible for their service and comfort.
>
> Taught me the direct correlation between especially considerate, professional service, and having satisfied customers.

Remember, "Everything can be a dead-end job if you're a dead-end guy" (Anthony Chaffo). By showing a connection as above, however, it suggests to a member of the hiring team that, if even in a part-time job you were especially good and careful with customers, you will probably not have problems with parents either. A good trait!

7. Perhaps you worked for the Ministry of the Solicitor General. Did you have to attend parole hearings? Under duties you could relate it to teaching by pointing out:

> Also required to attend Parole Hearings in a variety of Federal Penitentiaries. Working with people who had ended up in trouble with the law heightened my resolve to become a teacher and work with pupils to help them develop their potential in positive ways.

See, that shows your compassion and determination to help! Might you be more effective than most in a class of children with conduct disorders?

8. Even working in a department store is relative to the teacher's work. Under duties, you could say:

> –   This helped me to develop a caring and service-oriented attitude toward people.
> –   Good training in inter-personal relations.

or, if you worked in the warranty department:

> Gave me good experience in dealing with disappointed and concerned clients, working out satisfactory compromises and agreement.

REMEMBER

Hyphens or not: you must be consistent!

9. If there is just no way you can relate it to teaching, how about the ending of this one? You're not afraid of taking on a formidable task!

> Summer 1986   Student Labourer: Ministry of Transportation and Communication: Parry Sound, Ontario.
>
> Duties:
>
> Worked on crew maintaining concrete and steel bridges. Hard work, but I met the challenge.
>
> Reason for leaving: return to university.

10. This one isn't very closely related to teaching either, but the **Reason for leaving** is:

> 1984-86   Sales Assistant: Woods-Gunther Incorporated: Toronto, Ontario.
>
> Responsible for maintaining client and stock records, distributing information re: investment strategies, placing buy and sell orders. Used IBM on-line Security System.
>
> Reason for leaving: An exciting career opportunity, but I want to work with children.

Now isn't that a nice reason for leaving a job?

11. For one client who had left his religious vocation to make a lot of money, and then was leaving a very successful business to return to teaching in a religious university, I put:

> Reason for leaving: to get out of the (albeit financially rewarding) rat-race and to return to a career of lasting value.

Teaching may or may not be a similar calling, but this suggests the idea of moral conviction. You may want to be more traditional in the wording you choose. Instead of "rat race" you could say simply "to return to a career of lasting value." This person had sufficient accumulated competence that he could get away with the non-conventional cliché.

ON GUARD!

Use this format only under the conditions specified.

12. If you have had a lot of very different jobs which are unrelated to each other, and of short duration, and if the C.V. is already quite long, but if the items are somehow intriguing and thus might add a note of interest to the C.V., you might consider adding them thus:

> Other employment experience has included:
>   transport driver
>   assistant in funeral home
>   flower arranger
>   furniture salesperson

13. One of my former clients had never held a job, not even babysitting, nor had she won any awards, or really done anything! With a precisely worded and perfectly formatted C.V., however, she got a

teaching position! For her, after listing her degrees and saying that all her reports to date were attached and others would be sent and so on, I put:

> 1972 to present. Being the oldest daughter in a family of ten children, I have extensive experience in caring for, and, in an informal way, teaching, young children: siblings, nieces, nephews, cousins. This life experience has contributed profoundly to my decision to become a teacher.

Her C.V. then went directly to the **REFERENCES** section, and she had a nice one-page résumé. I can only assume that her competition had followed someone's advice and kept their C.V. to a single page and did not bother to list their relevant experiences, so she appeared to be their equal!

14. In a case like number 13, above, when you have very limited **EDUCATION-, SCHOOL-** or **CHILD-RELATED EXPERIENCE,** by putting the bit about "All Practice Teaching Reports received ... " under the general heading **EMPLOYMENT EXPERIENCE,** rather than in a separate category, you can avoid drawing attention to your limited involvement with learners.

PUBLICATIONS

1. For books published, just use a standard bibliographical format, without listing your name, e.g.:

    The Underwater Classroom: Bringing Shipwreck Archaeology to Inner-City Youths. Vancouver: Wayward and Jones, 1989.

2. If you co-authored it, list both your name and the other writer's in the order in which they appear on the book.

3. If you just edited it and or wrote an introduction, or whatever, then your name goes in square brackets following the description of what you did to it thus (pretend you are John Smith for these ones):

    Jacobson, Anna. *Selected Essays of A.L. Stonehouse.* [ed. and intro. John Smith]. Toronto: Rogerson Press, 1990.

4. If you translated a book:

    Lafrance, Michelle. *Lucian: Dialogues of the Dead and Related Fragments.* [trans. John Smith]. Indianapolis: Bob-Merritt, 1985.

    In this example it is not necessary to give the original title in Latin, because after the imaginary Michelle Lafrance edited and translated it into French, it was again translated by you and published in English.

5. If, however, you **wrote** it in a foreign language, you would give the title in that language, and the English equivalent in square brackets, thus:

    La Vie Sur la Flume: 1650-1700 [Life Along the St. Lawrence: 1650-1700]. Montreal: Lajamb et Legros, 1986.

6. If it was an article published in a journal or magazine, remember that the title goes in quotation marks:

    "Life Insurance Designed to Be Worn," *Outdoor Canada Magazine:* Toronto, June 1973, p. 26-29, 43-51.

"What greater or better gift can we offer the republic than to teach and instruct our youth?"
—*Cicero*

BIBLIOGRAPHIC STYLE

Note also that these examples are most appropriate for documentation of writing in the humanities fields: alternate formats (i.e., A.P.A.: see PART II) may be used more appropriately for mostly scientific publications. Whatever format you select, however, you need to be consistent!

or for a more scholarly tome:

"Attentional Deficit and Hyperactivity Disorder: the New Popular Diagnosis," *Journal of Applied Psychology*. vol XXXVI: July, 1991.

Note that if the magazine is published by a company of the same name as the magazine, the name need not be repeated; just the place and date of publication. This is illustrated in PART V.

Any library, especially one at a university, usually has a copy of a standard authority on bibliographical format.

If one of your works is published both in hard copy and on the internet, give both the traditional data and the URL, with the URL in angle brackets thus, <http://www.etc/>, to separate it from surrounding text and punctuation. (See MLA and APA examples in PART II.) A really excellent resource for accurate internet documentation is: *online! a reference guide to using internet sources* [sic], by Harnack and Kleppinger, (ISBN 0-312-15023-7).

PERSONAL INTEREST AND ABILITY AREAS

1. Don't forget golf. Although it is not usually a school-related activity, it is one which evokes images of "fellowship" and is an activity with which a lot of people identify.

2. Other possibilities include:
    - Theatre: acting, directing, choreography and costume design.
    - Soccer: was captain in high school: would be willing to coach or help with a team. Also refereed inter-school games.

3. If you have coached a great deal, it could perhaps go under **TEACHING-RELATED EXPERIENCE**. Then here under **PERSONAL INTEREST AND ABILITY AREAS** you could say:

    Badminton: very much enjoy coaching and would like to help with school teams.

4. Administrators are sometimes looking for someone who will just help without the presumed "status" of being coach. Perhaps there is a coach who retires in a year or so, whose long service precludes them being pre-empted by a young upstart. By offering to either coach or "help," you give the principal two options to integrate you smoothly into staff, while your listed experiences will attest to your ability and potential.

    Thus, either as: (a) part of your strategy, or (b) if you are not at a high enough level yourself to coach, you could say:

    Alpine Skiing: would be willing to help with a team.

    If you are functioning below that level of competence, you might say something like:

    Chess: recreational level only, but enthusiastic: would be willing to help with competitions or school teams.

TAKE HEED!

Don't ruffle the feathers of the coach!

"The worst evil of all is to leave the ranks of the living before one dies."
—*Seneca*

5. If you have expertise in a plethora of sports, you may want to break it into two sub-sections: "Sports," such as golf, swimming, biking, archery, and "Team Sports" such a volleyball, soccer, baseball, etc.

6. Is there something really unique or interesting in your experience? Why not describe it?

> **Swimming:** SCUBA diving and snorkelling: experience has included spear fishing off coast of Greece and in Black Sea. Also three weeks of volunteer work diving with Royal Ontario Museum team investigating and mapping remains of second century BCE ship-wreck off coast of Italy at Pompeii.

7. For crafts, etc., such as calligraphy, you could suggest:

> – would be interested in offering this as an elective.

Many schools are looking for those who can add variety to the skills-base of the staff, and who could help with the annual electives program. If this can help them break a tie in your favour, won't you be glad you put it in?

8. You should have worked it into your Cover Letter, and also somewhere closer to the first of your C.V., such as in one of your **EXPERIENCE** sections, if you have capabilities in I.T. This could also be the spot where you could fit in:

> **Information Technology Experience**:
> Reasonably competent in CorelDRAW III, IV and V, also with Microsoft Persuasion and Adobe Printshop.
> Reasonably competent in Windows environment, including Windows 98.

Please don't make the mistake, however, of leaving all mention of your I.T. capability until this late in your C.V. It is an unbelievably important skill to have right now! Let them know right near the first, and you could also add it here!

> "To condemn technology *in toto* is to forget gardens made green by desalinization of sea water, while to idealize technology is to forget Hiroshima."
> —*Stuart Chase*

9. If you say "Sign Language," don't forget to specify which one(s); e.g.: Amerind, Amslan, Bliss, Signing Exact English, etc.

10. Still nothing rings a bell? See if any of these are familiar: carpentry, plumbing, landscaping, did you build your own cottage, dock, canoe? Backpacking, cycling, poetry writing (have you been published?), jogging or sky diving may belong on your list. Or maybe you are "the best darn lumberjack since Paul Bunyan," but be careful with that one: like it or not, some people do not hold timber cutters in good favour these days.

> "It is not death that man should fear, but he should fear never beginning to live."
> —*Marcus Aurelius*

NOTES

PART IV

YOUR COVER LETTER: THEIR FIRST IMPRESSION

If the C.V. is your first introduction to a possible employer, the Cover Letter is the First First. This is your opportunity to make them want to read your résumé and you want it to make them want to meet you. If it does, you do! Let's look at a few desirable characteristics of a cover letter and work toward developing suitable ones for a variety of situations. This section will also address several things to avoid.

It is probably more important to avoid turning off a potential employer in the cover letter than it is to concentrate on wowing them. You are applying for a position in a profession where many administrators are politically responsive and will avoid at almost all cost hiring anyone who will upset the *status quo*. Canadian futurist Frank Ogden suggests that schools are the most traditional of all Canada's doomed Industrial Age institutions, now that the Information Age is past and the Communications Age is upon us! Regrettable as it may be, like almost all establishments which have been in existence for more than six months, schools—and their staff—too often seem interested mainly in their own preservation and that of the institution. You don't want to have the paranoid among them become even more cautious and concerned that you will, through unbridled enthusiasm, cause them additional concern. It's a balancing act: "enthused, but controlled and professional."

In a similar vein, it's not always easy to walk the line between aggressive and apologetic, but almost nobody is hired because they are objects of pity. If you remember that you have something really good to offer, but remember that you may be dealing with an anxious administrator who does not want his throne shaken, or his cage rattled, it may help you to be confidently assertive.

Make Yours Different

So how do we make your cover letter stand out above the rest? It needs to be brief. This really is not the time to tell them about everything you have already also stated on your C.V., but neither is it the time to miss mentioning **very briefly** your **exactly appropriate experience and training** (usually by referring to your C.V.—"as indicated on my Curriculum Vitae, attached, I have both training and extensive experience in ... "). Just let them know that the person described in detail on the next few pages does, indeed, have what they are looking for.

First, I suggest you get right to the point—"Please consider this application for the advertised position: Grade Two teacher at St. Philip the Worker Separate School." Don't be ashamed of applying and don't make them wonder why you are writing; you are looking for a job, not trying to sell junk bonds to them. Let them know right away.

KEEP IT SIMPLE

The guideline is simple: keep your cover letter short enough that they still have energy and interest enough to turn to your C.V., but be sure there is a "hook" in it that will grab the reader's attention and separate you from all the others.

INCREASE YOUR CHANCES

Be certain to make specific reference to the qualities and qualifications specified on the posting. Keeping their needs in mind is the foremost way to increase your chances!

You need to identify the position for which you are applying. Often boards advertise for several openings in the same newspaper, and this way they won't put your application into the wrong pile.

Especially if your C.V. is only a couple of pages (not very heavy) and if you have very little to highlight in your cover letter, you might want to tell them you are a qualified teacher and that you have attached your résumé. Believe me, they will get plenty of letters from unqualified people, with short résumés, who seem to apply to any job posting that interests them, and you don't want yours to end up in that pile.

Why are you a good candidate? Give them a very quick snippet of your experience with children, sort of like Mr. Jones did in the example following (see page 65). They need these facts supporting your claim of excellence: some even call it evidence! If you have really very little related experience, check PART III again; it may help you to think of something. (And, if you don't get this job, spend your time getting some related experience, even in non-paying or volunteer roles! You might even want to get yourself on their occasional teacher list, or even their classroom assistant replacement list, or their replacement lunchroom supervisor list; it all shows you are comfortable working with children and gives you experience and gets you known.)

OCR Scanning

NOTE: Electronic application is complex. For details, see APPENDIX 15.

You might want to give consideration to the fact that the wave of the future is electronic screening. If there are specific key words used in the posting (coordinating, leadership, experienced, responsible, active, assess, communicate, investigate, recommend, supervise, verify, collaborative, participative, goals, co-curricular, etc.), be certain to work them into your cover letter. Increasingly applications are scanned by an OCR (optical character recognition) program, and key word searches identify the applications which get on to the next step. Think about it; it's on the upswing.

You might even consider attaching a copy of your cover letter, C.V., and image files as corroborating documentation on disk. Then mention in your cover letter that it is there. This sets you apart and puts you in the I.T.-aware group! That's getting onto the "inside track!"

Some very large boards are going one step farther and requiring you to fill in a form which allows fewer than 200 characters (letters, numbers, spaces, etc.) in total. In this case, leave off dates, use short forms, and be certain to include the exact words used in the posting to describe your training or experience. Plan carefully. Do several drafts, just like in résumé writing. Every letter counts!

Highlight Your Information Technology Competence

"There has never been a statue erected to the memory of someone who let well enough alone."
—*Jules Ellinger*

Because I.T. is such a "saleable" skill right now, if this is indeed one of your attributes, you should be certain to specify early in the cover letter your abilities with Information Technology. It has become, since January 1995, almost a *Shibboleth* in its own right, dividing quickly and clearly between the winners and the others, and the best guess is that it will remain so for quite some time.

As stated elsewhere in this book, capability in I.T. is probably the single best asset you could posses these days when school systems are discovering that community and governmental expectations re: I.T. by very far exceed current staff conceptual, knowledge and skill levels. Most areas and individual schools are searching, almost feverishly, for someone who can lead them out of the woods with I.T. They need staff with both the conceptual skills around how I.T. can and should impact learning and teaching, and who can also quickly de-bug the systems when they break down. It is frustrating to have to wait for a technician to finally get around to tell someone on staff some simple command to get the computers running again! If you can show leadership and skills in this field, you have made it very easy for them to offer you a job and to defend and brag about their choice to other desperate administrators!

Be Specific

It is usually a good idea to mention something specific that you know about their school or board. Their most interesting topic of conversation is, after all, them! If you don't know anything about that school or board, except that it has an opening, you will not compare favourably with those who do have an "inside track" and a foot already in the door. Check them out and find out what is important to them. They want staff who believe in what they believe in. What are the "Goals" of that school and/or board. Do they have a "Mission Statement?" Can you, without being too obvious, work in a phrase or two of their "bizbuzz?" Research carefully; the investment of time will help put you on the "inside track" and your first cheque as a teacher will more than pay for the phone bill!

It will usually capture an administrator's interest if you provide a connection: if there is a mutual friend of theirs and yours who suggested you apply, or if you went to that school (and especially if you distinguished yourself in a positive way and the principal will remember you favourably), or your cousin did (and he's not in jail right now), or you went to a school in that board, or lived in that city, or have gone there on vacation regularly, or whatever. See another example in the letter at the end of this chapter.

If you can't approach them under the conditions above, try to give a reason for wanting to work for that board or school: their initiatives in implementing a particular direction or innovation, or their excellence in academics, or sports, or addressing special needs within the classroom setting, or in separate clinical settings, or their inclusiveness policy, or their direction in establishing strategic partnerships with community or business, or whatever—**Just be very specific in your comments.** Let them know that your philosophy or methods are consistent with theirs. If you don't know enough about that school or district to do so, then you really should find out as part of your preparation. If you not only have no knowledge of the area, but have not bothered to try to find out anything about the specific conditions or culture of the community, this will not reflect favourably and could well torpedo you at the interview stage.

Attachments and Openness

If you're a new teacher, it's worth mentioning in your cover letter that all your reports are included. That lets them know that you are not hiding anything. If you have taught in the exact grade or type of class listed, it sure helps to bring this to their attention. If you did practice teaching in their board, of course mention that, and identify the teacher and school by name! This is a great chance to grab their attention!

Then, as explained in detail below, you must formally give them the right to check your background. Then wrap it up and, especially if your

CHECK THE WEB

If their school or board (or city) has a web site, mention that you saw it on the 'net, and comment on it. They will be proud of it and pleased that you saw it. It will also, more importantly, reinforce your I.T. awareness!

CRIMINAL RECORD CHECKS

It is becoming increasingly common for boards to demand that candidates supply a copy of a Criminal Reference Check (CRC), either at the time of application or before being offered a position. These can be obtained, for a fee, from any police force. Expect the process to take two or three days. You will be expected to pay for this document (the board will not accept the charge for this) but if applying to several positions, you can make photocopies and just send the copy.

handwriting is like mine, type your name below your signature so they can read it easily, and in case this page somehow gets separated from the rest of your application. Now wasn't that easy, and you have a great, customized, cover letter! Of course one way to make it even better is to set it aside for a day or two (time permitting) and come back and read it again after it is no longer fresh in your mind. Have someone else read it aloud to you and listen to its tone. Then fine-tune it. It's the little things like that will help you stay on the "inside track."

Another little detail: if you use the term "résumé" instead of calling it a "Curriculum Vitae" or "C.V.," that's OK, but remember that it looks a little better if you spell the word as "résumé," not "resume." "Resume" is a verb meaning to return to, or begin again, as after an interruption. "Résumé" is a French word which has been assumed into English. While the use of the accents over the "e's" is becoming optional (especially over the first "e") it is still considered "more correct" to accent them.

If you are very experienced, your cover letter could resemble that of Mrs. Jefferson in PART V. If you are relatively new to the teaching profession, and have only limited related experience, your letter may resemble that of the phantom John Jones, next. **Remember: you don't have to have tons of experience to be a great teacher!**

Permission to Contact References

Somewhere in the letter, above your signature, you need to give written permission to contact the references you have listed. You should also give permission to contact any and all of your previous employers listed on the C.V. This relates to boards' need for information, set against legislation which limits checks to those authorized by the candidate. If you have one or two jobs in your history where things didn't work out, that is a risk you really must take; the other option is to risk alienating some boards.

Some boards have a policy that they simply will not interview candidates who will not allow complete background investigation. This is because there are some really troubled people out there, whose teaching certificate has not yet been revoked by their Minister of Education while all the legal appeals are being heard, and most boards believe that hiring one of them is too big a risk to take with children.

By freely and openly granting them legal permission to check you out, you are very effectively placing yourself among the desirable candidates. You are assuring yourself a place on the "inside track."

111 Seaview Crescent
Chilliwack, British Columbia
V7T 9W2

September 3, 1994

Mrs. Irene Bailey, Principal
H.M.S. Pinafore Public School
1955 Belaire Avenue
Abbotsford, British Columbia
V2L 7C7

Dear Mrs. Bailey:

Please consider this application for the advertised position: Teacher of Grade
Four at H.M.S. Pinafore Public School in Abbotsford.

As indicated on my attached résumé, I have just graduated from the B.Ed
program at Simon Fraser University. Prior to that I have been extensively
involved with children of Grade Four age in the Chilliwack Cub Scouts
and have taught a Sunday School class for children aged 9 to 12 for three
years.

Having visited Abbotsford many times, and having cousins who have gone
through your school system, and hearing of the innovative work your
board is doing with conduct disordered children, I am eager to join the
staff of School District 76. I am also eager to further my explorations of
the use of computers in addressing the needs of these as well as other
children. I believe my knowledge in both DOS-based and Windows-based
educational applications could also benefit the children in my class.

Attached please find all of my practice teaching reports, including one
reflecting my experience in a Grade Four class in Squamish. Please feel
free to contact those references identified on my attached curriculum vitae,
and any or all of my former employers or anyone else you feel may have
information which will assist you in your decision. Of course I would be
delighted if you would call any of the teachers in whose classroom I did
my practice teaching.

May I meet with you to discuss this?

Sincerely,

John Jones

John Jones

Now some options: let's consider a different type of letter, again from a relatively inexperienced teacher. If appropriate to your history, it could stress past employment experience and how it relates to teaching. (See PART III.) You could say: "As indicated on my attached résumé, I have extensive experience working with children of the Grade 4 age at ...," and give just a very few details about your work with kids.

If you are applying only for occasional work, say so in your letter, so it isn't put with the ones that are sent a polite "sorry but there are no full-time openings now" letter. You might even want to say that "I am aware of some of the implications of current fiscal restraint in education, and the limitations it has put on staffing, but want to keep myself current and ready for when a regular teaching opportunity arrives. Please consider me for work as a Replacement Teacher in your school. I would also be interested in offering to help as a volunteer. To whom could I speak about volunteering?" (See PART IX.) That question will entice all but the most hard-hearted of them to give you a call and set up a time to meet with them or someone on their staff. That will have you in the door; now parlay that into occasional work (see PART VIII), and then into a full-time contract! (See PART VII.)

If you have already been doing occasional teaching in some other schools, especially schools in the same area, you could send a letter such as this:

COVER LETTER

Sample 2

SALUTATIONS

A question that sometimes arises is: when applying to a female, and you don't know whether they prefer Mrs. McCarthy, Ms McCarthy, or Miss McCarthy, how does one word the salutation? It's easy. Accepted practice includes just not using any title; address it to "Dear Susan McCarthy" instead. This is also illustrated in the sample to Eleanor Thompson on the right.

Eleanor Thompson, Principal
J.M. Walters Senior School
157 McNulty Avenue
Saskatoon, Saskatchewan
R0F 2G8

Dear Eleanor Thompson:

Please consider this application for occasional teaching in your school. As indicated on my attached résumé, last year I did occasional teaching at MacNeil Memorial, Sprucedale, Southside and Martha Pratt Schools. I hope to broaden my horizons and experience base to include your school this year.

The success I experienced working with the children in these schools, as well as in my volunteer work with Girl Guides, has, I believe, helped me to start refining my techniques as a teacher. I hope to continue to learn and grow in my chosen profession.

Please feel free to contact administrators or staff at the above schools, or the references listed on my résumé, or anyone else you feel may be able to give you information about my attitude, performance or potential.

May I meet with you to discuss occasional teaching in your school?

Sincerely

etc.

Some Things to Avoid

Please let me take a moment and share a few of the more blatant samples from among my personal collection of really bad applications that I have received over the years. First, some of those in my file were obviously form letters, and the candidate in some cases made no effort to disguise the fact. In my personal collection of "gems" I have one where really thick globs of "white-out" were smeared on and the appropriate changes made by hand. Another has a blank line upon which the candidate had filled in with a pen the name of the position being sought: *"Teacher."* One is really, really bad handwriting scrawled in six cramped and uneven lines across the very top quarter of a page. I have one on a half sheet of paper torn from a three-ring binder. If they didn't care enough to take the time to prepare a cover letter, why did they believe the reader would care enough or take the time to interview them, I couldn't help wondering. But they do make interesting additions to my file.

One that I treasure has four spelling mistakes in the cover letter alone and includes a sentence ending with the rather interesting construction: "I would like to thank you for taking the time to consider me for any supply work that I may be given within your school, it greatly appreciated." Wow. She is also the first person I have ever seen shorten "Ontario" to "Onta."! What makes this application really qualify for my collection, however, is that in the "References" section of her C.V. (such as it is) the name of one of my colleagues is really grossly misspelled! (Admittedly, his name has lots of z's and k's—one of which is silent—but don't you think her version of it should have them, too?) When I mentioned it to her as I scanned her package, she blithely shrugged it off with "I always call him Phil." How careful an employee do you think she would be?

On another "gem" in my collection, the candidate had added a postscript: "Due to the cost of travelling to interviews, please do not call me unless you are really interested." Right away I saved him a lot of money by letting him stay at home. After all, it seemed to my suspicious little principal's mind, the question begged to be asked: why was everyone else who interviewed him, and then sent him home without the job, doing so? How many unsuccessful interviews had he travelled to before he ran out of money?

Another in my collection emphasizes his "bodyguard" training, and also states that he is "capable of killing and cooking most animals." Perhaps he was not sure if my school was located in the inner city core or really deep in the forest.

Hand-written or Typed?

Now, on a more positive note, one thing about cover letters that has changed over the years is that they are no longer expected to be hand-written. A few years ago this was used as a sort of a check to see that the applicant's writing was reasonably legible, or so I am told by older principals. (In years before that, the "district inspectors" even used to critique the handwriting the teacher used in the attendance register, but that is another story.) Instead, your letter should be typed (block or modified block format is simplest) on the same type of paper you used for your résumé. It just makes it easier to read, and a bit more "professional."

CAUTION

Some of these examples do make a quote of Publius Syrus come to mind: "It is a good thing to learn caution from the misfortunes of others."

"Hastiness and superficiality are the psychic diseases of the twentieth century."
—*Alexander Solzhenitsyn*

Getting Their Name Right

As was once pointed out in "New Yorker" magazine, had Descartes written "Cogito Eggo Sum (instead of "Cogito Ergo Sum") it could be—very loosely—translated to mean "I think, therefore I am a waffle." A single wrong letter can make a big difference! Please remember, it is a major turn-off to see your name spelled incorrectly. There is a big difference between Mrs. Hall and Mrs. Hell (or Brenda and Brendan, or Barlow and Barbara—I got that one once in response to an application letter I sent out many years ago). Our name is the one thing we hold most dear: the thing which represents our very essence. Witness the incredible impact of the names, simply inscribed, on the Vietnam Memorial in Washington D.C.! The price of a phone call to verify the spelling of a name or the exact title of their position is a good investment. Then get the postal code while you are at it and also the fax number.

To Fax or Not To Fax

While on the topic of fax numbers, if the application deadline is close, you might want to call and ask if you can fax them an application, indicating that a copy is also on the way in the mail. That way you meet the deadline, but if they are not interviewing for a while, your "good" copy on better paper can be substituted for the fax paper copy they have in the file. (Remember on a separate note in your "good" package to tell them that, with permission, you faxed a copy before the deadline, and ask them if they would be so kind to replace it with the "good copy.") Better, however, is just to get your final copy to them if you can in time by using a courier service. Please don't fax applications without getting prior permission. Some principals refuse to read them, apparently from what I can gather, on two grounds: (i) they are a curled-up nuisance, and (ii) it is seen by some as presumptuous; they feel you are forcing them to pay for the fax paper you use. (I didn't say principals always make sense!)

Wrapping It Up

You might consider not following the old line of "I would be pleased to meet with you for an interview at your convenience." Not only is it boring, it may also be presumptuous: who mentioned an interview? Secondly, of course if you are called for an interview you will go at their convenience! You know they are unlikely to re-schedule to fit your needs! So how about trying something just a bit different: "May I meet with you to discuss this?" says it all and (until too many people take this advice) is a bit different, perhaps refreshingly, without being radical.

Now this next bit may appear to be really pedantic, but your résumé should be paper clipped together (not stapled) and the cover letter set on top before it is placed into the envelope. I know that very often the first thing that happens is that the secretary opens the envelope, removes the clip and drives a staple through the whole thing, but the clip is "proper" and in case you run into someone who looks for that ...

Some people like to bind their C.V. or put it into an acetate folder with a plastic spine. My only comment on that is that it is really frustrating to try to stack a bunch of them—they are thicker at one side than the other, and are quite slippery, so they tend to make the whole pile fall repeatedly. After the fifth time of picking them all up, that plastic cover loses some of its appeal.

Now take a look at PART V, next, to see how the whole package together might look. In PART V there are samples from two different applicants. The first, from the imaginary Gerald Lavoie, represents what might be sent by a teacher new to the profession. Following that is an application from the mythological Mrs. Jefferson, a highly trained and extensively experienced teacher. If you are relatively new to the profession, do not be intimidated by hers: refer again to the cover letter, above, of the hypothetical novice teacher, Mr. Jones, and recognize that your C.V., like his—and that of Mr. Lavoie—will reflect the differences in qualifications and experience levels. Besides, with your relative inexperience can come a very sincere willingness to learn. Sometimes that is far more valuable!

"A rock pile ceases to be a rock pile the moment one single person contemplates it, bearing within them the image of a cathedral."

—*Antoine de Saint-Exupéry*

PART V

THE WHOLE PACKAGE TOGETHER

"There is something in each of us that resents restraints, repressions, and controls, but we forget that nothing left loose ever does anything creative. No horse gets anywhere until he is harnessed. No steam or gas ever drives anything until it is confined. No Niagara ever turned into light and power until it is tunneled. No life ever grows great until it is dedicated, focused, disciplined."

—*Harry Emerson Fosdick*

What follows are two sample résumés along with their accompanying introductory letters. The first example provided below is a résumé of a relatively inexperienced teacher; the second is a résumé where the teacher is highly experienced and qualified. These are intended as examples only. You should use them accordingly.

Your package needs to be perfect, or close to it. And, most importantly, the whole package needs to fit together in a disciplined way. You need to have controlled the data!

Headers and Footers: Some people suggest putting your name on every page in case the package gets separated and some of it is lost. It could, theoretically, be of use if the secretary or person who opened the envelope had not stapled the whole thing together—the chances of that oversight are, however, minimal. Neither of the examples that follows show this, as I have yet to hear of an instance where it was needed. Nevertheless, what a header, or better perhaps, a footer could do is add a bit of "difference" to your package and illustrate your comfort with word processing and page design. That could be a help. It could, also, in a really short C.V., help fill up the pages to make your package look just a bit more extensive. If you need this, go for it.

If you decide to use a header or a footer, I would suggest a divider line separating it from the text. The header or footer should consist of one line in small print, giving your name and the position applied for. That would be unobtrusive and look rather nice. You might even want to bold your name for effect.

For example, the following might appear at the bottom of your C.V. pages:

Natalie M. Cappabello: Application for Grade 3 position at St. Francis of Assisi School, Calgary, AB.

HINT

It really is worth it to spend the money to buy full-size envelopes so you don't have to fold your papers. Otherwise, they tend to come out of the envelope looking "pre-mangled."

Sample 1: A Relatively New Teacher

123 Counsel Drive
Saskatoon, Saskatchewan
S5J 2K9

June 19, 1998

Ms. Arlene Cangiano, Principal
Mission Valley School
548 Frances Avenue
Fort Garry, Saskatchewan
S7Y 6J6

Dear Ms. Cangiano:

Please consider this application for the position in your school: Teacher of the Grade 4/5 class.

The posting was passed on to me by Mr. Harold Albright, who taught me in Grade 7 and still teaches in your school system. As indicated on my attached résumé, I have recently received my certification as a teacher from the University of Regina and am eager to return home. I want to contribute to a school system which served me very well.

As also indicated on my résumé, I have recently taken additional training in psychological testing; I believe this could help me better to understand and accommodate exceptional learners in the class. I am also eager to get involved in your school's extra-curricular program. Might there be opportunity for me to help coach a team? As you can see, I have a reasonably successful background in team sports and am aware of your school's recent success in Track and Field.

I was able to gain some practical experience in a class for Grade 4 pupils during my teacher training. The report on my work in that class is attached, as are all other reports of my practice teaching. Perhaps my experience as a Teacher Associate in Brandon could also prove beneficial. I hope you will contact some of the teachers I worked with, and anyone else you think might help you in making your decision. Attached, also, please find a copy of a recent C.R.C. as required by your School Board.

May I meet with you to discuss what I might offer to your school and these pupils?

Yours very truly,

Gerald Lavoie

Gerald Lavoie

Sample 1 (cont'd)

RÉSUMÉ

Gerald Joseph Lavoie

123 Counsel Drive

Saskatoon, Saskatchewan S5J 2K9

Tel: (306) 345-8765

E-mail: glavoie@westnet.sk.ca

Personal Data

D.O.B.:	Jan 05, 1970	FAMILY:	2 children: grade 1 and Kindergarten
S.I. NUMBER:	778 876 234	LANGUAGES:	Fluent in English and French

INFORMATION TECHNOLOGY: Comfortable in Windows 98 and Windows 2000 environments

Education

1996   Course: Principles of Psychological Testing: University of Regina, Regina, Saskatchewan

1995   Degree: Bachelor of Education: University of Regina

1994   Degree: Bachelor of Science: Brandon University, Brandon, Manitoba

        Major: Psychology of Child Development

Teaching-Related Experience

1996 (May-Jun)   Volunteer assistant with Grade 5 class, Holy Family School, Regina, Saskatchewan.

Duties:

- Public speaking coach, helping pupils with speech preparation and presentation.
- also selected as district judge for High School category.

Reason for leaving: family move back to Saskatoon.

1994 -95   Reports of all supervised practice-teaching experience are attached, both those from Supervising Teachers and those from Faculty of Education Staff.

1992 -93   Teacher Associate: Msgr. Wingham Roman Catholic Elementary School, Brandon, Manitoba.

Duties:

- Assist teacher in Grade 6 class in modifying program for boy with Trisomy 21, and resultant developmental delay.
- Participated in decisions re: assessment, diagnosis, prescription and implementation of program.

Sample 1 (cont'd)

	– Also involved in parent conferences and conferences with other professionals working with this boy.
	Reason for leaving: enrol in final year of university prior to Education program.
1991(May-Jun)	Volunteer Assistant with Grade 7 class (evenings and weekends), St. Alban the Martyr School, Brandon, Manitoba.

Duties:
- assisting pupils with Science Fair projects.
- I was especially commended by the principal for my success in involving females in this program.

1989-92 Volunteer: Fort Garry Down Syndrome Association, Fort Garry, Sask.

Duties:
- respite care for families of children with Down Syndrome.
- fundraising coordinator, 1991.

Other Employment Experience

1987-90 Customer Service: McDonald's Restaurants, Fort Garry, Saskatchewan

1082 87 Sales Clerk: Seamless Books and Toys, Fort Garry, Saskatchewan

Awards and Honours

1992-94 Dean's List, Brandon University

1991-94 Member: A-Level Team, Men's Volleyball, Brandon University

1992-93 Selected to Manitoba All-Star Team, Men's Volleyball
1993 Champions: Western Canada Cup

1993 Member: A-Level Team, Men's Basketball, Brandon University

Special Interests

Team Sports: Volleyball, basketball (would like to coach or help with teams)

Individual Recreational Activities: Swimming, aerobics, weight-lifting, off-road biking, camping (would like to work with Outdoors Club or Aerobics Club)

Strategy Games: Chess, bridge (recreational level player, but eager to help chess club)

References

Coleen O'Brien, Principal
Holy Family School
349 5th Avenue
North Battleford, Saskatchewan
S9P 3Y4
(306) 934-8836   — school phone
(306) 934-8765   — fax
(306) 934-3656   — home phone

Mary Henney, Grade 6 Teacher
Msgr. Wingham Elementary School
8694 Lakota Drive East
Saskatoon, Saskatchewan
S3T 6H7
(306) 439-8587   — school phone
(306) 476-9876   — home phone

Dr. Albert Suzulah, Chair
Psychology Department
Brandon University
856 19th Street
Brandon, Manitoba
R7A 6A9
(306) 793-2376   — office phone
(306) 793-4583   — fax
(306) 793-8465   — home phone

Alison MacGregor, President
Fort Garry Down Syndrome Association
1252 March Drive
Fort Garry, Saskatchewan
S6T 7J4
(306) 493-8697   — office phone
(306) 493-8464   — fax
(306) 493-9742   — home phone

Sample 2: An Extensively Experienced Teacher

1234 Alderman Avenue
Orillia, Ontario
L3V 6J2

June 19, 1998

Mr. John Smithers
Superintendent of Human Resources
The Ottawa Board of Education
1259 Julienne Boulevard
Ottawa, Ontario
J1F 9RS

Dear Mr. Smithers:

Please consider this application for the advertised position: Teacher of the Behavioural Class at Waldo P. Quackenbush Memorial Junior School.

As indicated on my attached résumé, I hold both a Master's degree with concentration in behavioural psychology and the required additional qualifications to teach in a class of conduct disordered pupils. I also have a total of four years' experience in a similar class setting with my present board. As my references will attest, I have had a great deal of success and satisfaction in that sector of education.

For information regarding my past performance please feel free to contact the references listed on my C.V. or any of my other former employers or colleagues.

I am moving to the Ottawa area with my family because, having grown up in Ottawa, attended your board's schools, and since spent many summers vacationing there, we have all developed a deep appreciation for what your area offers. Also, my husband will be commencing doctoral studies at the University of Ottawa this fall, and those factors, coupled with what I have learned about your board's philosophy on addressing the needs of exceptional pupils, makes me very eager to join your staff.

May I meet with you to discuss this?

Yours very truly,

Georgette Jefferson

Georgette Jefferson (Mrs.)

Sample 2 (cont'd)

CURRICULUM VITAE

Anne Marie <u>Georgette</u> Jefferson

PERSONAL DATA

ADDRESS: 1234 Alderman Avenue
                           Orillia, Ontario L3V 6J2

E-MAIL: jefferson_g@leacock.scbe.edu.on.ca

TELEPHONE: (705) 286-1397   home
                           (705) 288-4556   school

FAMILY: Married, three children: 13, 11, 9.

HEALTH: Excellent

SCHOOL SUPPORT: Public

LANGUAGES: write and speak: English, French, Spanish;
                           speak: German, Esperanto, some Japanese and Slovak

S.I.NUMBER: 574 830 724

INFORMATION TECHNOLOGY: Competent in both DOS and Windows platforms,
                           some familiarity with Mac

D.O.B.:   55 04 19

EDUCATION

1993   Degree: Master of Arts (Behavioural Psychology): McGill University: Montreal, Quebec.

          – concentration: Behavioural Psychology.

          – thesis: The Consistency-deprived Child in the School.

1992   Certificate: Standard I First Aid: St John's Ambulance: Windsor, Ontario.

1990   Specialist Certificate: Special Education: Faculty of Education: Brock University: St. Catharines, Ontario.

          – option: Education of Gifted Children.

1989   Additional Qualification: Teaching the Conduct Disordered Child: Faculty of Education: Simon Fraser University: Vancouver, British Columbia.

1989   Degree: Master of Education (Counselling): School of Graduate Studies: University of Windsor: Windsor, Ontario.

1987   Certificate: Special Education: Core II: Faculty of Education: Queen's University: Kingston, Ontario.

          – option: Teaching the Trainable Child.

1987   Certificate: Primary Education Part II: Faculty of Education: Queen's University.

1986   Certificate: Primary Education Part I: Faculty of Education: University of Toronto: Toronto, Ontario.

1984   Education in the Intermediate Division: School of Education: Lakehead University, Thunder Bay, Ontario.

1983   Certificate: Special Education: Core I: Faculty of Education: Brock University.

Sample 2 (cont'd)

1980	Degree: Bachelor of Education: Faculty of Education: Nipissing University College: North Bay, Ontario.

     – certified to teach Primary and Junior Divisions.

     – option: Education of Native Canadians.

1979   Degree: Bachelor of Arts (Honours): University of Ottawa: Ottawa, Ontario.

     – Double major: Psychology and Philosophy.

1975   Honours Secondary School Graduation Diploma: Colonel Bye Memorial Secondary School: Ottawa, Ontario.

1974   Bronze Medallion: Red Cross Society: Toronto, Ontario.

TEACHING EXPERIENCE

1992-to present. Teacher of class for Conduct Disordered Pupils: Steven Leacock Memorial School: Orillia, Ontario.

Duties:

- teach group of eight full-time and six part-time integrated pupils: all have been formally identified as having severe-to-profound conduct disorder.
- develop and implement Special Education Plans.
- supervise therapy assistant.
- maximize integration opportunities by maintaining excellent working relationship with and support of colleagues in regular classes.
- liaise effectively with homes to optimize progress.

1991-to present. Part-time Off-Campus Instructor: Computers in the Classroom: Advanced Applications: Faculty of Education: University of Toronto.

1991-92   Primary Resource Teacher: Susan Alexandra Miller Public School: Windsor, Ontario.

Duties:

- provide assistance re: strategies and materials to teachers serving exceptional pupils.
- Chair: In-School Services Team.
- Volunteer Coordinator.
- reason for leaving: move with family to Orillia.

1987-88   Teacher: Grades One and Two: McAullay Street Elementary School: Leamington, Ontario.

Duties:

- pilot project, involving exceptional pupils mainstreamed into regular classes, as part of board's move toward more complete integration.
- member of System Advisory Committee on Special Education.
- member of Family of Schools Resource Committee.
- reason for leaving: studies toward degree: Master of Education.

Sample 2 (cont'd)

1985-87   Teacher: Grade Three: Wolf Valley Public School: Leamington, Ontario.
Duties:
- member of playground committee.
- coached Junior Boys' Basketball to city Championship.
- reason for leaving: to accept position combining Primary Education and working with Exceptional Children.

1983-85   Teacher: Junior Basic Class: King George V Public School: Leamington, Ontario.
Duties:
- taught class of pupils identified Exceptional, most of whom were multi-handicapped: intellectually and behaviourally.
- led Primary Choir to regional finals.
- helped coach Chess Club.
- member of In-School-Resource-Committee.
- reason for leaving: transfer to a position in Primary Division.

1980-83   Teacher: Grade Three: Robert Alcroft Elementary School: New Haven, Ontario.
Duties:
- taught Grade Three all subjects except Physical Education; also taught Grade Four music, on rotary system.
- helped coach Junior Girls Basketball, and Intermediate Cross-Country Skiing.
- led Primary Choir.
- staff representative on Parent-Teacher Association.
- reason for leaving: husband transferred.

TEACHING-RELATED EXPERIENCE

1982-89   Sunday School Teacher: New Haven and Leamington, Ontario.
Duties:
- taught variety of classes, children aged 4-15.
- 1987-89: Assistant Superintendent.
- reason for leaving: to finish graduate studies.

1973-79   Volunteer: Civic Hospital: Ottawa, Ontario.
Duties:
- in Paediatrics ward: read to and with children.
- organized art activities.
- assisted hospital Play Therapist.
- typed reports for staff Paediatric Psychiatrist.

1974-75   Assistant Swimming Instructor: Ottawa YMCA: Ottawa, Ontario.
Duties:
- assisted Aquatics Director in lessons for physically and intellectually handicapped children.
- coordinated Special Olympics Swim Competition: Ottawa 1975.

Sample 2 (cont'd)

OTHER EMPLOYMENT EXPERIENCE

1973-75   (weekends and summers) Clerk: Nepean Dry Cleaners: Nepean, Ontario.
           Duties:

- public relations.
- checking in orders, cash balance, training other part-time help.
- as this business practised equal opportunity, it gave me some experience working with exceptional people (developmentally handicapped) as fellow-employees. This helped to interest me in Special Education.

1970-72   (summers) Waitress: Lotus Flower Dining Emporium: Ottawa, Ontario.
           Duties:

- seating guests, taking orders, serving.
- occasionally helped kitchen staff.
- excellent experience in working with public.

AWARDS AND HONOURS

1990   David Ambrose Award for Outstanding Scholarly Contribution in an Academic Field of Study: University of Windsor: Windsor, Ontario.

1990   Dean Juvette Award for Student Leadership: University of Windsor.

1989   Teacher of the Year Award: Royal Canadian Legion, Branch 459, Leamington, Ontario.

1979   President's List (for academic excellence): University of Ottawa: Ottawa, Ontario.

1975   Ontario Scholar, and Valedictorian: Colonel By Memorial Secondary School: Ottawa, Ontario.

1973-75   Most Valuable Player: Girls' Basketball: Colonel By Memorial Secondary School.

PUBLICATIONS

"But This Is Where He Belongs." *OPSTF News*: Toronto: Ontario Public School Teachers' Federation, vol. 5, no.2 [October 1991], pp.27-31.

"Learning Disabled or Teaching Disabled: Myths, Anyone?" *MacLeans*: Toronto: 1989, pp. 7-11, 29-32.

Grandma and Me. [J. Doe, illust.] Toronto: Children's Press, 1988.

"The Zen of a Black Spruce Swamp." *Outdoor Canada Magazine*. Toronto: Canadian Sportsman Shows Press, July 1984, pp.17-19.

"What's Right About Your Child's School?" *Toronto Today*: Merriweather Press, July 1983, pp. 37-8.

PROFESSIONAL AFFILIATIONS

Council of Teachers of Exceptional Children: London, Ontario.

Curriculum Council of Ontario: Toronto, Ontario.

Outdoor Writers of Canada: Hamilton, Ontario.

United Brotherhood of Movie Projectionists: Montreal, Quebec.

Sample 2 (cont'd)

SPECIAL INTEREST AND ABILITY AREAS

Sports: Basketball, Volleyball, Swimming, Field Hockey.
           – would be willing to coach or help with teams.

Music: Play Piano and guitar (self-taught).
           – not talented, but pupils seem to appreciate it.

Chess: Average, but enthusiastic player.
           – Would be willing to help with a chess club.

Writing: Would like to start or help with Young Writers Club.

REFERENCES

Mr. Henry F. Smith, Special Services Coordinator
Middlesex Board of Education
1220 Hyde Park Road
Hyde Park, Ontario
N0M 5Y2
Office   (519) 288-4352, ext. 53
Fax   (519) 289-8634
Home   (519) 267-3479

Ms. Susan M. Chambers, Principal
Susan Miller Public School
257 Avery Road
Windsor, Ontario
L5T 2W1
Office   (519) 288-4894
Fax   (519) 288-9657
Home   (519) 245-7890
E-mail   schambers@miller.exbd.edu.on.ca

Mr. Tom Landry, Principal   (former principal: McAullay Street
Silverleah Senior School   Public School)
679 Leasman Drive
Chatham, Ontario
P7Y 6F4
Office   (519) 675-9854
Fax   (519) 677-3750
Home   (519) 622-7878

Dr. Melody Guschlak, Supervisor of Studies
Department of Graduate Studies
University of Windsor
1200 Espolade Avenue
Windsor, Ontario
K9J 6G6
Office   (519) 278-9834, ext.961
Fax   (519) 279-8531
Home   (519) 877-2589
E-mail   gusch@windsu.edu.on.ca

PART VI

THE INTERVIEW

Congratulations! This is your chance to present yourself "in person." The interview will usually be structured to elicit information about you in two major areas: (a) what you are like as a person and thus as an employee, and (b) what you can do for the pupils and school. The members of the committee will want to know what kind of person you are because, no matter how hard you may try to fit another mould, who you are determines what kind of teacher you are: how efficiently and diligently you work, how well you get along with others, your attitude toward the pupils, their parents, the school, the community, extra duties which you may be asked to fulfil, and the list goes on and on. Teaching is a human relations profession and who we are, and how well we teach, cannot easily be separated.

Experience and the research literature clearly indicate that when teachers consistently fail to excel, it is rarely because of a lack of basic technical skills or training; it is usually because of one of two other factors: a lack of motivation or the inability to get along with other people. (See APPENDIX 11: Personal and Professional Characteristics of Effective Teachers. This appendix gives additional guidance on how to present your characteristics, attitudes and skills.)

> "The man who makes no mistakes usually does not make anything."
> —*Edward John Phelps*

GETTING READY

When you are called to an interview, make whatever plans are necessary to free your mind of any extraneous worry while you are concentrating on getting the job.

Brush up on information you have gathered about that school or board or area. If you haven't done so already, you might check the internet to see if they have a home-page. Review your general answers to questions likely to come up related to the job advertised. See the sample questions below.

Then plan your method of transportation. Will you drive yourself, or will navigating in a strange city just give you extra stress? Will a friend drive you there? If they do, will you worry about keeping them waiting while you are inside? If you are like me, that is all you would need to be really distracted!

But no matter how well you could do in the interview, you have to be there, physically. Remember the power of punctuality. Plan to arrive at the building well ahead of time. This will avoid the classic problems of slow traffic, missed busses, delayed flights and taxis (or your own map skills) which take you to the wrong part of town. (I remember once interviewing a candidate who arrived, very flustered, twenty minutes late. Despite our best effort, it was difficult for everyone involved.) Best of all, find the building the day before.

> "All the world's a stage,
> And all the men and women merely players;
> They have their exits and their entrances,
> And one man in his time plays many parts."
> —*As You Like It,* Act 2, Scene 7

JOB FAIRS

The "Job Fair" scene is very similar to any other interview situation: there are the same expectations for dress, conduct, preparedness, knowledge of the Board or school and knowledge of what you want to say about what you have to offer, prior scouting, note-taking and follow-up of contacts (get business cards for spelling and addresses). There are, however, a few extras to consider. Don't allow yourself to be lulled into excessively casual behaviour with the recruiters; it is still seriously professional, even though it seems like a midway. This is not the time to carry food around from stall to stall. You will need to bring several copies of your résumé, rather than just one, and a case to carry all the handouts you will pick up. Go first to the displays of those Boards in which you are most interested; budget your time, but meet with representatives of as many opportunities as you can—it is an opportunity that will be gone tomorrow. You might also want to attend any free seminars which are part of the Fair. If they seem irrelevant, you can always leave and continue with your "direct contacts." The job fair is a unique opportunity for you to do some "comparison shopping."

Then it usually works well if you arrive about fifteen to twenty minutes before your interview. More than this tends to be too much. Less than fifteen minutes can call into question your ability to arrive places (like the classroom) ahead of time. You also want to allow time in case there is advance information for you to consider, or in case they give you the questions ahead of time. Also, although rare, sometimes the interview before you will run short and the committee members are pleased that you are there so they don't have to waste time waiting. Again, you are making it easy for them to feel good about you and about giving you the job.

SURVIVING THE INTERVIEW

There is a cornucopia of books on the self-help market dealing with surviving the interview process. Some are excellent, others are less reliable in the specific field of education. In some, you will find advice which is directly opposed to success in this profession. You should read one, or several (depending upon how confused you wish to become). See PART IX for suggested further readings.

The following are a **very few**, **very basic** suggestions. There is no attempt here to be all-encompassing regarding the interview or to deal either extensively with the topic or to address all possible contingencies. So here are a few ideas, not usually addressed in other books, that may help; they come from my experience, both interviewing, and being interviewed!

Some General Tips

This is your time to make your best impression. This is the time to be calm and relaxed. As Mark Twain pointed out, "Courage is resistance to fear, mastery of fear—not absence of fear." Take comfort, too, in the fact that it is not necessary to perform flawlessly in an interview. I know one Personnel Director in a very large educational institution who, after he has interviewed someone who has done unusually well in the interrogation, always asks himself where they got all the practice!

Do your best. Another force in your favour is that many administrators realize, as Samuel Feinberg so eloquently pointed out, "Many top businessmen would be out of a job if they had to take personality and capability tests given applicants for employment or promotion in their own companies." Just do the best you can; except for you and me there are very few perfect people out there!

Read all documentation. You may be given a list of the criteria for the position while you wait, or a list of those on the interview panel or other documentation; some board policies require interview committees to provide this. If you are given anything, be sure to read it right away. If you are not, however, don't ask.

Would you like a coffee? Sometimes you will be offered coffee after you go into the interview room. Some experts advise against accepting it because of the danger of spillage, but that applies more in an interview where you would be moving and demonstrating artwork or technical drawings. That does not apply to our profession except in specific circumstances. So if everyone else has a cup (and theirs are not empty) you might want to take it and thank them even if you don't usually drink it. (If you ask for only half a cup and double milk it tastes less terrible, and you only have to hold it occasionally; you don't actually have to drink it. It gives you something to do with your hands, though, and builds a feeling in the room of collegial togetherness.) What you are trying to do here is avoid appearing to reject their hospitality. The danger of asking for water instead is that it may require them to go to extra effort to fetch you some and, once you have made the request, they will feel obligated to follow through. The exception would be if no one else has a cup in front of them: then consider declining with thanks. The key is that with these little things you want to be unobtrusive and "be like them." Francois Voltaire said, "To succeed in chaining the crowd you must seem to wear the same fetters." With this silly little stuff, you can only lose by being different!

Don't smoke. Even if they ask you if you would like to, don't. Most schools in Canada are now recognized and posted as non-smoking areas, and there may be just one person on the committee who detests second-hand smoke. Imagine if their vote is the one which breaks a tie.

Take samples of units you have prepared. They can illustrate the type of work you do and how you approach your teaching. Having them with you can also make you feel just a bit more confident. It's usually best if you don't pull them (or your letters of commendation) out of your file folder until they are needed, however. If some on the committee are insecure, you really don't want to be seen as sitting behind a spread of papers, intimidating them.

Have a pen in a pocket or in top of your case. You may be invited to jot notes. Also have your list of questions ready to ask when invited to do so. Consider, as well, taking a duplicate copy of your application package in case you (or they) want to refer to something.

Be polite and observe formalities. You will be shown where to sit. General rules of politeness apply, of course: it's not usually "correct" to sit until after they do; shake hands if they initiate it (but don't appear "pushy"). Make eye contact with everyone. You don't have to glue your eyes to theirs until they blink first, like one candidate I remember, but look them in the eye and make definite contact. Usually a few opening comments will be made after the introductions, usually on the topic of weather. (It is one of the few "safe" topics free of gender, racial, or religious bias—unless of course God is blamed for it.) It is important to read the formality level as soon as possible and comply. There is a real risk in assuming that the interview is less formal than some on the team might want it to be. Join in any humour which arises, of course, unless it is in bad taste; then, if it is, it helps to look directly at someone else who is also not smiling right then and add some detail to your last answer while the group gets past the sensitive spot.

RELATING TO FIVE DISTINCT TYPES OF COMMITTEE CHAIRPERSONS

In determining how to relate to the committee members (and especially the chair), it might help to remember that there are, more or less, five types of interviewers. They could be called: the "**sergeant-major**," the "**nice-guy**," the "**contemplative**," and the two ineffectual types—the "**mouseburger**" and the "**super-hero**."

The *sergeant-major* will want to get on with the interview. They may ask a very few supplementary questions but will always be in a hurry to get on with the next "official" question. They will have little time for humour and no tolerance for getting off-track. With this type, it is usually best to be serious, logical, linear and direct. Their questions will be mostly those which require a reference to factual information or clearly-stated opinion.

"It is no exaggeration to say that the undecideds could go one way or another."
—*George Bush*, former US President

"My dad had taught me there are times in life when you just don't want to miss a good chance to shut up. This was clearly one of those times."
—*Dr. Phil McGraw*

83

"You will find it a distinct advantage if you know and look as if you know what you are doing."
—*IRS Training Manual for Tax Auditors*

The "**nice-guy**" will want you to like them. Douglas McGregor referred to this as the "country-club" management style. Remember to smile and nod affirmation to his/her questions or comments. They want to know they can get along with you; that you will fit the personality mould that they see for the ideal teacher—someone who is loyal, open, friendly, "on-side" and trustworthy. They want to be comfortable with you. They usually don't want anyone with too many new ideas. Their questions will tend toward relationship issues and questions of group- or team-work. They want you to agree with them. "Pleasant" and "comfortable" are the watch-words.

The "**contemplative**" will ask mostly process-oriented questions. They like to go "perhapsing" around on all topics, chatting and reflecting about the latest fad for the salvation of education. They see, and want you to see, the big picture, the ideal, "how it could be." The one risk here: don't let them know if you don't believe in it! Your research ahead of time on the extent to which the chairperson personally verbalizes commitment to the Board or School Goals will let you know how often you need to refer to them. If they talk about them constantly, you really need to let them know that you are right on-side with them. This type, too, will tend to be very team-oriented and consensus is often, though not always, a key component. They tend to be "feelings-oriented," and time tends to have very little meaning to them. Don't rush them; it's up to them to keep the interview moving along.

The final two types are both ineffectual, though for very different reasons. They could be divided into their sub-categories based upon their degree of self-knowledge: the "**mouseburgers**" are aware of their short-comings, are not quite sure what to do and are afraid someone will see their mask slip—but may present some symptoms of paranoia—and the "**super-heroes**" are those who know they are really God's gift to educational administration, and can't understand why the rest of the world won't listen and realize this. These, latter, are completely filled with confidence.

Both of these last types will want you to be very respectful and subservient, the first because they are intimidated by everything, including you, and the latter because they just know they deserve your humble adoration. Mouseburger ineffectuals will appreciate it when you bail them out by giving the process some direction. In their interviews there may be a noticeable lack of crispness and/or control. They may well tend to ramble and, in extreme cases, even whine. There will possibly be little observable theme to his/her questions. They may mumble a bit, they may even seem to avoid eye contact, and you may find uncomfortable pauses.

Don't hesitate to take more control in these interviews, but if they interrupt you, stop immediately and go on with their topic or direction. Try very hard not to say or do anything to threaten or intimidate or upset them; they are uncomfortable enough.

"My grandfather once told me that there were two kinds of people: those who do the work and those who take the credit. He told me to try to be in the first group; there was much less competition."
—*Indira Gandhi*

Super-hero ineffectuals will often reflect the behaviour of the sergeant-major in an interview, in that their questions will be sharp and staccato. The difference is that they may have very little time to listen to your responses and may even do most of the talking. They will glow when you agree with them, as long as your agreement takes nothing from their right to radiate wisdom. Be very respectful and in awe of them: let them feel good about letting you know how good they are!

Arguably, the best interviewers combine a bit of each of the first three. It will help you a great deal if you are aware of each of these archetypes.

Even better, if you know administrators who tend to fit into these various types, ask each of them for a "trial" interview "just for practice." They will usually be flattered, and it will help you refine your repertoire of skills.

Although there are exceptions (and you will definitely need to modify your responses to meet the needs of whoever is asking the question at the time), you will usually find that in a committee there is one predominant paradigm. The committee is usually hand-selected by the chair, and thus the members reflect his/her own dominant behavioural type. This is especially true when the administrator in charge is not particularly skilled in interviewing and is feeling less than confident. It is most especially true when they are overcompensating for their lack of experience or expertise and want no-one to disagree with, or challenge, them in the decision (Mouseburgers).

ANSWERING QUESTIONS

There are a few general guidelines to consider when formulating your responses to questions right in the interview.

First, there may be times when you do not understand the question. It's OK to ask for clarification or to have the question repeated. This will help you to answer the question being asked instead of one you might think was asked. Remember, "People, like boats, toot loudest when they're in a fog." Frequently, nebulous questions are asked intentionally to see how you deal with ambiguity or stress. Will you be astute enough to obtain clarification on the job? Also, asking for clarification can give you thinking time or help you subtly control the tempo of the interview.

Second, it's easy to become caught up in answering the wrong question. If you are asked how you feel about corporal punishment, it might not mean they want to discuss human and individual rights and the criminal code and protecting society and capital punishment. They may just be asking how you develop self-discipline in your pupils! Asking them to re-state the question can help focus on what they are really looking for.

Third, answer all questions thoroughly. Consider for a moment these two contrasting true-life situations:

(a) When being interviewed for a position, the candidate was unaware that the large committee was composed of several trustees and community members of an advisory committee, in addition to only two professional educators. At this time the Ontario government had just re-organized its various Departments into Ministries, and the Department of Education had thus just become the Ministry of Education. In response to a question, the applicant had made several references to the Ministry of Education and was faced by blank stares from several committee members who eventually asked what "the Ministry of Education" was. Instead of registering shock or amusement, the candidate very politely and simply explained the recent government changes; then the interview went on with no one's feelings hurt. She got the job!

(b) Contrast that with another true-life situation where a candidate who was eminently well qualified was being interviewed for a specialty subject position that he had wanted for a long time. He was, in fact, better qualified and much more experienced than any other person in the district for that position. When he was not selected, in an attempt to see what had misfired, I asked him how the interview had gone. Within a few moments, I was not surprised he had been unsuccessful; his response was that the interview was "farcical." The questions were far beneath his level of

BE POSITIVE

Above all else, no matter what the type of interviewers you meet, think positively and be positive. You have something unique and valuable to offer. It's OK to tell yourself now and again that you are doing well.

"Never worry about the bullet with your name on it. Instead, worry about the shrapnel addressed: 'To Occupant'."

—*Murphy's 10th Military Law*

OVERLAPPING QUESTIONS

Sometimes there will seem to be an overlap in the questions asked. This is usually because your answer to a previous question sort of expanded to answer the next one. Sometimes a committee will see that and skip it; but, if they ask, they expect you to answer anyway by adding to your previous response.

knowledge and competence and he intimated to me that the questions had been beneath his dignity as well. Why, he wanted to know, was someone of his professional stature not asked questions of a more challenging level? You can guess what happened. The committee didn't like having their questions treated with contempt. Despite his having excellent qualifications and years of directly related experience, another candidate was selected, and he was left to languish in a position he did not like and could not leave. He eventually took early retirement, as it was evident he was going nowhere. His attitude got in the way of his progress!

Fourth, don't allow yourself to be manoeuvred into a negative mode. If they ask whether you had difficulty finding their place, don't mention the traffic or bus transfers or obscure and unmarked country roads. They live there, and probably even like the area.

Again, be positive! "Life is a grindstone. Whether it grinds you down or polishes you up depends on what you're made of" (Jacob M. Braude). I know of one candidate who drove seven hours to get to an interview and was really exhausted when she got there. She had planned well and had about an hour to relax, freshen up and change her clothes, but was feeling far from prime. (Have you ever tried to change your clothes in the washroom at a gas station? She probably should have driven up even earlier in the day and had a rest in a hotel room, but her budget was tight, so she did what she could. What would have happened if she had had car trouble though. She had not considered that!) The first thing she was asked upon entering the room for the interview was whether the trip had seemed long and if she was exhausted. I am certain her comments on how beautiful the day was, so sunny and warm with the first leaves of spring bursting from the branches, instead of mentioning fatigue, gave the committee the image of an upbeat positive person, rather than one who wanted pity for being tired. After all, the committee members were tired, too; the interview was after their long day of work. They wanted to have their spirits picked up, not dragged down further. She got the job!

Fifth, expect some questions to induce stress. It is usually planned that way; in our profession, stress is never far away. The ability to deal with it can be the difference between successful and unsuccessful teachers.

Sixth, as indicated above, you should expect to be interviewed by a committee. When answering a question, while it is a good idea to glance around at the others (thus drawing them into the conversation), direct most of your attention to the person who asked that particular question. Frequently, the various members of the interview committee will take turns, but don't make the mistake of addressing all your comments to the person you believe is in charge. Even if you have successfully identified the "main person" (the one responsible for making the final decision), don't leave the others out or they will not support you. Most administrators and teachers prefer team players rather than those who attempt to "play up to the boss." Besides, you may have guessed wrong about who is in control. Excessive attention to "the boss" can also make her/him uncomfortable.

Seventh, don't let them see you sweat. About the "conversation" aspects of an interview: usually an attempt is made to pretend that this very formalized activity is really a pleasant conversation among a group of professionals. Try to keep your doubts to yourself. If you let them know how stressful you are finding it, that can really create discomfort in the others. I think back to one candidate who kept saying she was nervous. Her tension eventually spread to us, and we couldn't wait until the interview was over!

"A fool shows his annoyance at once, but a prudent person overlooks an insult."

—*Proverbs of Solomon*

Eighth, be as direct and open as you can. There can be a strong temptation to "add flavour," but don't let it become too close to inaccuracy. If it is an inaccuracy about qualifications, it is reason for dismissal. If it is one of philosophy, you will soon be seen to be out of sync. This is your chance to let them know what you will add to their school, but be careful not to go too far.

Finally, walk the talk. You won't add much to your candidacy by telling them how enthusiastic, sincere, tactful, professional, courteous, eager and motivated you are. Instead, show them. You can do this by being well prepared and by your attitude and answers. That will keep you on the "inside track!"

Dealing with Inappropriate or Illegal Questions

You may sometimes be asked questions which you know are not acceptable: questions about your height, weight, marital status, birth name, dependants, information about a spouse or companion, willingness to transfer, second income, insurance beneficiaries, relationship of a person to be notified in case of emergency, plans to have children, child-care arrangements, ethnic origin, age, non-criminal offences, etc.

You are quite within your rights to refuse to answer these questions and to indicate that you are reporting the whole committee to the Human Rights Commission. It is also damning to do so. Instead, why not consider deflecting the question: if it is about your age, you can simply say "I have found maturity to be a definite benefit," or "I have found that my youthful enthusiasm and willingness to learn is a benefit." If they press about your ability to do the job, you can say something like, "I have no shortage of energy; in fact, I find that I am learning how to work smarter each day." If it is about child-care, you could just say: "I have excellent arrangements. My family will not detract in any way from my ability to do this job very well." If it is about your religion or creed, and you are not applying to a parochial school, you can simply say that you are very respectful of all spiritualities and lifestyles, and that yours will not impinge upon your ability to be an excellent teacher. (They can, however, ask if there is anything which will prevent you from teaching the regular school calendar. If your creed necessitates special holidays, contact other teachers of your faith and find out how they handle it. In most cases, you will not have a problem. In the interview, you could simply say that you understand you will have to take (2 or 3) days off without pay, but you will be careful to make arrangements so that the program continues effectively.) If it is about your physical size, you can make a joke: "I find I am tall enough so that my head and my feet are both firmly attached to the rest of me," or you could say, "I find I don't blow around in the wind." If they ask about offences such as speeding tickets, this might again be the time for humour: "I don't do a lot of driving in the classroom" said with a grin can get past the hurdle. They will take the hint. In each case, the key is to answer pleasantly so they can't be diverted into thinking it was you who made the interview go off track. Like Henry Louis Mencken's quote about democracy, an interview "is the art and science of running the circus from the monkey cage."

Yes, it would be nice to confront them, but diplomacy can win in the situation, and your best revenge can be success! Give them time; they'll get caught!

KEEP COOL

The interview will be a very stressful situation, of course, so don't lose your cool or your concentration. Think of this comment by a champion racing driver:

"It is necessary to relax your muscles when you can. Relaxing your brain is fatal."

—*Stirling Moss*

"No one can take advantage of you unless you let them."
—*Ann Landers*

"I am a great believer in luck and I find that the harder I work the more I have of it."
—*Stephen Leacock*

"It ain't over 'till it's over."
—*Yogi Berra*

IT'S NOT SO BAD

Going to an interview is not really too bad, at least not when stacked up against other activities such as those described in the *Tibetan Book of the Dead:*

"Then the Lord of Death will place around thy neck a rope and drag thee along; he will cut off thy head, tear out thy heart, pull out thy intestines, lick up thy brain, drink thy blood, eat thy flesh and gnaw thy bones; but thou wilt be incapable of dying. Even when thy body is hacked to pieces, it will revive again. The repeated hacking will cause intense pain and torture."

See! Compared to this, the interview is not bad at all!

WHEN YOU KNOW YOU WON'T GET THE JOB

Now a "sticky situation": what should you do if you are called to an interview and you suspect, or absolutely know, that the position has been promised to someone else, or that those in charge fully intend to award it to someone in particular and have decided this in advance of the interviews? Let us first deal with the suspicion scenario: if you don't know, there might still be a chance for you, so go and do the very best you can. Secondly, if you do really know on excellent authority that the competition is already "sewn up," without getting into discussions of the professionalism or wisdom of either the administrators involved or those who spread the information, the worst that could happen is that you are getting real experience in being interviewed, and that can't hurt. More importantly, however, you have a chance to make a favourable impression on them, and the likelihood is great that they will think of you next time a position comes open!

Frequently administrators do have a good idea who will be the best candidate, judging by the résumés and reference checks, but it is incredible how often someone other than the expected one is chosen after the interviews are completed! If you really want a teaching job, you cannot afford to take the chance of missing an interview or failing to make your mark in their minds for future occasions. Also, Occasional Teachers are often chosen from among those who have made a positive impression during an interview, and you can read in PART VIII how you can make that situation lead to a full-time contract!

TAKING CONTROL OF THE INTERVIEW

You will benefit from developing ahead of time some sound educational responses to questions, such as the ones on the following pages, and being familiar with them, so you don't have to do so much creating on-the-spot. Some questions will be designed and asked in a fashion intended to force on-the-spot thinking, but if you are comfortable with your responses to these questions, you will be ready for most eventualities. You may sometimes be given the actual interview questions ahead of time, but certainly not always. As you go through these, please note that although some of these questions are similar to others in the list, they tend to require a slightly different slant or emphasis in your answer.

In the interview, just listen carefully to the question being asked, even ask for clarification if necessary. As suggested earlier, you may even want to request a few seconds to think, but be careful not to do so for every question or you will seem unnecessarily hesitant. This is the "passive" part of the process, and it is vitally important.

There is also an "active" part: this is where you exert some control over the flow of the process. You will need to do this, too, or you may not adequately communicate that you are indeed the best choice. To do this, you need to consider what information the committee already has about you (though you can never be certain that they have all read even your cover letter) and decide on two or three things they really need to know before you leave. If you can't work these points into one of your answers, you may be able to put them into a brief summary at the end. Be ready for this; have the wording loosely planned—you want to have a good idea what you will say, but be ready to relate it to the conversation which has gone before. There is a fairly good chance that the questions you are given will not elicit everything you want and need to say to separate you from the other applicants; many interviews are conducted by those who are pathetically unskilled in this important process! Your concluding statement could come either when they ask you if there is anything else you would like to add, or when they ask if you have any questions; either time will do. Don't make your summary last more than sixty seconds, reassure them that you are very interested in working with them (now even more than before), and leave them with the one or two most significant reasons why they should hire you.

"It usually takes me more than three weeks to prepare a good impromptu speech."
—*Mark Twain*

SAMPLE QUESTIONS

The types of questions you are likely to be asked are divided into categories dealing with: General Overview, Personality, Discipline, Classroom Management and Developing Self-Discipline, Dealing with Pupils with Special Needs, Dealing with Parents, Programming and Curriculum: General and Specific, Questions Related to Classes Up to the End of Grade 3, Questions Related to Classes From Grade 4 to Grade 6, Questions Related to Classes From Grade 7 to Grade 9, Questions Related to Classes in Grade 10 and After, Teaching in a Specialty School, Teaching in a First Nations School, Teaching a Second Language, Record Keeping, Innovations and Creativity, Public Relations, Your Extra-Curricular Potential, Initiative, Team/Co-operative Activities, The Use and Potential of Information Technology in Your Classroom (and in the education field in general) and Wrap-Up Questions.

Many of these questions could fit into more than one of the categories, as they cut across several topic boundaries. Good interview questions will do that. That is why you may want to go through some of the questions in sections not directly related to the position you are seeking; that will decrease the possibility of your being surprised. Robert Frost is quoted saying: "I'll discuss anything—I like to go perhaps-ing around on all subjects." You might even want to organize your thoughts by jotting down some points.

Please note that in the following sample questions quotation marks are omitted. The information following some questions offers a suggestion on how you might consider such a question.

GENERAL OVERVIEW QUESTIONS

- **Why are you the best candidate for this position?**

  Refer in your answer to your training, experience and personal characteristics. Be ready to address each of these areas succinctly, but thoroughly. Let them interrupt with questions if they wish.

- **What are your teaching interests: grade, subject, specialty?**

  Give the one applied for, of course, but also name several others so they could consider you for one of them as well.

- **Why do you want to join us at this school or board?**

  Have two or three specific reasons ready: is it some special philosophy you share or some initiative they are involved in that you are committed to? Why/how are you "like them"?

"If I didn't start painting, I would have raised chickens."
—*Grandma Moses*, famous American folk-artist, began painting at age 78

"When I stand before God at the end of my life, I would hope that I would not have a single bit of talent left and could say: 'I used everything you gave me'."
—*Erma Bombeck*

- **Do you have any specific interests in working with children outside the classroom?**

  Are you committed to children or just involved? This is the time to mention work with Scouts, Guides, church groups, teams, Big Brothers/Sisters, etc.

- **What are your views about children today?**

  This one is wide open. You may wish to ask for clarification. If you do, they will probably want to know about one or more of the following: (a) your philosophy of education, (b) your discipline code or procedures, (c) how you believe children learn best (i.e., active versus rote or drill versus Socratic learning and the appropriate times for each), (d) the role of the teacher, or (e) the purpose of homework (for "e" see APPENDIX 13).

- **Of the following, what is most important to you: (a) your family, (b) your career, (c) your own personal/spiritual development? In other words, how would your prioritize them?**

  This is a tough one, which cuts across many categories of questions. It is also a minefield. If you say "family" is most important, it looks like you lack commitment to your career. If you say "career," it looks like you are uncaring about your family and your personal development and are someone who is not interested in life-long learning. If you say your "personal/spiritual development," it looks like you are a dreamer who is not action-oriented. So how to win? In cases like this, explain that you believe in a balance and that short-term priorities can change depending upon circumstances. You might explain that sometimes for short periods of time any one area can assume more energy than its share, but balance in the medium-to-long term is what matters. You might want to refer to Steven Covey's work (*First Things First*) for a matrix of the categories "urgent" and "important." It divides issues or opportunities or circumstances requiring decision among the following four categories: "not urgent and not important" (the "who really cares and even though maybe you 'ought-ta' do it you'll never really miss it" stuff), "urgent but not important" (the pressing, pestering, trivial stuff), "not urgent but important" (the long-range stuff) and "urgent and important" (the "get at it immediately or suffer the consequences" stuff). You might also refer to Bolles' book *The Four Boxes of Life* (see PART XI). Just don't fall into the trap of simplistically picking one item as highest priority and letting your answer go at that.

- **Could you start in this position immediately? Or, it may be asked as: Are you prepared to accept this position today if it is offered to you?**

  If you are already under contract you must, by law in most provinces, notify your present Board within a specified number of hours that you have signed a new contract. In Ontario, for example, it is within twenty-four hours of signing; contact your Teachers' Federation/Society/Union/Association—listed in PART X—for specifics. This is very important to avoid breach of contract! If under contract, you must gain a release either by mutual consent or by giving the required notice (this, too, is specified in most provinces. Again using Ontario as an example, for the agreement to terminate December 31, notice must be given by November 30, and to terminate the agreement August 31, notice must be given by May 30). In either case, you cannot start right away. Unless you are presenting difficulties in your performance, most boards will not want you to leave half-way through a term and may refuse to give you "mutual consent" leave; it is their contractual

"For your information, I'm going to ask you a few questions."
—*Sam Goldwyn*

right to do so. Also, you may want to wonder whether it is a trick question: they may not want to hire someone who will drop what they are doing and leave without warning. You can, however, accept a position with the definite and clear understanding that it will commence after the legal termination date of your current position, but you must then notify your board within a prescribed time that you have done so. (See APPENDIX 8 for details of contract termination by province/territory.) Of course, if you are not presently employed, you won't face these restrictions.

- **What is your perception of the position being offered?**

Especially if it is a bit unusual, they will want to know if you cared enough or are a sufficiently thorough person to bother finding out before the interview. This can be a genuine indicator of later professional performance and conduct and can be seen as a "predictor." Although it is a good question for any interview, you may encounter it more frequently when applying for an unusual position: Special Education, Corrections Facilities, etc.

- **What are your negative points?**

This may be asked point-blank, or may be phrased more tactfully; e.g., What are your areas that you hope to improve? I prefer to ask bluntly. The way a person reacts to this quasi-attack is a good predictor of their ability to respond in a rational manner to similar affronts from parents and others. Think up one that lets them know you know you are a little less than perfect, but don't list one that will eliminate you! Then present your identified area of weakness calmly and professionally, and if you are working to improve in that area by independent reading or taking courses, etc., be sure to say so! One former principal I knew explained her most serious flaw as sometimes expecting too much of herself and then being disappointed when she just couldn't achieve her goals.

> "If one throws salt at you, you will not be harmed unless you have sore places."
> —*Marcus Porcius Cato*

- **What is the most useful thing you can teach these pupils?**

Needless to say, this may well depend upon the type and level of pupils being considered. They will most likely want a very practical answer: keep it brief, but you can talk from the heart. You might want to consider that the "Public Agenda" writers in the U.S. (Johnson and Immerwahr, New York: 1994), in *First Things First: What Americans Expect from the Public Schools*, listed as top priorities "safety, order and basic skills." Could this be a starting point? Would Canadians want the same? Without disparaging Americans, make it clear that you are not using their priorities to set standards for Canadian schools—some administrators are quite sensitive to that—and then go on to show how development of self-confidence and self-discipline, and an enquiring mind, can contribute to these. At the risk of quoting another non-Canadian, Malcolm Forbes made an insightful comment: "The purpose of education is to replace an empty mind with an open one."

- **What materials and activities would form the basis of your curriculum in the month of September?**

Again, this will depend upon the type and level of pupils being considered. Be prepared to give them a brief outline of the September part of your Long Range Plans you will implement if you get that job.

- **What emergency situations have you experienced in the work place?**

Injuries, disruptions from non-custodial parents or those under restraining order, etc., are good examples. Losing a child on a field trip is probably not the type of emergency you want to describe!

> "When I filled out the form that said 'In case of emergency notify _____.', I wrote 'My doctor'. After all, what's my mother going to do?"
> —*Anon.*

"A closed mind is like a closed book; just a block of wood."

—*Anon.*

- **What did you do to contribute to the successful conclusion of the emergency?**

  These two may be more frequent in a Special Needs classroom or high risk area: Technology and Design, Conduct/Behavioural, etc. Perhaps you can consider the quote of Publius Syrus: "Anyone can hold the rudder when the sea is calm," but don't make yourself sound so self-important that they are turned off. A bit of self-deprecating humour along with a comment such as this can, however, have a great effect, if you can pull it off!

- **What are the responsibilities of the teacher when dealing with medical emergencies?**

  Be aware of *The Good Samaritan Act* but don't try to be all things in all situations; you are not a physician. It will, however, help if you mention your first-aid training. You might also want to be sure you know the board's policy on administration of medications.

- **Would you be willing to take (or maintain current) First-Aid training if you accept this position?**

  Of course you would—if you have not already. If that's all that keeps you from a job ...

- **Do you support the Goals of this Board of Education?**

  You really do need to find out what particular, specific initiatives that board or school is involved in— a specific curriculum area, public relations, assessment, a particular instructional philosophy or instructional method, some specific approach to the change process or whatever—and pick up some of the "buzz word" bits of colloquialism that go along with it. Be ready to say how you could support and contribute to those objectives or directions! Comment on how they relate to your teaching. The Board Office, or any school secretary, could give you a list. (On a cynical/realistic note, remember that these words can change frequently; often "the last gasp of an expiring organization is to publish a new set of old rules." *Kaiser News.)*

PERSONALITY QUESTIONS

- **Think of one of your previous supervisors (or they may narrow it to your immediately previous supervisor). How were you and they different?**

  Remember: don't denigrate them. Just describe how you were different in a positive and very professional way. If you were very similar say so and how. They will then usually ask you to pick another. They may also be trying to find out if you can co-operate with others.

- **Another way it is sometimes asked is: How were you treated by your former administrators?**

  This is a minefield. Are you perhaps unduly sensitive?

- **To what extent have you been involved with fellow staff members in planning, observation and feedback from activities? What role do you see other staff members taking in the day-to-day activities of your classroom?**

  Peer coaching, team teaching, etc. Again, they may be trying to find out if you can co-operate?

For an overview, see APPENDIX 11: *Personal and Professional Characteristics of Effective Teachers.* These are the characteristics you are wanting to demonstrate.

- **Without giving details that would identify the person, tell us about a success you have had in eliciting co-operation from a colleague everyone else thought was "impossible to deal with."**

  This one, too, could go under the "Team" heading. Be positive; this is your chance to show your diplomatic skills. Do you use the method of William Ury *et. al.*—as described in the absolutely fabulous books: *Getting To Yes*, and *Getting Past No*? If so, mention this method by name: "Principled Negotiation."

- **Intelligent people think; thinking people have opinions; those with opinions differ. Describe, without identifying the persons involved, a serious difficulty or disagreement you have been involved with on the job and tell how you solved the problem.**

  This is a variation on the one above. Have a scenario in mind.

- **Do you have an analytical mind?**

  What do you think about your own thinking skills, and how do you relate your perception of your own to that of others?

- **What part of your teaching positions in the past have you enjoyed the most?**

  A little enthusiasm, if you will. If it was similar to the job being offered, so much the better, but don't fabricate.

- **Every job has a few negatives. What part of your teaching positions in the past have your disliked the most?**

  Be honest. If your "hate list" is like a job description for what they have in mind for you, better to find out now. To keep it unabashedly positive, however, you could quote James Thurber: "There is, of course, a certain amount of drudgery in newspaper work, just as there is in teaching classes, tunnelling into a bank, or being President of the United States."

- **What responsibilities or results have not come up to your expectations? We would like to know about things you hoped to accomplish and did not. Perhaps you could even call them "little disappointments."**

  Remember, it takes as much courage to try something and fail as it does to try something and succeed. It is possible to fail magnificently and only because one has set one's goals at an unattainable level. John Milton set about to "vindicate the ways of God to men" and failed; instead he succeeded only in writing a monumental and timeless masterpiece: *Paradise Lost.*

- **Most of us can think of at least one important decision we would make differently if we could do it all over again. What is the biggest mistake you have made?**

  Fortunately, this question is rarely asked of teachers, especially new teachers. It is usually saved for experienced administrators looking for a new position. If you are asked, mention something not too damning, and something which you have since corrected and/or actually done differently.

"It often happens that I awaken in the night and start to think about a serious problem, and decide that I must talk to the Pope about it in the morning. Then I awaken fully, and realize that I am the Pope."
—*John XXIII*

"A strong, positive self-image is the best possible preparation for success."
—*Joyce Brothers*

"I've read about foreign policy and studied—I know the number of continents."

—*George Wallace*, 1968 US presidential campaign

- **What is the last professional book you have read? When did you finish it?**

  Is professional reading one of the ways you strive to improve your craft? In what area are you interested in improving? (Don't say this book! It would be good advertisement for me, but you don't necessarily want them to know you are "coached.")

- **What is the last professional development course or training you have taken? Why did you choose that one?**

  Are you taking advantage of this option to improve? In what area? How about Rory McGreal's comment: "The learners inherit the earth; the learned are equipped for a world that no longer exists." Be careful, though. If the members of the committee seem to want to impress you with the fact that they are awesomely "learned," stay away from that one. There's no sense in rocking their boat until after you have a permanent contract! To help you be gentle with them, you might also want to think of an observation of Kurt Vonnegut Jr., when you are facing a "learned" person in a position of authority. He writes in *Cat's Cradle*, "Beware of the man who works hard to learn something, learns it, and finds himself no wiser than before ... He is full of murderous resentment of people who are ignorant without having to come to their ignorance the hard way."

- **Why did you choose to become a teacher?**

  Limit your response to what you feel you can contribute because of your past. Be specific.

- **What personal characteristics do you have that make you a good teacher?**

  Be self-assured, but not braggadocio.

- **Are you interested in research?**

  Have you been involved in any research, formal or informal? It doesn't have to be Ph.D.-level research. Do you work with others to try new ideas or approaches, and carefully monitor results, considering the extraneous variables, etc.? That's research, too!

- **What is the single most important thing you have learned from experience?**

  Do you learn the lessons life offers?

- **In your undergraduate education, which course did you like the best? Why?**

  They just want to see the "warm" you.

- **Why did you choose that university?**

  Do you have an overall plan for life?

- **When did you choose your major?**

  Early or late in your educational career—do you have a global plan for life? If not, you might want to be ready to defend its apparent absence by explaining that while you have a general direction, you move "incrementally" and try very hard to remain open to opportunities which lead further toward your overall goal. You may then be asked what that goal is: perhaps it is

"I am part of all that I have met."

—*Alfred Lord Tennyson, "Ulysses"*

administration or a position of added responsibility, or simply being the best teacher, or perhaps research or writing in the education field. You pick what it is and have a good, brief, positive way of describing it.

- **Did you change your major field of interest or studies during your program?**

- **What do you want to be doing two years from now? Five years? Ten years?**

1. They may want to know your interests and motivation, i.e., positions of added responsibility or whatever, or see whether you have any idea of where you are going in your career. Or they may be wanting to know if you are seeing this position just as a stepping stone rather than one you plan to fulfil well, even if only for a short time. This is especially relevant to positions usually considered undesirable, as some try to use them just to open the door to other opportunities. While there is no harm in change, let them know you will do every job well.

2. On a slightly different angle, let them know that you are not afraid of change. In this time of government cutbacks, change has been described as the only constant. One popular cliché is: "Change is not optional—growth is." What about considering an extension of this: "Change is not optional— growth is, but growth is not optional if we want to survive."

- **How many hours a day, excluding class time, do you think a teacher should spend on teaching-related work? Why do you say that?**

Be honest; don't over- or under-estimate. A comment that comes to mind is from John Oliver Hobbes: "A man with a career can have no time to waste on his wife and his friends; he has to devote it wholly to his enemies." I definitely don't think it is one you should use in an interview, but to my perverse mind...

DISCIPLINE, CLASSROOM MANAGEMENT AND DEVELOPING SELF-DISCIPLINE

- **Recognizing the individuality of each child, what is your common thread, or philosophy, or creed, of dealing with children?**

They want to know what drives you—in a positive way. Is it respect, or self-discipline, or the enquiring mind, or the need for efficiency or what? Perhaps it is the desire to encourage pupils to follow your example in accepting ownership for one's own actions. Perhaps you believe that free thinkers are free to make choices and are free to accept responsibility for them.

- **What are some methods you would implement to help develop self-esteem in a Grade 6 (or other level) pupil? Describe for us a bit about the background and presenting symptoms of this hypothetical pupil, and describe what you would do.**

Or they may give you a full case scenario and ask for your response, but have one sort of sketched out in case. You might also want to have a look at a Canadian Education Association publication—also referred to in PART XI—called *Building Student Self-esteem*, available for $8.00. Their phone number: (416) 924-7721.

"A disciplined mind is not necessarily a good mind—that is, a moral mind—but without discipline we are barbarians."
—*Howard Gardner*

"Example is not the main thing in influencing others, it's the only thing."
—*Albert Schweitzer*

"Discipline is like cabbage. We may not care for it ourselves, but feel sure it would be good for somebody else."
—*Bill Vaughan*

"Discipline is necessary for wisdom, but not sufficient."
—*Howard Gardner*

- **What are your methods of pupil discipline?**

  Know that board's policy and the school's discipline code. This should be part of your pre-interview investigative work. In some provinces, all schools are required to file a copy of their discipline procedures with the board; you may be able to get a copy there. In any discussion of discipline, be certain to emphasize separation of the person from the behaviour. We can intensely dislike the behaviour while we still like the child. By the way, one method that almost everyone forgets to mention is "proximity control," yet it is very simple and immensely effective! How about mentioning the importance of keeping children busy right from the first. I know an experienced teacher—with a well-deserved reputation for excellence in classroom management—who claims she doesn't give her pupils 30 seconds of free time for the first three weeks in September. The same could apply to the time of your arrival in the classroom part way through the year, perhaps. This may, moreover, confirm in their minds that you have high standards for performance, that you see commitment to school work as valuable, and you believe that what can be accomplished during the remainder of the year is important.

- **What is your philosophy with regard to the development of self-discipline in pupils at the Primary level?**

  Or Junior or Intermediate or Senior or Elementary or High School levels, too, depending upon what you are applying for. It doesn't hurt to be ready to be asked about another level, as you may be considered for another position if you are their "second choice" for this one.

- **Please describe your method(s) of classroom discipline in the Early Primary/Primary/Junior/Intermediate/Senior classroom, or variously: the Design and Technology/Special Education/Conduct Disordered/ Learning Skills/A.D.H.D./Core French or whatever classroom.**

  Each of these will require a different approach. Have your overview ready and rehearsed.

- **How would you deal with a physically aggressive pupil?**

  Re-direct? Preventative measures you would take? When would you involve other professionals and who?

- **How would you deal with a pupil who continually slams the door, or pounds his fist on the table, or throws things or otherwise seriously disturbs the classroom?**

  See preceding question.

- **What would you do if that didn't work?**

- **And, what if that didn't work?**

  These are the times when you bring up your next line(s) of action.

- **And, what if that didn't work?**

  In addition to knowing your intermediary steps, they will want to know when you would involve the vice-principal or guidance personnel.

"Likely as not, the child you can do least with will make you the most proud."
—*Mignon McLaughlin*

- **Here's a scenario for you to consider. A boy in Grade 6 (or up) has been for the past six weeks teasing a girl in his class and making rude and crude sexual comments about her within her hearing, and directly to her. She has reported this to you on several occasions. What would you do?**

The process needs to be progressive. First, speak to him and tell him you have heard the allegation, and that it needs to stop. You probably should mention that sexual harassment is a serious offence. Next time it is reported, assuming that you have supporting evidence that it occurred, you might assign a punishment such as an essay and/or written apology and, at this point, notify the vice-principal, in writing, of the offence and your actions and keep a copy for your documentation—**sexual harassment of pupils is that important**! Request that the vice-principal inform his parents, or do so yourself, keeping documentation of the phone call or a copy of the note to them. The next time she reports it, refer her—or better yet, take her—to the vice-principal, relate the course of events as you know them and your involvement to date, and request suspension of the offending pupil. (The principal may not do it, but you have requested significant action, and he or she may now be more inclined to take the issue seriously.) Again, document. If the harassment continues, notify the vice-principal in writing, keeping a copy of your note. You can depend on the fact that it will escalate, and you will need your evidence of the action you have taken.

- **Now, the scenario continues: One day as they are entering your class, from sheer frustration and continued insult, perhaps, she retaliates by kneeing him. He falls down and is taken to the hospital where he is found to have sustained significant physical injury. Now his parents are demanding to know how she will be punished, are contemplating a charge of assault, and are considering allegations that you have failed to provide a safe environment for their son. She has never been in trouble before. What do you do?**

With the adjacent disclaimer in mind, you could: refer it to the principal, tell the parents that you have done so, and direct them there. *Say as little to them as possible. At this point, you won't help and will only complicate the situation by talking to them!* Fill out an accident report for insurance purposes. **Contact your teachers' federation or union: at this point it is "going legal!"** The girl will probably be suspended, but at the end of legal proceedings this can be expunged from her records, at the principal's discretion. If the police become involved, you may be required to provide details of your documentation, but you might want to talk to your union for advice first. A charge of assault may be laid. This is, however, a police decision and you should not attempt to interfere. You will probably be required to testify regarding details of strategies you used to attempt to halt the harassment as it will, no doubt, be raised to demonstrate extenuating circumstances. You will survive, or not, based on your documentation and the reasonableness of your actions, both corrective and pro-active, which you have taken: (a) to attempt to prevent a "poisoned environment" for the girl, and (b) to help the boy stop offending. These are part of your duty as a teacher, and that of the principal and board. The girl's parents will probably subpoena you as a character witness and to confirm the extent of the on-going psychological abuse of their daughter, if there is civil litigation by the boy for injuries sustained. Her family, too, may commence court action against the board, the principal, the vice-principal, and you for failure to fulfil your fiduciary duty to maintain a safe environment for their child while

"What we have here is a serious failure to communicate."
—*Strother Martin in "Cool Hand Luke"*

NOTE: This response is a recommendation only, it is not legal advice. For authoritative guidance, consult your teachers' union's legal department or other legal counsel!

at school. Be prepared to realize that the Canadian Criminal Justice System does not operate in the manner one might expect. Please remember to keep in close contact with your teachers' union's legal counsel, and/or your own counsel, and follow their advice!

• **What place do rules have in the classroom?**

Are there rules for just pupils, or for you, too? Are the pupils involved in developing classroom expectations? Do pupils understand why there are rules?

(An excellent book, for both new and experienced teachers, on the whole field of discipline and developing and nurturing self-worth in the classroom, is *Discipline With Dignity* by Curwin & Mender. You may want to read it, or a similar one or two, before you go to interviews.)

• **What is the role of democracy in the classroom?**

You may want to point out that, while you recognize your ultimate responsibility for organizing the activities of the classroom, you do attempt to allow many questions of preference to be decided democratically— although you decide which things are truly optional—and that you attempt to provide opportunities for pupils to practice the thinking required to live in a democracy where no one tells you what you must think. If you do want to talk about the limits of democratic principles in the classroom, you might want to quote no less a person than Robertson Davies, who said, "The ideal of democracy has no place in the classroom." Then, I would encourage you to indicate that you do not go so far as he does, but merely that you realize that there must be a balance.

• **How do you balance the demands of structure versus creative expression in your classroom?**

Does your curriculum reflect the need for children to have variety of activity? How can you modify the environment to permit creative action within permissible bounds?

• **How would you react when a Grade 7 pupil swears in class, shouts "I hate Math," and refuses to work?**

Is this another time to re-direct and later work on finding out the motivation or stimulus? If this is part of a much larger issue, how can you be certain it is dealt with, effectively and sensitively? Is there something you can do to modify the program to make it more enjoyable, or at least tolerable, for the non-traditional learner? What about the crisis-intervention techniques you would use? Let them know that you would be sensitive to the earlier indicators of the problem, and what you would do to avoid it getting to this.

• **What do you mean by the word "respect?"**

Is it a two-way street? What are some symptoms of a respectful relationship? Is the "Golden Rule" relevant here? Barbara J. Ayers of Montana State U. and Deborah L. Hedeen of Idaho State U. wrote a brief (3 page) pithy article in the Feb. 96 (vol 53, no. 5) *Educational Leadership* magazine of the ASCD, titled "Been There, Done That, Didn't Work: Alternative Solutions for Behavioural Problems." It is definitely worth a look—very practical, with examples of situations. The thesis: your carefully planned and implemented demonstration(s) of flexibility (within boundaries you can live with!) and the respect you show can have significant impact on pupils'

"We're here to protect democracy, not practice it."
—*Gene Hackman in "Crimson Tide"*

"Notice the difference between when a person says to themself, 'I have failed three times', and what happens when they say 'I am a failure'."
—*Samuel I. Hayakawa*

behaviour. Request the whole issue; it also has some great intellectual and yet practical articles on inclusion of exceptional pupils. This will add to your readiness in this era of "inclusion."

HINT

Professional magazines can really add depth to the insights and responses of less experienced teachers!

- **You are beginning this position in the middle of our year. How are you planning to make this a smooth transition for your pupils?**

  This one applies if you are coming in to replace a teacher going on leave, etc. It should be answered from a programming perspective, a parent-relations perspective, and a teamwork perspective, as well as discipline. Don't forget to mention that you would talk to the teacher being replaced, if possible, and to other teachers in that grade in that school. You would also probably check the teacher's long-range plans—a copy will be filed at the office. Another part of this could be finding out by a classroom discussion how the pupils interpret the classroom routines—you'll have to watch for cons, of course (the " ... no! Really! Mr. Smith just let us do anything we want!" sort of thing) and then try to minimize change to the rules and routines. Some ill teachers may even want to co-plan with you, if there is a chance they will be back before the end of the term. Are you open to this? This might, likewise, be the time to mention that, except in emergency, you believe changes to routines should be made very slowly.

"Of course, 'behaviourism' works. So does torture."
—*W.H. Auden*

DEALING WITH SPECIAL-NEEDS CHILDREN

- **The social skills of some pupils with special needs are very weak. How would your program accommodate these needs?**

  Time spent on role-playing, situation analysis, modelling ... that's a start. You might even want to consider a comment by Judith Martin about not just "special needs" kids, but every young person: "Teaching etiquette is the kindest thing you can do for your child. It predates law and everything else in getting along with other people. You can't get away without etiquette any more than you can decide not to use language."

- **What are some record-keeping devices you would use?**

  This is an especially relevant question for either regular pupils in Early Primary, or for a Specialized Program, where pupils are functioning at a less mature level; i.e., Special Education, especially working with severely and profoundly delayed children. It can, however, apply very well to any class. Name or explain what ones you use, whether your own, or "recognized" ones.

"The biggest disease today is not leprosy or tuberculosis, but rather the feeling of being unwanted, uncared for and deserted by everybody. The greatest evil is the lack of love and charity, the terrible indifference towards one's neighbour who lives at the roadside assaulted by exploitation, corruption, poverty and disease."
—*Mother Teresa of Calcutta*

- **What are your beliefs regarding the role of specialized personnel in dealing with children with special needs?**

  Can you co-operate? Also, do you favour the Corrective or Preventative model? What do you see as the responsibility of the regular classroom teacher and that of external experts? Do you understand co-operation and collaboration?

"It's a pity to shoot the pianist when the piano is out of tune."
—*René Coty*

- Describe your experience in working with auxiliary personnel or, if you have no experience, explain how you would use auxiliary personnel. See also APPENDIX 14.

  How would you utilize a regular volunteer or long-term placement student (i.e., Co-op Program Student or College Placement Student) in your program to maximize the benefit for your pupils?

- How do you feel about working as a member of a multi-disciplinary team rather than alone in your classroom?

  Team-teaching or with a para-professional or with other professionals such as behaviour therapists.

- How do you view the role of the paid, trained, para-professional or Educational Assistant in your classroom and program?

  Know your Teachers' Union's policy, but be ready to show you would delegate/empower and how you would keep the relationship positive; i.e., one of mutual respect. You might also want to look at APPENDIX 10.

"Our theories determine what gets measured."
—*Albert Einstein*

- The assessment process in a class for exceptional learners is an on-going one. Explain its complex role in this class.

  How will you keep track of what they can do, are learning to do, and need to learn to do next? Checklists? What ones? Informal assessments? Formal assessments are good, but are cross-sectional rather than longitudinal. Also, see the questions in this section on "Record Keeping."

- Are you aware that this position requires you to help the pupils with personal hygiene?

  This would apply if there was a severely disabled pupil in your classroom.

- Are you willing to toilet-train or change diapers on pupils?

  This would apply only to severely disabled pupils. If you are male, respectfully decline; you don't need allegations of sexual misconduct. Like it or not, this is reality. Males are the most frequent perpetrators of sexual abuse and are, therefore, more suspect. Courteously explain that because of your knowledge of current societal attitudes, you simply will never allow yourself to be in a compromising situation, but you would help with other tasks usually considered unpleasant or not part of a teacher's usual role or would "exchange duties" with another teacher or staff person. As society changes, this is also becoming less likely to be required of a female teacher; a Health-Care Assistant would do it. But then again, as boards are trying to cut back on staff ...

- Can you lift children or push wheelchairs when required to do so?

  This question must reflect a "bone fide occupational requirement" (BOR); i.e., are there likely to be such demands in the classroom. If it is a BOR, simply say "yes" unless you can't.

- Have you ever conducted clinical Behaviour Modification programs?

  By "clinical" they mean under the specific direction of a psychologist or psychiatrist.

"'Do' or 'do not'. There is no 'try'."
—*Yoda, "Star Wars II"*

- **Have you ever implemented any physiotherapy/speech therapy, etc. programs for pupils?**

  Don't be afraid to say "No, but I am willing to learn." If you have, tell them when and how.

- **How do you feel a teacher should deal with a pupil's physical self-abuse?**

  This could apply to severely disturbed pupils or to regular pupils who have a drug or alcohol problem.

- **Although you have not met these pupils, let's assume that you have read their School Records. What steps would you take to program for them?**

  This will depend on the type of exceptionality, but could include gathering learning resources to meet their needs, establishing networks with specialists in the various fields, drawing up lists of their specific needs and attempting to set some general and some specific objectives, perhaps even calling the parents and introducing yourself and asking them what their objectives for the year are.

- **What differences do you see between these pupils and the ones you are working with now?**

  See also the questions under *"Questions Related to Classes Up to the End of Grade 3,"* following.

DEALINGS WITH PARENTS

This has always been a very important (though unfortunately usually undervalued) part of our job. It is, after all, our parents and pupils who are our customers. It is they, directly and indirectly, who pay the bills. It is they who decide whether or not to buy the product we are selling: "excellent education." Unless they are satisfied, it is increasingly easy for them to find an alternate supplier. This has become especially evident in recent years when more parents are inclined to "shop" for their children's school, rather than just accept the one closest to their home. This unwillingness to accept what they do not approve will extend exponentially as "on-line" and satellite education become more easily and inexpensively available in the next five years. Increasingly in Canada we will see the rise of private schools, with contractually guaranteed close contact with parents and the exclusivity and standards of behaviour and progress which parents have been shouting for over the past many years. There is no longer a monopoly in education. And the competition is only starting to develop!

Another source of increasingly significant impact by parents in major decision-making is the advent of Parent Councils, Advisory Councils or School Councils. Since the NWT suggested these, to return local control of education away from "southerners" and to aboriginal peoples, BC and the Yukon codified their role (1989 and 1990). Now all provinces and territories have similar legislation, and their role is being strengthened. In fact, in the Yukon, the chair of the School council receives a copy of a new teacher's contract! The final question in this sub-section speaks directly to these groups.

The aphorism holds: *"If we don't look after our customers, someone else will!"*

TIP: TALKING TO PARENTS

Remember: If you can get a cup of coffee into their hands, you are half way there. It is very difficult to fight while being fed.

- How would you deal with parents who have refused to believe that their child is not functioning at the "average" level and have been very reluctant to have him tested when now, after finally getting their permission, the test results confirm that he might benefit from extensive specialized intervention and help, perhaps even placement for much or all of his day in a specialized class, now or in the future? Talk to me as you would to this parent, please. Manufacture details of the protocol and profile to suit yourself.

  Do just that—talk to them as to a parent: kind, considerate, informative, caring, open to them.

- How would you maintain contact with parents? How would you keep them informed of what was happening in your classroom?

  What will your newsletters include? You may even want to bring a couple of samples of your "Letters to Parents." How about things like an introduction, a brief description of what you hope your pupils will gain or learn this year, an invitation to them to meet or call you, a description of your open-door policy—make sure it is congruent with the school's policy—a bit of information about you that might make you more "personable" such as if you have any kids of your own, your favourite subject in school, why you chose to become a teacher, etc. What about a special "program night" when parents are invited to come and hear about your classroom curriculum and procedures and ask questions? Do you stay late one night a month so parents can "drop in" and talk to you?

- How serious would a situation have to be before you contacted the parents of a child?

  If you would contact each parent every other week, for example, just to keep them up-to-date, this would be a great spot to mention this as well. How often do you contact parents to give them good news? Do you believe that giving them positive contact first will help your calls to be less intimidating? This could be by either sharing good news or just a pleasant introductory call, couldn't it? Will this make them more likely to want to work with you as a team?

- What role might parents have in your classroom/program?

  Volunteer, skills reinforcement, out-of-class activities, etc.? Be creative, but don't breech union or federation guidelines. See APPENDIX 10.

- What roles have parents played in your classroom?

  If you are a new teacher, see next question.

- What role do you feel comfortable with concerning parents in your classroom?

- What have you done to make other staff, or parents, especially welcome in your classroom and of genuine benefit to the pupils?

  If you have no experience, how about something you did when practice teaching, or even what you think you would do?

- How do you foster the kind of relationship you like to have with parents?

  Name several specific ideas and practises beyond the usual generalities! One aphorism you might want to keep in mind is "when we suddenly need parents' support, it's six months too late to get it."

"Love your neighbour, but don't tear down your fence."
—*German proverb*

• **What would you do about a parent who, when volunteering in your classroom, disturbs other pupils, looks on your desk for confidential information, interrupts your lessons, etc.?**

Re-direct. Then, remind them of the right of their child and all others to confidentiality but, at this point, you might question their suitability as a volunteer in a classroom. It may also be good at this point to talk to the principal or v.p., and definitely document both the activity of the parent and what you did about it.

• **What if that did not work?**

Refer the situation to the principal!!!!

• **Some provinces, as well as the Northwest Territories, are empowering parent committees to take a much more active and legally powerful role in determining school curriculum, personnel selection and ratios, budget allocations and so on. How would you try to work with them, both (a) genuinely to learn from them and be responsive to their concerns and (b) to keep them supporting you even when hard decisions have to be made and your training and experience tells you very clearly that their preference would be for a course of action which would in the long view not be wise.**

Talk about how you build and maintain trust. Know your Board's or Ministry/ Department's guidelines on these groups! You might want to mention Stephen Covey's advice to make early "deposits" in the "emotional bank account" so the relationship of trust is already established before it is needed.

PROGRAMMING AND CURRICULUM: GENERAL AND SPECIFIC

• **How would you know when to revise groupings of children for instructional activities?**

• **Effective use of space is essential to programming. Identify and discuss some of the needs and/or implications of spatial arrangements in a classroom of Grade 1, or 2, or 3, or 4, etc. (or a combined-grade class: 2 and 3, for example).**

• **"Language is more than vocabulary. It is a dynamic interplay of sound, syntax and semantics, formed and developed by interaction among young people." With this in mind, how would you provide opportunities for effective language development in your classroom?**

You might mention opportunities for group work and group discussion interspersed with opportunities to listen to you and to listen to classmates, opportunity for large and small group sharing, activity centres designed to maximize language, and ways you would arrange the room's furnishings and equipment to increase the number of fellow-pupils with whom each would co-operate each day.

"Make happy those who are near, and those who are far will come."
—*Chinese proverb*

"Everything you've learned in school as 'obvious' becomes less and less obvious as you begin to study the universe. For example, there are no solids in the universe. There's not even the suggestion of a solid. There are no absolute continuums. There are no surfaces. There are no straight lines."

—R. Buckminster Fuller

- We often use the word "readiness" when discussing reading, writing and math. What do you believe it means when a pupil is "ready" or "not ready"?

  Readiness can be an issue for a child starting a new section of work, or for issues of promotion or retention.

- Under what conditions would you recommend to the principal that a pupil be retained/failed/not promoted?

  As well as academics, include consideration of parents' role in the decision!

- "Mathematics ... helps us to understand, analyze, and communicate both qualitative and quantitative ideas about our environment." *(EPJD)* How can a program be modified to ensure that such development takes place?

- There is a tendency when discussing a math program to focus on computational skills. What are the benefits and limitations of emphasizing these skills in a total math program for the Intermediate Division (or Junior, or Primary or Elementary or Secondary etc.)?

- It is our school's philosophy that pupils in mathematics should: (a) use calculators as often as possible, (b) use computers as often as possible, (c) not use a textbook on a daily basis, and (d) have math for at least 60-75 minutes per day. How would you design your math curriculum to meet these expectations?

  This would most likely be the case in a Grade 4 and up classroom. Unless you have really strong feelings against this, accommodate your beliefs to theirs, and emphasize areas of overlapping objectives and methods. It's not wise to risk alienating them by discussing differences; this is probably the time to be "similar."

- How would you encourage higher level thinking skills in your everyday program?

  This is a curriculum differentiation issue. Give several specific examples in different subject areas. Talk about variation in types of questions, especially those designed to elicit analysis, synthesis and evaluation. If you live in Ontario, you might want to enrol in the E.T.F.O.-sponsored P.R.I.D.E. course, and other unions may have similar training courses which emphasize skilled questioning techniques. Ask.

- Why is it valuable to extend the learning environment beyond the classroom to field trips, etc.?

  Know the board policy on Field Trips and/or High Risk Activities, if they have one.

- "Freedom to use the arts in their own way, so that they are able to participate fully and spontaneously in an experience, is important for children." *(EPJD)* How would your program reflect this need?

  How would you integrate the arts across the curriculum? Also, we are accustomed to differentiating academic curriculum to meet individual needs. How would you differentiate the fine arts program to address the needs of those who are not traditionally considered "artistic."

- How would you integrate the theme "Animals in Springtime" into your lessons in Language Arts, Environmental Studies, Math, etc.?

- How would you use a thematic approach in your Math program?

  Obviously the answer to this will differ in each grade and division. Don't forget to include how you will address the differing needs of pupils as well.

- We hear the term "Whole Language" used a lot. What do you feel is meant by "Whole Language" in a Grade 1 (or 3 or 5) classroom?

- The "Whole Language" approach is being adopted by many teachers and is now being rejected by increasing numbers. Could you describe what you might observe happening in a "Whole Language Classroom, or Program," and what you would not see happening?

  Describe the positive things you would see, and a couple of areas for improvement or potential pitfalls, and perhaps suggest how you would address the need for mastery of phonetic decoding skills; that is often a sensitive point.

- What experience have you had with programs such as "Reading Recovery," or "Early Literacy Intervention" and how do you see these programs working in your classroom?

  This is a fancy name for intensive individual teaching over a short period of time and involves a very detailed analysis of the reading process. It used to be called "good teaching" before the worst aspects of a misunderstood application of "whole language" took over. It's becoming an important trend.

- Give us your definition of "Activity-Based Learning."

- Identify the steps necessary to make the transition from a "traditional" classroom to one which focuses on the child and his/her development.

  This can be a dangerous one; remember the current shift from "child-centred education" and "child development" and "continuous development" toward measurable "benchmarks" or "standards."

- One difficulty which seems to cause problems for teachers is changing the focus of schooling from "content" to "child development." How would you address this potential concern?

  The above two questions could be a major minefield, especially the latter. For many years we, in education, have been dragging ourselves, and any convenient others who we hoped to influence, kicking and screaming toward the idea of "continuous development." Now, several loud—and official— voices (for better or worse depends upon degree, perhaps) are pushing back the other way toward pre-determined standards of competence, and are being heard! Harris and Graham, (1994, 95, 96) in several of their publications suggest that for "constructivism" as they refer to "whole language," "the research base is insufficient to draw even the most tentative conclusions" regarding its effectiveness with special needs children, and go on to say "[n]or can clear conclusions be drawn for other students" (1996). The best warning to you is to "go easy" on criticizing that approach, however, at least until you can see "the lay of the land." Another of their

"Keep your fears to yourself, but share your inspiration with others."
—*Robert Louis Stevenson*

"Change! Change! Who wants change? Things are bad enough as they are!"
—*The Earl of Sandwich*

SETTING OBJECTIVES

A really excellent book on setting useful objectives, and ones related to the evaluation to be used, is Robert F. Mager's *Measuring Instructional Results, or Got a Match?* (Centre for Effective Performance: Atlanta, GA, 1996). Another good book by the same author is *Developing Attitude Toward Learning.*

comments sums up many administrators who are committed to "whole language": "[w]hen people who subscribe to one approach are incapable of examining it critically, and when their behaviour is insular, they may well ignore the knowledge gained by practitioners of competing or alternative paradigms" ("Memo to Constructivists: Skills Count, Too!" ASCD, 1996). Don't tread on their corns, however; many administrators are still stuck in the simple (simplistic?) past

- **One difficulty which seems to cause problems for teachers is changing the focus of schooling from "child development" to "content." How would you address this potential concern?**

  This is the opposite to the one above; be ready for both. Discuss setting of objectives in terms of student outcomes or competencies—behavioural objectives, in other words—and how you would provide enrichment for those at both ends of the continuum.

- **How would you accommodate a wide range of ability and achievement levels in a split-grade class in the Junior division? (Or other division)**

  How would you combine and separate the class and differentiate the program? How would you juggle time?

- **Identify some of the most effective means of student evaluation. Briefly discuss some of the features and limitations of each.**

  Standardized, teacher-designed, summative, formative, self-evaluation, norm-referenced, criterion-referenced, longitudinal, cross-sectional, objective, subjective, random sample, etc.

Again, a Mager book: his *Analyzing Performance Problems* gives a unique perspective on planning.

- **Effective planning implies making the best use of resources, both human and material. Discuss some resources which you consider most effective.**

  This could also be part of the *Dealing With Parents* section, i.e., use of volunteers.

- **In what ways has your planning improved in the last two years?**

- **How many hours of homework per night/week should a child in the ___ Grade be expected to do?**

  Have an idea for the grade applied for and be prepared to defend it. If you don't have a lot of teaching experience, ask for guidance from experienced teachers at that grade level. Also, see APPENDIX 13.

- **Sometimes you will be given a whole batch of questions ahead of time which build on each other, such as the following:**

  Pick something from your experience and pretend that you are developing a unit on it. What would you consider to be the most important and most appropriate learning objectives for that unit?

What would you see as the levels of growth related to those objectives?

Describe the different levels of learning you would expect in each grade, in the unit described above.

Tell us how you would arrange the classroom and the activities in it to meet the objectives described earlier.

What skills of yours would be required to enable the pupils to meet the objectives in that classroom you described?

How would you sequence the learning objectives in the unit?

How would you motivate the pupils to acquire the new learning?

How would you introduce new concepts?

How would you have them consolidate the new learning?

How would you monitor the ongoing activities?

How would you evaluate the learning?

How would you evaluate your teaching strategies?

For this, scan the list of questions and choose your "topic" unit with care so you can address the rest of the questions. It needs to be something you are comfortable manipulating in your mind, therefore, something you have fairly extensive experience with; don't try to "invent" or you will run out of details, and you will possibly end up boxing yourself in because it's hard to see the end from the beginning, so to speak.

• Phillip Schlechty said: "What is wanted is a school system that can ensure that all children will learn to read, write and cipher and that at the same time all children will learn how to think. That is the challenge that has never before faced public education." How would you ensure that all children will learn to think?

Teach thinking skills, perhaps using resources such as de Bono's *Lateral Thinking* or some of the children's books put out by MENSA, have a special "Thinking Question" for the class every day, encourage open debate, etc. Of course your answer will vary depending upon the age level of the pupils, but let them know that you understand that thinking is a skill that can, and needs to, be learned; it does not happen naturally. Also you will want to address such things as Bloom's taxonomy of cognitive learning.

QUESTIONS RELATED TO CLASSES UP TO THE END OF GRADE THREE

• Keeping in mind the levels of physical development for 3-, 4- and 5-year olds, how would you set up a gymnasium for a half-hour of free play?

This question could be applied to any age group; here it applies to Junior and Senior kindergarten.

"We've been working on the basics because, basically, we've been having trouble with the basics."

—*Bob Ojeda,* baseball pitcher

"Good teaching practice insists that knowledge does not fall into neatly separate compartments and that work and play are not opposite but complimentary."

—*Plowden Report*

- **If teaching the concept of conservation of volume, what type of activity will address the three levels of pupils in your class?**

  Tell them how you would differentiate the lesson to meet the needs of the slower learners while still challenging the more advanced.

- **What is the role of the educator in a learning centre environment?**

  What will you do before the pupils arrive and while they are there to ensure that the activity is purposeful, and they learn and meet your objectives? You might want to factor into your response the origin of the word, pedagogy. The Greek παιδαγωγος *(paidagogos*, literally a "child-conductor") was one, usually a slave, who had the responsibility of guiding the child as they developed into an adult. Only when the child became an adult did the responsibility of the paidagogos end. How will you guide the children and "conduct" them along the *curriculum* (Latin: the running path; i.e., race track) of learning? What "pedagogy" will you use?

- **How does play fit into an early education program?**

  Do you know the benefits and, perhaps more important, the limitations of play activities?

- **In a child's early years, it is important that the teacher work more closely with parents than may be the case as they go into higher grades. How do you see the parents as team members within your classroom?**

  Volunteers? You might want to mention ways of including them: formal and/ or informal "Drop-In Days," newsletters, special evening meetings where your program is presented and questions answered, sources of information about their children, etc. To what extent would you invite their input?

- **What skills/knowledge/attitudes can be taught with the following activity centres: (a) sand centre, (b) block centre, (c) water centre, (d) science centre, (e) paint centre, (f) family skills centre; i.e., housekeeping, dolls, dress-up?**

- **How can the early childhood educator foster an atmosphere of trust and structured freedom which promotes development of initiative and self-reliance?**

- **How would you use puppets in a primary classroom?**

- **Nutrition is especially important to children in the younger grades. Children, however, often do not like their lunch and tend to eat only what appeals to them. At home it is easier to deal with this, yet at school they are expected to eat what they have. You will occasionally (or every day) be on lunchroom duty. How would you make sure each child eats a good lunch?**

- **How would you organize the lunch hour for a Kindergarten class, considering that every pupil must be supervised at all times, yet some children eat more quickly than others and get restless while waiting? What would you do to stop the problems that result from this "idle time" so that lunch can be both controlled and yet a social time?**

"Everyone's task is as unique as his specific opportunity to implement it."

—*Victor E. Frankl*

- **What strategies could you use to assist a child who is experiencing difficulty with letter reversals?**

  Remember that this is reasonably normal in the early primary child, but have a strategy or two ready.

- **What strategies could you use to assist a child who is experiencing difficulties with using contextual clues?**

- **Ontario's *Common Curriculum, Provincial Standards: Language*, 1995, says "Writing helps students to learn the skills necessary to become effective readers." How do you see writing helping a child to learn to read?**

  While recording ideas, the conventions of phonics and how letters create sounds are reinforced. A pupil has the opportunity to see different letter structures being used for different or similar sounds. The various topics being written about, different tenses, modes, audiences, etc., all provide opportunity for practice in using and learning to understand conventions in language. Writing reinforces context as a clue to meaning; this can transfer to reading. That's not a bad start in answering one like that.

- **Why would you, or would you not, encourage the use of temporary spelling in a Primary classroom? ("Temporary spelling" just means "sound spelling" but it does not upset parents as much as the older term "inventive spelling.")**

- **What role does Information Technology (I.T.) have in your program?**

  This question can be applied to all levels and subjects! See also the questions under the I.T. section and also the sections in PART IV **Your Cover Letter: Their First Impression** that apply to I.T.

  For classes up to the end of Grade 1, your use of I.T. in the program will probably consist mostly of their exploring the computer as a learning tool, using some multi-media programs (CD ROM's) for data retrieval (research) and non-complex internet searches assisted by a volunteer or older student. With a little help, however, pupils can begin to use the computer as a publishing tool right from Kindergarten, adding script to picture stories.

  It should not, however, replace printing, painting, etc., as those activities are very necessary for the development of fine motor control in young children!

  Work with a mentor (volunteer or older student) will establish in the pupils' minds a sense of empowerment with the technology and help give them a sense of what it can do. Pupils up to Grade 3 will also quite willingly use a computer, fully engaged for hours, on practising basic math and spelling. If reasonable programs are chosen they are having so much fun they don't know they are learning. (I have frequently seen pupils—up to Grade 5—beg to stay in at recess to practice spelling, when they can use an interactive program!) By Grades 2 and 3, they should be becoming comfortable using the internet as a source of information—using teacher-selected sites. Formal instruction in keyboarding should begin in Grade 3.

"Don't think there are no crocodiles because the water is calm."
—*Malayan proverb*

"Every man who knows how to read has it in his power to magnify himself, to multiply the ways in which he exists, to make his life full, significant and interesting."
—*Aldous Huxley*

"Be a person on whom nothing is wasted."
—*Socrates*

QUESTIONS RELATED TO CLASSES FROM GRADE FOUR TO SIX

- **The Junior Division (Grades 4-6) has been identified as the "Golden Age of Reading." How would you ensure that your pupils get the very best from their middle elementary school years?**

- **How would you teach reading to this class, given that: (a) many of the pupils "hate" reading, and (b) one-third of the class is not at grade level in basic reading skills?**

  This situation is not as unusual as we might imagine. Talk about how you motivate pupils to enjoy language as a whole, and reading in particular, and some methods you might use: buddy reading, "high-interest / low vocab." books, material tuned to their interests, daily oral reading to them from an interesting story, author studies, etc.

- **"Up to Grade 3 pupils learn to read. After Grade 3 they read to learn." Do you agree?**

  How would you deal with a pupil whose reading level did not allow him to learn from reading?

- **"In all subject disciplines, activities should be designed to allow each child maximum opportunities for engaging in oral discourse ... Children need experience in exploring talk ..."** *Ontario Assessment Instrument Pool: Junior Division Language Arts, Book I: Assessing Language Arts*, **1991. What opportunities for various types of talk can be provided to children, and how could you maximize these opportunities by manipulating the physical arrangement of the classroom?**

  1:1, small group, large group, presentations, provide time to talk and time for listening and time for quiet work.

- *Science is Happening Here* **(1988) states that at the Primary and Junior level "science is seen, not as a separate subject, but as one component of a balanced and integrated program." How would your program reflect this integration of experiences and allow this to happen?**

- **What role does Information Technology (I.T.) have in your program?**

  During these years pupils should be refining their keyboarding skills—both in speed and accuracy—and extending other skills. They should, for example, be able to load programs, and save data and retrieve it from disk. They should be introduced to Boolean search logic—AND, OR, NOT and NEAR—for internet research, and they should be developing a sense of the need for determining credibility of internet sources. They are also ready to begin using the computer as a multi-media reporting tool. By the end of Grade 4, they should be using I.T. to learn, more than learning to use I.T.

"The most exciting phrase to hear in science, the one that hails new discoveries, is not 'Eureka', but 'that's funny ...'."
—*Isaac Asimov*

QUESTIONS RELATED TO CLASSES
FROM GRADE SEVEN TO NINE

• How would you address the needs of all levels of pupils in
your (whatever subjects you will be teaching) class? How will
the homework you assign reflect your awareness of individual
differences? (Or: How would you accommodate the needs of
the various levels of learner, from those functioning at the
Grade 12 level to those reading at the Grade 3 level, in your
Grade 9 Science—or whatever—class?)

• *The Ontario Curriculum* (1997) states that "Students must learn
when it is appropriate to use a calculator and when it is not",
i.e., when estimation or mental math is more suitable. How
would you help pupils develop that judgment?

Teach basic calculation without calculators, then practice working on
problems with them and decide for each whether or not a calculator is
needed? When they experience doing easy calculations in their head
faster than they can punch in the numbers, they will be convinced.

• It is sometimes said that "older executives use paper-and-
pencil to check their calculator's answers, while students use a
calculator to check their paper-and-pencil calculations."
Discuss how you would develop your pupils' confidence in
their computation abilities.

Mention how you would work with them on learning estimation skills,
and also how you would affirm them in their abilities.

• Students "must learn from experience ... when to estimate and
when to seek an exact answer and how to estimate answers to
verrify the plausibiltiy of claculator results." *Ontario
Curriculum, 1997: Math*. Comment.

See above.

• What can be done by the classroom teacher to facilitate
transitions for pupils who are already going through a lot of
changes just because of their age?

This question can be adapted to fit any of the transitions faced by
pupils in their school years.

• What role does Information Technology (I.T.) have in your
program?

It is not unreasonable to expect that by this level your pupils can be
refining their presentation skills; their keyboarding should be around 30-
40 words per minute—correct—and they should be developing a fairly
clear understanding of how to access data that is more likely to be
credible. This is another part of "media-literacy." They should be familiar
with documentation methods relating to I.T. sources. All of their reports
should now contain references to electronic sources—CD encyclopaedia
and the internet. It would also be appropriate for them to start using
animations and hyperlinks in their reports—depending upon what
hardware and software are available to them—and they should be
becoming comfortable with LAN and WAN use, including remote printing
and e-mail.

• How do performance standards for pupils relate to transitions
between elementary education and high school?

SOME THINGS ARE MORE
SERIOUS THAN OTHERS

Children need to learn not only
how to estimate, but when to
estimate and why they should
estimate. They need to be
taught that there is a
continuum of priority in
exactness that does not
impinge upon excellence and
how appropriately to locate a
problem along that continuum.

As Robert M Hutchins put it: "It
is not so important to be
serious as it is to be serious
about important things."

"Nothing in life is to be feared.
It is only to be understood."

—*Marie Curie*

SENIOR, OR SPECIALIZATION, YEARS: GRADE TEN AND AFTER

[Questions here will tend to be a combination of subject-specific ones (which enable you to demonstrate subject knowledge), some which will elicit your extra-curricular potential, and a combination of questions of a more general educational nature, such as those listed earlier in this chapter. To a very great extent, teaching is teaching, and learning is learning at whatever level.]

- **Some recent studies and articles are suggesting that traditional math: geometry, algebra and calculus—those subjects which have been described as "gatekeeper courses" for further studies—are no longer relevant to students and are almost never used in the workplace. Instead our students will require logic, probability and measurement. How will your Grade 12 (or whatever) program reflect this?**

  Find out what the school offers in materials and hardware. Discuss how you would implement results of Edward De Bono's work on lateral thinking, perhaps, or how you teach Boolean search techniques, or even classical and applied logic. Dr. Willard Daggett has written some neat stuff on this. He supports a taxonomy, quite different than Bloom's, that goes like this: (1) Knowledge; (2) Application within a discipline; (3) Application between disciplines; (4) Application to real-world predictable problems; (5) Application to real-world un-predictable problems. Thus you might do well to stress the applicability of your content and how you teach its application, rather than over-emphasising the acquisition of knowledge.

- **Referring to a taxonomy of "applied" rather than more abstract learning (see above), how could you modify your subject area to ensure that it teaches students the applicability of what they are learning, and how can your subject be used to teach the skills of application of knowledge in real-world un-predictable situations?**

- **"Good instruction in measurement should not only teach skills, but also expand the student's ability to learn and understand mathematics,"** *Common Curriculum.* **How would you ensure that the development of skills in measurement helps develop skills and concepts in other areas of mathematics?**

  Use measurement in active problem solving. Compare, order and then measure. Manipulate models, both tangible and in the abstract. Provide lots and lots of chances to explore relationships and identify generalizations from observed patterns. Frequent exposure to opportunities to use measurement will help. Use estimation as a corollary skill. Stress the importance of estimation when using a calculator. Also discuss the whole area of making math cross-curricular by co-operating with other teachers. Discuss how to make math, and especially measurement, real-life relevant: graphing, statistics (and manipulating them for fun), probability, analyzing and interpreting data, formulating hypotheses, and devising testing procedures and controls. Use student experiences and incorporate them as well as structure them.

"I studied the lives of great men and famous women, and I found that the men and women who got to the top were those who did the jobs they had in hand, with everything they had of energy and enthusiasm and hard work."

—*Harry S. Truman*

- The *Common Curriculum* identifies as an important outcome, students developing "Understanding of Form in the Arts." Why is it important for students to develop the ability to analyze form in the arts?

  Students discover ways in which materials, elements, techniques, balance, unity and variety contribute to the structure of a whole work, then they understand how to create impact or emote specific responses by their art. This knowledge may help them develop the skills to express feeling. They can also, by understanding form, transfer understanding of form from one art to another.

- How might you in a Grade 11 class deal with the fact that 60% of your students have used the same non-standard grammar structure (such as split infinitive, or non-agreement of noun and verb) in their writing in the past week?

  How about a mini-lesson for the whole class, then review the lesson one week later with the group of those still experiencing difficulty. Encouraging peer editing might also be a technique.

- Describe some of the characteristics of an adolescent.

  Hormones going crazy, search for identity, self-esteem issues, need for recognition, need for independence together with need for support, etc. *Answering the Call*, listed in PART XI, has a good section on this.

- Do males and females have different adolescent experiences?

  If you think not, you need to broaden your reading. Do, however, be certain you don't appear sexist!

- What in your training or experience especially equips you to work with adolescent learners?

- What, other than hardware shortage, would limit your use of I.T. in your program?

  By this point in their education, pupils should be using I.T. seamlessly, as another research and reporting tool, across platforms and programs, choosing the best format for developing and presenting their work. All of their written or multi-media reports should be expected to include accurately annotated electronic sources. If they can't by now, they are almost too late.

"Those who educate children well are more to be honoured than parents, for these only gave life, those the art of living well."
—*Aristotle*

"I'm too old to know everything."
—*Anon.*

"By these methods we may learn wisdom: first, by reflection, which is noblest; second, by imitation, which is easiest; and third, by experience which is the bitterest."
—*Confucius*

TEACHING IN A SPECIALTY SCHOOL

[This could be a school of a specific faith, a school which subscribes to a particular teaching methodology (Montessori, Waldorf, etc.) or a school serving one specific cultural group.]

- **What training or experience have you had specifically in (this faith, methodology, culture) ?**

  Let them know you are well prepared to meet the needs of their pupils and the requirements of the school's supporters; you have background and understanding of their objectives. Give them evidence of your expertise: classes you have taught, outreach programs or youth groups you have organized or helped with, study classes that you have taken or led, etc. Be certain to include as at least one of your references someone who has a position of repute in that community: a respected member of the faith or a clergyperson, a respected authority in that field, local or national, depending on who you know.

- **Why is this methodology superior to others?**

  They want to know that you are committed to what they are committed to. They believe with all their heart in what they represent; do you? Don't put other people or methods down excessively but let them know you are positive about theirs. To get a feeling for the idea of the difference between "involvement" and "commitment," consider a breakfast of ham and eggs. The chicken was involved, the pig was committed.

- **What is your vision of the role of the teacher in (*Roman Catholic, Baptist, Islamic, Hebrew, Montessori, Seventh-Day Adventist, etc.*) education?**

  Talk to them about the concept of teaching by precept and example, how it is important for the teacher to walk the talk, and how it is a lifestyle as well as intellectual content which is being taught.

  The above question could also be asked about "public" educators. Here, your answer would reflect the fact that public education teaches children how to think, rather than telling them what to believe. It also teaches respect and tolerance for divergence of opinions and permits differences to co-exist.

TEACHING IN A FIRST NATIONS SCHOOL

- **How have you lived your culture?**

  They will want to know if you have taken or taught native language classes, are you fluent in their aboriginal language, have you helped with youth counselling, what work have you done to support the band or council, etc. In other words, do you walk the talk? If you are a non-aboriginal person applying to teach in a First Nations school, be ready to answer the same question: what have you done to learn of and to support their culture?

- **To what extent are you "capable?"**

  This is a really neat word used by the Dené to describe someone who is able to look after him/herself in nature, in the old ways, and to help others to do so, too. It is someone who has a good and secure comfort and relationship with the spiritual world, the community, the land and him/herself.

"It takes few words to tell the truth."
—*Chief Joseph* of the Nez Percé

- What do you see as the importance of the control by First Nations people of First Nations schools?

- How would you awaken the interest of youth in our culture and values?

  Do your homework on this one and have a plan with several practical ideas, preferably ones you have already found effective! They have heard all the platitudes too many times. Your talk will need to match your walk. How have you shown respect for the elders, and how have you shown respect for yourself and your heritage? Now, what will you do to be an example that young people will want to follow?

"We are an island in a lake. We must stand together, or they will rub us out separately."
—*Tatanka Yotanka* (*Sitting Bull*, Great Chief of the Sioux)

FRENCH AS A SECOND LANGUAGE
(OR OTHER SECOND LANGUAGE)

Expect to be asked some questions in French and be ready to respond in French. Don't worry if you think not everyone on the committee understands; you might be surprised, and if not, that's OK, too.

- How would you accommodate split-grade programming, considering that language acquisition is a progressive or cumulative process? For example, if you have those in the same class now who have a different number of years of French instruction; i.e., Grade 3's in with Grade 4's.

  Teach in groups, just like any other class!

- How would you go about developing motivated, self-directed learners in a second-language classroom?

- How would you modify your program to accommodate both gifted learners and the learning-delayed pupils in your French program?

- The *Common Curriculum Provincial Standards: Language*, 1995, states that "First-language literacy is important for second-language learning. It helps students grasp key concepts more easily and influences general academic achievement." How would you modify a language immersion, or a second-language program to accommodate the needs of students in the early years who have not yet developed first-language literacy?

- Referring to the above quote from the *Common Curriculum Provincial Standards: Language*, 1995, how do you justify starting second-language instruction before Grade 5?

- How would you establish "achievement standards" for your students?

- When is it important to explain something to a pupil in his/her own language rather than in the language being taught?

- What other subjects could you integrate with French to build and maintain enthusiasm?

- **How can you use Information Technology (I.T.) in your French program?**

  Start with enrichment and remediation. There are a lot of good FSL computer programs now.

RECORD-KEEPING

- **How would you keep track of the progress of each child in an activity-based program? Or it could be asked as: What are some record-keeping devices you have used or would use in this classroom?**

  Give specific examples of how you organize your record-keeping. If you use a recognized method or set of assessment instruments, name them. This question may also be asked when applying for a position with Special Needs learners.

- **Do you feel a program should be "Developmental?"**

- **What role should use of "Benchmarks" play in determining the program for pupils in your class?**

  This is especially important in today's "accountability-rich" environment.

- **How would you improve the report card used by this school/board?**

  Know what it is, have an idea or two, but don't be excessively critical.

THE USE AND POTENTIAL OF INFORMATION TECHNOLOGY IN EDUCATION AND YOUR CLASSROOM

- **Describe your knowledge and skills with computers as they relate to the classroom.**

- **What is the future of I.T. in education?**

  Have a pretty good idea of futurist thought but moderate your enthusiasm by knowing what hardware/software the board or school has or is likely to acquire. Also know the philosophy of the administrators; they control the pursestrings, and no-one ever said I.T. is inexpensive, although many have said we can't afford not to include it along with reading and writing.

- **"Children up to the end of Grade 3 learn to read; after that they read to learn. Children up to the end of Grade 4 learn to use I.T.; after that they use I.T. to learn." What are your comments on this suggestion?**

- **How would you go about accessing World Wide Web sites that would be relevant to your children?**

  There are many good lists already prepared, such as "Compass for the Internet"—a commercial one. You could also mention the search engine(s) you use—Alta Vista seems to meet the needs of most teachers for complex as well as simple searches. You could mention a few of the sites you have found particularly helpful, as well, and even mention why they meet your criteria of a good or useful site. Don't be shy; tell them enough to let them know you know where you are going on the 'net.

See also APPENDIX 16.

- **What are some WWW sites you have used in your classroom?**

  List several and discuss their specific benefits and positive points, as well as a few of their limitations.

- **What computer programs have you found useful working with pupils in math (reading, spelling, environmental studies, FSL, or whatever) at the _____ grade level?**

  Compile a list for each curriculum category so you can offer a few you are familiar with for the level you are applying for.

- **How early would you start to teach keyboarding.**

  You could mention that you are aware that voice-activated equipment may well reduce the need for keyboarding, but let them know you see it as an important skill, at least until then. If you would use a specific teaching program, such as Almena™ or Dr. Mario Teaches Typing™, mention it or them by name.

- **What can you do to make children I.T.-literate with the equipment we have?**

  Find out what there is as part of your pre-interview research and then come up with a plan. Tell them what it is. Sounds simple; it isn't, so please spend some time working on it. This whole topic of I.T. in education is an area which will do more to sell you than any other, right now! I don't know how to say that strongly enough! Please, just believe me and prepare yourself by acquiring as extensive a knowledge in this as you possibly can! See PART IV for a brief discussion of this.

INNOVATIONS AND CREATIVITY

- **Describe an initiative you have taken or an innovation you have introduced which demonstrates your creativity.**

- **What is the one change you have made in your school or class of which you are most proud?**

- **How do you go about creating change?**

  Let them know that you are not the type who is so busy making people grow, and helping people grow, that you don't let people grow. Also, discuss how you share a vision and tend to act your role in getting others to see the need for change, how you get them on-side, how you focus the group energy, and how you help to maintain the pace of change. A quote from Edgar A. Guest might help: "He started to sing as he tackled the thing / That couldn't be done, and he did it." On the whole topic of eliciting and focusing the energy of a group, and effective use of "strategic humility," a book which does an excellent job of contrasting effective and ineffective styles, and a really "good read," is *The Genius of Sitting Bull: 13 Heroic Strategies for Today's Business Leaders*, by Emmett C. Murphy and Michael

Another really excellent book on this topic is *The Fifth Discipline: The Art and Practice of the Learning Organization*, by Peter Senge.

117

> "We judge ourselves by what we feel capable of doing, while others judge us by what we have already done."
> —Henry Wadsworth Longfellow

Snell, published by Prentice Hall. It's aimed at business leaders but applies exactly to teachers and school personnel! A "must read" for those who want to influence the direction of change.

- **Why do you tend to change jobs so frequently?**

  This will only apply if it fits, so to speak; e.g., if you didn't list on your C.V. your **"Reason for leaving"** for each of your previous jobs or your reasons were not convincing. If you are the creative type who thrives on change, including change in location, while being careful not to give unintentional affront, you could possibly suggest that, personally, you agree with Ellen Glascow's point of view: "The only difference between a rut and a grave is their dimensions." You will then have to explain, however, that you are referring only to you liking to move to keep out of a rut; you know others keep themselves fresh in other ways. (Don't ruffle their carefully preened feathers.) They will next, probably, want to know about how long you intend to stay in this job, and so on. Thus the best approach is to be very careful in demonstrating a plan in your career path. Some people have been known to use creative re-construction, a little blending of serendipity and perspicacity, otherwise known as "only afterward, recognizing the astuteness of your decisions."

PUBLIC RELATIONS

> "The first and possibly commonest error in public relations is to regard them as a form of first aid, to be applied only in times of trouble."
> —Rex Harlow

- **What are some public relations activities you have implemented, or would like to implement, to make a school better known and to increase its repute in the community?**

  Go beyond the simple, usual ones. Inspire them but don't suggest things that cost money!

- **Dr. William Purkey divides teachers and schools into four categories: (1) intentionally uninviting, (2) unintentionally uninviting, (3) unintentionally inviting, and (4) intentionally inviting. Tell us about something you have done in the recent past which has made your school "intentionally inviting."**

YOUR EXTRA-CURRICULAR POTENTIAL

- **What do you do to relax?**

  What is it that you are not only willing to do, but like to do, that you could share with your pupils?

- **Besides being an excellent teacher and colleague, what can you add to this school as a whole?**

  It is no longer enough to be just a great teacher.

- **What special abilities can you bring to (a) this position, and/or (b) the school? or it may be worded as: What can you offer this school? or What extra-curricular activities can you offer the pupils of this school?**

  Name several and be prepared to tell how you would implement them.

> "Nothing is so contagious as enthusiasm."
> —Samuel Taylor Coleridge

- What hidden talents do you have?

- How have your life experiences (or hobbies, or personal skills, or activities out of school) made you a better person in ways that you can now share with children?

"Where there is no vision, the people perish."
—*Proverbs of Solomon, 29:18*

INITIATIVE

- What job would you choose if you could have any position in our board right now? Why?

  Show interest in the job applied for but also very briefly sketch out your planned career path. Be certain, however, that they are not given the idea that you are just using this position as a stepping stone. They need to be reassured that you will fulfil this position well!

- Do you feel you have done the best work of which you are capable?

  This one could be dangerous: are you smugly resting on your laurels, or still striving, or have you been more laid-back than you might have in past positions, or what? Plan your response carefully. Are you still improving?

- Tell us about something which illustrates your initiative.

  Be careful not to go too far; personal initiative without control is anarchy.

- Our board is in the process of implementing several important initiatives; e.g., math assessment, transactional writing, etc., etc. How could you as a member of staff contribute to these areas?

TEAM/CO-OPERATIVE ACTIVITIES

- Describe some cross-divisional or inter-class activities you have co-operatively planned and implemented in your school.

- Most schools encourage planning as a Divisional Team. Discuss ways in which you can encourage this to happen.

- What have you done to include other teachers, parents, or pupils in your planning?

- Describe in detail (but without identifying individuals) what you personally have done in a planning group to "draw in" or include a colleague whom other staff wanted to exclude, either because their input was not considered valuable or because they were considered too domineering.

- How can you make sure that a team you are on is successful in meeting its objectives, or delivering on its mandate?

  Help keep them focused on the goals, facilitate rather than obstruct, keep positive, praise the contribution of others and, perhaps especially, attempt to help eliminate or at least limit interferences such as constant changes of format, direction, process, etc. You might even want to remember a mid-

"I have found it advisable not to give too much heed to what people say when I am trying to accomplish something of consequence. Invariably they proclaim, 'It can't be done.' I deem that the very best time to make the effort."
—*Calvin Coolidge*

"A man has at least a start on discovering the meaning of human life when he plants shade trees under which he knows full well he will never sit."
—*Elton Trueblood*

first century AD quote from Gaius Petronius: "We trained hard—but it seemed that every time we were beginning to form into teams, we would be reorganized. I was to learn later in life that we tend to meet any new situation by reorganizing. And what a wonderful method it can be for creating the illusion of progress while producing inefficiency, confusion and demoralization." By contrast, Shiddle once commented that "A group becomes a team when each of its members becomes sufficiently confident in his own contributions to praise the work of others." That idea will take you a long way!

A good quote to use in an answer on this whole area could be one attributed, by the classical author Arrian, to Alexander the Great: "Upon the conduct of each, depends the fate of all." Why not work it into your response if you can make it fit?

See also the "Special Needs" section.

WRAP-UP QUESTIONS

- **In light of the selection criteria we are using, and of which you have been given a copy, (note: you do not always get this) do you have any questions for us, or is there anything you wish to clarify?**

  Now is the time to bring out your list of questions. See below for suggestions.

- **We want to make our decision as soon as possible. Some of those you named for references we could not contact. Could you provide the name of one or two other persons who could give a reference?**

  Have one or two ready, perhaps even written out for them on a piece of paper just in case. That shows preparedness: a good quality in a teacher!

- **Are you able to participate in frequent after-school functions: co-curricular activities, staff meetings, in-service training sessions, school and board committee meetings, etc.?**

  Are you a member of the "3:31 Track Club?" Remember: if you regularly need to go to physiotherapy and can only schedule it at 4:00, this will be a decided problem! Then offer to work at lunch time.

- **Is there any reason, except for illness or bereavement, why you will not be able to work every day of the established school year?**

  This is the only legal way of asking if your religious obligations will interfere with your teaching by requiring special holy days off work. You probably won't be asked but, just in case, find out how others of your faith handle it. What sort of a deal do they have with the board?

- **Why do you want to work for our board?**

  What did you find out about this board? Don't let them think it is just one of three dozen to which you applied.

- **This is your last chance. Is there anything you wish to add to what you have told us?**

  They mean exactly that: don't hesitate now!

"He who asks is a fool for five minutes, but he who does not ask remains a fool forever."
—*Chinese proverb*

You will almost always be given an opportunity at the end to ask your questions. Don't feel you have to hide your list. Asking a few insightful questions now is a good way to indicate sincere interest in them and the job. It helps show that you are not just "comparison shopping." You may want to consider such questions as: very specific details about the community and area, local service clubs, and if it is a term-definite position, the starting date, etc. This suggestion I owe to Prof. Jack Jones of the Nipissing Faculty of Education: "be careful not to ask questions which are answered in the board's literature!" On the same vein, general questions such as extra curricular activities in the school, school teams, special initiatives of the school or board, etc., they will expect you to have found out as part of your research; you could, however, ask very, very specific questions on these. You may even want to mention some success their school has had recently to show you do know about them, and follow their fortunes! You aren't telling them you are interested; you are showing them! Then briefly summarize the two or three key points that you want them to remember, smile, and they will ask for clarification of what you have just said if they want it, and/or let you know the interview is over. Then thank them, and the receptionist on your way by, and leave gracefully.

IMPRESSIONS

It is best at this time to avoid questions about pay, benefits, etc., as we want our interest in children to be the final impression we make on the committee. Besides, you can obtain that information from your Teachers' Federation/ Union/Association/Society office. (See PART IX.)

AFTER THE INTERVIEW

Though very rarely, it is sometimes acceptable to send a brief note to the "contact person" thanking the committee for their time and interest in you, whether you have not heard yet, or know you didn't get the position. Not only can it be polite if they were especially accommodating to you, but under some circumstances it can help to keep you in their mind. It may also be useful if you want to add a maximum of one piece of information you missed presenting. It can, too, be a mine-field: be certain to judge the climate of their personalities; are they likely to see such a contact as an attempt to manipulate or pressure them? If there is even a chance they will, don't contact them at all! Except in very specific circumstances, your best option is to sit quietly and wait.

If, however, you decide such a note will be the right thing to do, keep it very, very, very short. Just thank them and mention the additional information; do not say anything about "hoping to hear from you"—they don't need and won't appreciate the pressure. It should simply say something like:

Dear Mr. Smithers:

Thank you for your time, and that of the other committee members, at my interview yesterday. I am now more than ever convinced that I want to work in your school.

One thing I forgot to mention in the interview was that I have worked with my present board developing a unit on Archaeology for Primary Aged Pupils. I would be pleased to provide details if you wish.

Yours truly

etc.

"I'll be back."
—*Arnold Schwarzenegger* in *"The Terminator"*

PATIENCE IS A VIRTUE

It is difficult to sit and wait after an interview, but there is nothing to be gained by calling them. Sometimes decisions take time.

In the interview you showed them your vision; now show them your patience!

Then sit and wait. Unless at least two weeks have gone by, there is nothing to be gained by phoning them. If they are going to hire you they will let you know. If not, what do you gain? If they are just trying to make up their mind, they won't appreciate a call and won't be more inclined to hire you.

Regrettable as it may seem, some administrators take a lot of time to make a decision. Personally, I try to contact all the candidates that same day, unless there is a reason why the decision cannot be made immediately, but not all principals are the same. It is uncomfortable to be kept waiting, but sit tight and consider going to other interviews if they are scheduled. You might be able to "buy some time," but remember that if you even verbally agree to accept another position, and then the earlier one is offered to you, you have a verbal contract and you are committed (except in Alberta, see APPENDICES 8 and 9). It is a gamble, but there is just no way out of it in our profession. You alone can decide when it is worth turning down one on the chance that the other may be offered.

If you are unsuccessful, you may wish to ask for comments on your interview. This is usually called a debriefing, if it is done formally. You could discretely request a debriefing by asking if there are courses they recommend which would better prepare you, or is there something in the way you present yourself in an interview that needs attention. It is usually best to avoid directly demanding a debriefing as this can raise fears of grievance or litigation in the minds of more anxious or less secure administrators, and there is usually nothing to be gained by alienating them. They talk to other administrators!

Perhaps this is the time when you could also ask them if they know of other openings coming up in their school or board. That is a good way to prevent their consideration of you from being limited!

With this extensive groundwork you will do much better than you think! We have covered a lot in this section, but your preparation will pay off. You are now well on the way!

PART VII

ACCEPTING A POSITION AND SIGNING A CONTRACT

So, you have made it: they're offering you a position! Now there are a few things to remember, including the fact that even a verbal agreement is a contract, and thus is binding (except in Alberta, but there is another technicality that can catch you; see APPENDIX 8). In our profession you do **not** want to be in breach of contract!

Frankly, if you are hoping and waiting for a particular offer and meanwhile you receive an offer for another position, you can ask for a day to think about it (although there is a very real possibility that this will result in the offer being withdrawn and given to someone else). But there is totally and absolutely no way you can ethically or legally play one against the other. If you accept, you are bound; if you don't, they are free to offer the position to someone else. (The exception to this is in Saskatchewan where you have four days to accept or decline an offer of a position.) Some boards formalize the agreement by having an Acceptance of Position Form signed pending the preparation of a contract and until you provide to them necessary documentation. In provinces and territories without formal "contracts," the "Acceptance of Position" form confirms the agreement. See APPENDIX 9 for samples of each.

If you accept a position, you are bound until the agreement is terminated, either by you or the board. Note, however, that time-definite positions are limited; they are not permanent contracts and, unless both parties agree to extend the agreement, these positions terminate as planned. For other contracts, there are for each province and territory specific cut-off dates or requirements for advance notification by which notice must be given if either party intends to terminate the contract. See APPENDIX 8. You and the board must adhere to these dates or restrictions; you cannot just not appear in class some day and later tell them that you have moved or decided to extend your tropical vacation! I once worked (briefly) with a teacher who did that!

In addition to specified periods or dates for notification of intent to terminate, at any other time the contract can be broken only by "mutual consent" (except in cases of firings, or termination "with cause," as it is called). Be assured that mutual consent is rare indeed; although I know of exceptions, few principals and boards are willing to release what they perceive to be an excellent teacher part way through a term. I know of many more examples where the teacher was required to continue to teach until the legal termination date, just as a teacher would expect the board to continue to pay them if the board wanted out of the contract.

Note that terminations initiated by a board can be for different reasons: (a) for layoff (which involves in most areas an obligation with respect to recall—Quebec has an especially "sweet" deal) or (b) for misconduct. The

"Too many people quit looking for work when they find a job."
—*Anon.*

"Nothing in fine print is ever good news."
—*Mickey Rooney*

"What's past is prologue."
—*The Tempest*, Act 2, Scene 1

latter type of termination occurs when, for reasons considered appropriate (just cause), a board terminates a contract with full intention of replacing the terminated teacher with another; it is not a case of the position being no longer available. "With cause" terminations can occur at any time during the year; lay-offs usually occur at the end of a year or the end of a term.

For a detailed look at the requirements of each province and territory for notification of intent to terminate a contract, see "APPENDIX 8: **Dates, Details and Deadlines for Termination of a Contract, Contract Types and their Durations**." Remember, though, it is a guide; for detailed specifics or for help out of a difficult situation, or to avoid getting into one, your best help is your provincial or territorial teachers' union, association, society or federation. See PART X for their phone numbers and call them!

For your reference, and to illustrate the vast diversity among them, find in APPENDIX 9 a few samples of contracts from various geographical areas, and a few notes on them.

"There is a tide in the affairs of men
Which, when taken at the flood, leads on to fortune;
Omitted, all the voyage of their life
Is bound in shallows and in miseries.
On such a full sea are we now afloat,
And we must take the current when it serves,
Or lose our ventures."
—*Julius Casear*, Act 4, Scene 3

PART VIII

"OCCASIONAL TEACHING": AN ALTERNATE ROUTE TO A FULL-TIME POSITION

One very viable option which can be used while you decide what level/grade you want to teach, or in which school, or until the job you like comes up, is, as it is variously known, the Supply or Casual or Occasional or Replacement Teacher route. It does provide an interim way of almost keeping the bailiff from seizing all your assets to pay your debts and, much more important, it is an excellent way to get into schools, get known and show them how good you are! It can be an alternate route to a full-time position you want.

After you have taught several times in a school, if you have become comfortable with the principal or vice-principal, you could even invite them to pop in for an informal appraisal—"to offer some suggestions"— so you "can improve your skills." If they like what they see, it will help your chances! You might, also, eventually ask if you can use them as a reference; they will have more credibility than an "outsider."

GETTING ON THE LIST

So, how to do this? Different boards handle this differently. In some, the principal selects those to be on that school's Occasional Teacher List; in others, they are selected centrally; in still others, they are interviewed in the schools and then their names placed on a central list; some boards have a policy of "if you apply you are on the list until you are deemed unacceptable or get a full-time job"; and there are probably other methods as well. Then, in some boards they are called by the principal or VP of the school as needed; in some boards they are called by a central dispatch person, and so on. It is impossible to generalize. You simply must check and see how the board(s) you are interested in conduct this whole procedure. Any school secretary is a good person to ask for a accurate answer on almost anything, including this!

Before you get on an Occasional Teacher List, you will probably be called to an interview, either at a school or the board office. Increasingly, boards and principals are becoming more careful into whose care they put their children. When you contact the board to discover their procedures, also check the timeline. This is very important as many boards have application deadlines and/or ceilings on the number on the list. Your vigilance will be rewarded!

A bit of advice: when required to fill out an application form, avoid the temptation just to put "see attached résumé" and hope they will do the cross-match! **Remember, it is worth it to make it easy for them!** It is a good idea, however, also to attach your résumé unless specifically instructed

"One can no more judge a person by the actions of an hour than the climate of a country by the temperature of the day."
—*J. Petit-Senn*

not to. Referring to your résumé will help you remember to list all your qualifications; you don't want to miss out because you forgot to mention that you have some particular course or qualification they are hoping for.

NEW GRADUATES

New graduates often wonder if they can do replacement teaching between their graduation and the end of the school year. Check with your Teachers' Federation/Union/Society/Association as the ruling on this varies by province and territory. In most jurisdictions, you are not deemed a qualified teacher until the Ministry or Department of Education, or College of Teachers, for your area has actually granted you the "paper," or "registered" you (upon the "recommendation" of a Dean of Education is how it is officially done). Some areas are taking a very conservative view and are holding to the letter of the law. In areas where there are fewer replacement teachers available or in a school where your "practice-teaching" distinguished you, however, you may well find that the rules bend a little. It's worth the chance. Each jurisdiction will have its own interpretation, and even the rules are subject to change, seemingly without notice.

SHORT- AND LONG-TERM POSITIONS

There are essentially two types of "Occasional" or "Replacement" or "Supply" teachers: "Short-Term"—sometimes called "Casual"—and "Extended" or "Long-Term." The former are hired usually by the day to replace teachers who are ill or away on leave, etc. The latter are hired to replace those teachers who are to be away for an extended time: long-term illness, pregnancy, and in some provinces, death during the year, etc. (Check APPENDIX 8 for details on contracts for less than a full year.)

You may start your career in a short-term position more easily than in a long-term one, as the latter are usually posted and those on contract with the board already (perhaps in a part-day position) have first opportunity to apply. But a day here and a day there is the way to get known and to build experience so you do especially well when a better opportunity arises. Surprisingly often, occasional teachers are those who are hired for an upcoming position—they have already demonstrated their proficiency through (depending upon the number of days they have been in) a 5- or 10- or 30-hour "interview!"

Whatever the manner, it is advisable to get yourself on the list as soon as you can. If you are a new graduate, you can call and find out about whether they will take an interim application pending receipt of the certificate. It helps immensely if you get around to the schools; meet the person who is in charge of replacement teachers and make it your business to become aware of the school procedures for these teachers. You can then pick up a copy of their "School Handbook" and "Occasional Teacher Handbook," too, so when you do get called you know the school routines. You may also want to request a copy of their Behavioural Code. Don't be afraid to drop around again in about a month if you haven't been called. Sometimes it helps to jog their memory that you are still available! After about three visits and no calls, however, you probably might as well let it go—they obviously are not interested.

One way to decide which board you should do replacement teaching for may be: have they hired teachers recently with qualifications similar to yours? Can you can get to their schools by public transit if you have no car? Remember, when it comes to the application process, the board that

PROCESSING FEE

Don't be surprised if there is a "processing fee" of five to twenty-five dollars when you apply to a large board.

Sure, it's a blatant attempt to augment their budget. But, if you ask and the local union reports a high demand for replacement teachers, you can re-coup that!

makes it hardest may be the one with the best chances for you, if it thus discourages others. If you can get another job which will allow you freedom to cancel there and be replaced whenever a teaching job comes up for a day, that may be a determining factor. I have known people with such an arrangement to pay the bills until the full-time teaching job they wanted became available. And, as the teacher surplus is disappearing and teaching jobs become more plentiful in Canada, the ultimate question might be: "Do I really want to live in this area?"

A FEW BLUNT "DO'S" AND "DON'TS"

A few words of further advice from someone who has spent frustrating hours calling occasional teachers: **you will do well if you don't limit yourself to the "close" schools.** Be willing to travel. But do be reasonable in large boards: can you really get to a school almost sixty kilometres away in forty-five minutes if you have not showered or dressed when the call comes in. Then gently offer to negotiate: "I would like to, but it is 55 km from here so I couldn't get there until almost 9:30." If the person calling is in a difficult spot she or he may accept that; in any case, they will recognize that it is a legitimate problem, see that you are trying your best to be accommodating, and will be inclined to call again when they have more "lead time."

Please be careful not to turn down opportunities because you are going shopping or fishing or have a hair appointment. (Or, at least, don't let them know that is the reason you are not available.) Again, from the caller's perspective, I have to tell you that it is very frustrating to hear excuse after excuse as an administrator tries to get replacement teachers lined up for the day. It is a good idea, if you have already been called to another school, to tell them the school you are going to (at least if it is in the same board) it shows that you are the sort of replacement teacher who is "in demand."

Remember, too, if you decline you may be setting yourself up for a wait; in boards where replacement teachers are called in rotation, it may be a while before your name comes up again; in boards where they are not called in any order, the ones with a history of being "ready and willing" get called over and over. How do you get onto and stay on the "inside track?" **Let them know you take their school seriously, and they will take you seriously.**

Another point to consider: it is really not a good idea to specify on the forms that you want to be called the night before. Not only does that limit your calls but, as indicated above, by being flexible and willing to help out when they need you suddenly, they will then think of you in more relaxed moments as well. **Make it easy for them to give you the job.** Even though it is extremely short-term, it could (and very likely will, eventually, if you are really outstanding) lead to a permanent position. Once you are in the door, you can start to impress everyone with your competence. And you would not believe how often a "one-day" call stretches on when the teacher being replaced realizes they are more seriously ill than they thought! You are now working your way toward exactly the job you want!

Please remember always to be professional; it is very important that you make a good impression on them! Dress for comfort, but be appropriate. Don't discuss problem students in the staff room, even if others are doing so. Don't criticize the school routines or policies. Don't try to tell the principal (all on the first day) all the things she or he is doing

INSIDE TIP

Be sure to answer the phone yourself in the mornings. Think of it from their position: a principal, vice-principal or dispatcher just does not have time to talk to a four-year old, trying to explain to them why it is so necessary for them to tell their mommy or daddy right away that the stranger on the phone really needs to talk to them.

BE APPROACHABLE

Not all staff members are friendly; make the best of it by being professional and friendly yourself. Bring your own coffee mug, and ask if there are "designated" chairs in the staffroom. Be approachable, without gushing.

wrong. (I've seen that done, too!) Don't gossip about other schools or compare them to the one you are in. It just does not put you on the "inside track."

Don't criticize the teacher's work or plans (or lack thereof). I know one school system, in Nebraska, where Substitute Teachers are asked to fill out a report on the absent teacher's lesson plans and organization! Questions include: are the day-plans clear? are they easily followed? are they complete? are materials readily available? is the class list up-to-date? is the daily schedule available? are supervision duties outlined? and is the rules/discipline plan available? They then are expected to hand their report to the principal for his or her signature!

Be aware, though, that in addition to that being profoundly unprofessional—by Canadian standards—in their system the replaced teacher is also asked to fill out a report on the occasional teacher! Areas for comment include: are you respected by the pupils and did you maintain classroom control (exactly how they are supposed to know, I don't know, but I guess they can guess)? did you follow lesson plans outlined? did you do the extra supervision duties required? would they like you back in their classroom? and the big one, did you maintain confidentiality? You might want to ask yourself whether they will report favourably on you, and want you back, if you break confidentiality by "tattling" to the principal that you don't like their lesson plans! You might consider, also, that the principal might not be too impressed with someone who is critical of an experienced (and possibly favourite) teacher. **Survive! If you can't be positive, be non-committal.** The argument can be made (to yourself, at least) that if the principal wants to know about that teacher's lesson plans, she or he can check it out on their own. It is not your duty to document another teacher's performance!

Now a suggestion which ought to be absurd, but unfortunately isn't: if you are using the photocopy machine and another "regular" teacher comes along and needs to use it, you can score points by stopping your work and letting them. Then continue on with your own photocopying after they use the machine. (I know that a line can form; you have to be the judge of when it becomes ridiculous!) Doing so can, however, promote your "positive and co-operative" image.

This is one more reason to arrive as early as you can and to make up the "class sets" of replacement copies for use at your next school at the end of the day before you leave. Don't forget to mention to the secretary— just in passing, as it were—that you are doing so to replace ones you brought with you. I know this may appear pedantic, but it can be a little misunderstanding like that that can get you kicked off the "inside track."

A FEW MORE SUGGESTIONS FOR SUCCESS IN OCCASIONAL TEACHING

You may want to have a lunch made up the night before or make one up and keep it in the freezer (one that needs very little preparation is best; the staffroom microwave may be busy). Also, I have been told it helps to have appropriate clothes chosen and set out the night before. In winter, as a long shot, you may wish to take a change of clothes and a kit of toiletries if you are teaching far from home. If a sudden storm hits, you may need to stay in a hotel that night instead of going home. That way you are fresh and available for the next day if needed and, more important, safe. I know of those who do so, but that seems to be a rare requirement even in a snow belt.

You really need to have a briefcase or box packed with a complete day-plan for each division you may be called to teach. Sometimes teachers take their day-plan book home, and then become ill, so you have nothing when you arrive. The office will have a schedule of their gym times, and such, but you may be on your own for the rest. Include a selection of surefire lessons for the variety of different age groups. Those intended for other age groups can help address, on short notice, the needs of exceptional learners at each end of the developmental continuum.

Be sure to include a Physical Education lesson which is fun, complete and requires no unusual entry skills or equipment; an easy-to-teach art lesson which is effective but demands few unusual materials; an interesting "extension" math lesson; and a reading lesson complete with materials including handouts and questions or a response guide. Most schools, if you ask them, will let you make a class set (or even two) of copies of materials you have used, ready for your next call, and many will see that as commendable preparedness.

A collection of slides of a trip you took may well initiate a brief self-contained unit on Geography, Multiculturalism, Man and Society, Conservation and Ecology, etc. Bring along an interesting item—an animal pelt, a bear's claw, a dog harness with photos of a team in action, an autographed baseball, an interesting bit of rock, a wasp's nest, an item of very old clothes (such as a high button shoe), a piece of cultural art, etc.—and let the pupils feel and explore it. I remember one occasional teacher who had lived in Ethiopia for a couple of years, teaching in the International School in Addis Ababa. The two days he spent in my school were very enlightening and exciting for that class, as he showed pictures and artifacts and regaled them with stories of the culture, history, politics, customs, food, industry, and so on of that country. I would have hired him for the first opening I had (not just for this; he was an excellent and creative teacher), but he went back when the civil war there ended, and last I heard he was running a children's circus in India!

Find out the basic school routines, and let the pupils know that you know!

You may want to include the class in planning the day, especially if there is no plan. Ask them for suggestions, give them options within which you can live, and let them help decide how much time will be used effectively on each area. It is, however, important that you make certain the time is used effectively all day and that activity is purposeful, and obviously so to the pupils. You do not need parents hearing that the day with you was less than profitable and having them reporting such information back to the principal!

Consider including in your "Box" a selection of games, puzzles, brainteasers (these can make math interesting even to pupils who usually hate it), story-books, etc. Be sure to include a variety of stories so some are suitable for each age level. These can be useful "contingency" items in case the VCR doesn't work when it is supposed to.

At the end of the day, you will want to record for your own future information what you taught that class; a "special lesson" loses effect the second time you try to present it to the same group! It will help you to build your collection of lessons and to improve and modify them; it will help you keep track of teachers who could help you in various curriculum areas (networking); it will enable you to refresh your memory before you

PHOTOCOPYING TIP

If you need a lot of copies made of a variety of handouts, talk to a principal you know. Most will tell you to just go ahead or, if it's not for use at their school, will ask you to supply the paper. That beats paying 6 to 15 cents a copy.

"I don't think much of a man who is not wiser today than he was yesterday."

—*Abraham Lincoln*

go into that classroom next time, so you are even better prepared! It also helps you keep track of what levels and schools you have taught in, so you can relate this when you are asked at an interview. (Later you might even want to take to the interview a copy of units you have developed and taught; when your experience is limited, use what you have.)

You could use a recording form like the one provided below (with the compliments of John Stephens, a principal with the Near North District School Board and long-time Teachers' Federation Executive member) or make up one of your own. Another copy of this, ready for photocopying, is included for you in APPENDIX 3.

SUPPLY TEACHING INFORMATION RECORD SHEET

School: _____ Date(s) _____ to _____

Class/Subject(s) taught: _____

Name(s) of teacher(s) replaced: _____

Lessons taught: _____

Exceptionalities or peculiarities of the class or school: _____

_____

Unusual or unlisted school routines: _____

_____

Potential network persons, and their areas of expertise:

_____

Does the school have a copy of your résumé?   ❏ YES   ❏ NO

Has Principal or Vice-Principal observed teaching?   ❏ YES   ❏ NO

Before you leave, mark all assignments for that day, unless the teacher's instructions tell you not to. Please be sure to leave the room and the teacher's desk or work area as good as, or better than, you found it. Complaints about this from the returning teacher—or custodian—can quickly bump you off the "inside track"; you are not asked for by name, and it often seems to cause questions to arise in the principal's mind about your organization and classroom management skills.

One little "extra" that Susan Jennings—a really excellent replacement teacher—suggested to me, and I have observed her do it in my school, (until she got a full-time job teaching her "dream-grade"—I didn't have an opening on staff soon enough to snag her ahead of another principal) is that before she left she made up a day-plan for the next day, based on the regular teacher's daybook and left it with the note "Just in case Mr. X is not back." She received several compliments on it from teachers. Then, if the regular teacher was back, but not feeling prime, they appreciated having something to start from; it showed where the class had left off and where they could reasonably go. Perhaps more importantly, the ill teacher soon learned that he or she did not have to worry. Even if a different Replacement Teacher was called in because, for example, Sue was pre-booked at another school for the next day, they could rest at home, getting better, and depend on Sue to have left a reasonable plan! If, however, the regular teacher returned and did not want to use Sue's plan, no problem. Yes, it was a bit of extra work, but that is the type of replacement that teachers ask for by name!

In summary, then, the following might serve as a possible "Check-List" for the day:

LEAVE NOTES

It is really important to leave detailed notes for the regular teacher about what you did: what parts of the day-plan were or were not accomplished, notes on any specific behaviours or referrals to the office, any information which may help them to answer questions about the day from parents or the principal (no-one likes to be blind-sided), and leave your full name and phone number in case they want to contact you, or better yet, recommend you!

A photo-copy-ready sample of this Checklist is provided in APPENDIX 4.

CHECKLIST FOR THE DAY

Night Before:
— map of area schools near phone
— pencil and paper for messages near phone
— family instructed not to answer phone in morning unless you are in shower
— clothes selected and ready for next day, including those suitable if on outdoor yard duty
— car filled with gas and ready to go (if it is winter, be sure driveway is shoveled)

When Called:
— record name of school, be certain you already know route to it, and name of teacher you are replacing, and subjects (if applicable) _____
— load appropriate emergency lesson plan, materials, etc., into box and *into the car*
— are you on yard duty?   _ YES_ NO
   If yes, when?_____

When You Arrive:
— arrive at least 30 minutes before start of classes
— check in at office with
      _ Principal/Vice Principal, and
      _ Secretary
      _ Department Head (if appropriate)
— get school routines
— any special events today? If Yes:_____Time: _____
— confirm duty schedule if any: _____

When You Enter the Classroom:
— check day-plan book
— check for a list of special instructions for an occasional teacher
— organize, into order required, the work left by teacher
— in absence of above, get own plans and materials ready
— gather any necessary materials or equipment
— duplicate any required materials
— find seating plan
— print your name on board or chart-paper, if unknown to class
— introduce yourself to teachers in adjoining rooms

TIP

When you are new at it, why not make copies (from APPENDIX 4) and check off each item as your day progresses?

USEFUL TIP

Remember to check the staffroom bulletin board for job postings!!!

When Pupils Arrive:

— greet them in the hall with a smile (By standing very close to the doorway, you can supervise both hall and classroom)

— follow opening exercises routine

— spend a few minutes confirming classroom routines (washroom, pencils, monitors, "special person of the day," etc.)

— confirm names as on seating plan, or make name tags for each desk

— take attendance, record it in day-plan book and send copy to office if required

Throughout the Day:

— record *in detail* all work accomplished and assigned from teacher's day-plan

— get to know the rest of the staff and be willing to ask for suggestions or to accept and record offers of help in your career

— check bulletin boards for job postings!

— demonstrate willingness to be flexible, without being exploited

— constantly recall to memory significant behavioural strategies you are intending to use, and use them as required

— find out about extra-curricular programs, or other program areas, in which you could contribute to the school and make yourself indispensable

— be alert for a classroom you could gain volunteer experience in, if you will benefit and/or learn from it

After Final Dismissal:

— do all marking

— finish recording what was or was not completed of teacher's day-plan

— finish recording *in detail* what else was taught

— make specific comments about how the day went, including any concerns or issues which might need to be addressed when the teacher returns

— if you enjoyed the class and would like to be called back, say so in your note to the teacher

— make certain room is clean (keep the custodians from black-listing you) and the teacher's desk is neat, but don't move their stuff!

— leave your name and phone number for the teacher when he/she returns

— write up a "contingency" day-plan for the next day

— say "goodbye" to the principal or vice-principal, and the secretary, and let them know you are available again tomorrow, "if needed"

When You Get Home:

— fill out your *OCCASIONAL TEACHING INFORMATION RECORD SHEET*

— pack another lunch

— replenish your box of lessons

Now you are ready for the next day!

AFTER YOU HAVE STARTED OCCASIONAL TEACHING

Some collective agreements allow registered Occasional Teachers to receive the advantages of the board's benefits package: dental, hospital, savings plans, etc. Check it out! Some contracts specify that those on the approved Occasional Teacher List can apply for openings as "internal candidates" who already work for the board. This means you don't have to wait until everyone else on staff has had a chance to decline an advertised position, and you don't have to wait until the posting goes "external" to the general public!

Another side-benefit you should be aware of: many contracts specify that if you are in a position replacing a teacher for twenty consecutive days (or four, or five or ten; it varies by area), you get regular teacher's salary, retroactive!

One more suggestion: if an administrator suggests you take an upgrading course, it might mean that they anticipate an opening in that area. You could ask them if they "foresee a need in the board." That more general approach will relax them so they don't feel they are committing any opening in their school to you. It is usually useful to try to keep administrators from feeling you are putting them into a corner. If they don't feel pressured most of them will be more forthcoming, but under pressure they tend to become very cautious. (It's part of the acquired paranoia!) Perhaps then, depending on what they say, it might be worth getting that qualification, if at all possible, and being ready for when the job comes up. Also, if they see themselves in a mentoring role with you, there is a tendency for them to try harder to look after you, and this can include hiring!

Remember that volunteering is one good way to get known and to gain valuable experience. It is, however, considered unethical and a contravention of Teacher's Federation/Society/Association or Union policy in most jurisdictions to volunteer in a classroom if you are replacing a teacher who would otherwise be paid, or if you "volunteer" with an understanding of any pre-condition for preferential treatment in future. (See APPENDIX 10.) Do be careful to remain professional, but don't stay if those you are working with don't treat you like a professional too! See PART IX: The Value of Volunteering: Its Benefits and Limitations, next.

THINK AHEAD

Be certain to get yourself enrolled in the Teachers' Pension Plan as soon as you begin to do "Occasional Teaching." In some provinces, if you work a specified number of days you can get service credit which will advance your date of retirement with full pension. Simply let the board know you want deductions toward the plan. Your board or teachers' federation can give you details and addresses.

NOTES

PART IX

THE VALUE OF VOLUNTEERING: ITS BENEFITS AND LIMITATIONS

Once you are on the official Replacement Teacher List, one question sometimes is: "How do I get known so that I get called to do occasional teaching in the school I want?" Many teachers these days are finding an alternate route into occasional work: **volunteerism**.

Taking into consideration a few precautions, volunteering has proven to be one successful route for many in an increasingly competitive work environment. Unfortunately, the way you sometimes feel might be reflected by Lewis Carroll's description: "Now here, you see, it takes all the running you can do to keep in the same place. If you want to get somewhere else, you must run at least twice as fast as that!" Volunteering done wisely, however, and with carefully considered choices, can help you get "somewhere else,"—that is, onto the list of the "hired!"

POTENTIAL BENEFITS

Why is volunteering so effective? There are many reasons. It gets you into classrooms, in a semi-official capacity, and allows you to interact with children and other staff members in at least a somewhat professional manner. It gives the teachers and administrators a chance to see you in action. It gives you a chance to show them how good you are! It lets you paint that picture that is worth a thousand words! It allows them to respond with growing respect to you and your abilities.

It also allows you to get to know the programs and pupils in a teacher's class, or those of several teachers' classes before they start to ask for your help. In many cases, volunteers have found that the teacher will then specifically request you to replace them because you know their classroom situation, and they don't have to write miles of detailed instructions for you, as they might for an uninitiated replacement. At this point, you have developed "extra value."

There are many other advantages to using your "waiting time" this way. Volunteering in a school can provide you with experience, if yours is limited, and with that experience will come confidence. You now know you have more to offer! It will also help you to have more real-life examples to draw on when answering interview questions. You will see how a variety of teachers meet the daily challenges of the classroom. You will not be afraid to jump right in and get involved, and confidence is contagious! It can allow you opportunity to experiment and confirm what grade levels you are most comfortable with.

Volunteering can also keep you up to date in your knowledge base, and in your practice working with children. It also keeps you aware of any postings for openings in the system (check the staffroom bulletin board). Another major benefit: being with children can help keep you firm in your

"Knowing is not enough; we must apply. Willing is not enough; we must do."
—*Johann Wolfgang von Goethe*

"We ought not to judge a person's merits by their qualifications, but by the use they make of them."
—*Pierre Charron*

GETTING FAMILIAR

Being in the school as a volunteer is also a really good way to get to know where the photocopier is—without having to ask—and where the class supplies are kept. Then when you are called the first time, you just blend in with the other staff—you are already "one of them."

commitment to be a teacher. This contact with them can help stave off discouragement if you are having trouble finding a job in your chosen profession. "It kept me going. Being with the kids reminded me of why I still wanted to teach," I was told by one teacher who used this stepping stone.

Volunteering can also permit you to be in proximity to the decision-maker(s) when the decision is being made about calling a replacement. If you are there and ready, they are more inclined to think of you as a possible solution to their temporary teacher shortage; they don't have to try to reach someone on the phone. You have made it easy for them to think of you and easy to give you (albeit for a very short term) a teaching job and, as indicated much earlier, those often lead to more frequent, and more long-term work. You are on the "inside track." These, then, are some of the very considerable "benefits."

DEMONSTRATING YOUR CAPABILITY

And how does one find out if there is an opportunity to volunteer? If you know a teacher, ask them if they need help. (They will then clear it through the administration.) As an alternative, some schools have volunteer coordinators. The secretary can tell you who it is. If there is not one for that school, again the secretary can advise, but you are probably best to contact the vice-principal or principal. They can steer you in the right direction. And remember: in every province and territory in Canada volunteers are legally under the authority of the principal, so she or he should be made aware that you are in the school.

So how does one develop into the quintessential volunteer-*cum*-replacement teacher? Among specific requirements listed by classroom teachers are: (a) flexibility and the willingness to adapt to sudden changes in routine and expectations, (b) willingness to make a weekly commitment of one-half to one day so that the teacher can plan effectively for the deployment of adults in the instructional environment, (c) absolute discretion and respect for confidentiality, (d) willingness and ability to fit in with staff, so that the teacher you are working with feels comfortable with you and, instead of staying in the classroom with you, is free to take you to the staffroom at breaks, (e) good teaching skills, (f) the ability to bring extra skills to the classroom: your interest and ability areas which will enrich the curriculum, (g) willingness to do whatever is required, including taking the whole group for short periods so the teacher can do observations, or be willing to work with the class on practising for a concert or "tea" while the teacher works on decorations, etc., (h) ability to do "the impossible" such as take over the afternoon before Halloween (when you pull this off you really go up in their esteem), (i) the ability to get by with a minimal sketch of plans (like in normal replacement teaching duties, one person told me), and (j) reliability—they can always count on you either to be there when expected, or to let them know well in advance if you have to cancel.

As you can see, these are really just a list of the requirements for a good teacher, so you are already headed onto the "inside track!"

THE LIMITATIONS

So what is the "downside," the "limitations," to the volunteering process? There are, unfortunately, several. Each of these described below are real-life examples, shared here to confirm for you that, as you move further along on the "inside track," you are not alone; others have, regrettably, experienced similar things and they too, at first, felt disempowered.

One downside is that it can be rather difficult for an experienced teacher to have to resort to volunteering to prove, once again, her or his worth. "I had taught Grade Two for seven years [in my former board], and here I am giving my time as an unpaid helper for someone who has no experience but has the job," one volunteer told me. You are not alone when you feel that it can be especially demoralizing when you have, perhaps, moved from an area where your expertise was recognized and respected and are now expected to volunteer with a substantially less qualified and experienced teacher, just to get a foot in the door. This is especially the case where you feel that your help is not seen as a gift to the school and the children but as "partial payment" on a debt you didn't create! It makes you feel like they think you somehow owe the system and haven't paid your dues. These circumstances and some others of these "downsides" could also be seen as very clear signs that you are not on the "inside track" there, and it would be more profitable to move on and volunteer in another classroom or school. In each situation, you will have to decide, but remember, you cannot be taken advantage of; without your consent and compliance, they can only try.

A strong sign that you are not on the "inside track" is when you feel you are wasting your time—you feel that you are not really being used effectively and frequently feel as though you are just being tolerated, and are even in the way. That's not a nice way to be treated. Although there are exceptions, and some relationships take time to build, it could, perhaps, be argued that there is limited likelihood that a relationship such as this will develop into one of trust.

Another sign is your being sent on more than your share of yard and lunchroom duty. While it is reasonable occasionally to accompany a teacher on duty, or occasionally to relieve them to attend to emergent tasks, you will probably recognize when you are being exploited. No one exploits persons they respect, and teachers usually do not ask for, and administrators usually do not hire, those they do not treat with respect.

Something you might reasonably expect in a school where your volunteering is likely to be rewarded is this: the person in charge of replacement teachers makes time for you. When you first arrive, they may even take you around and introduce you to each of the staff. That is a very good sign. After you are there a while, they will want to talk to you, to find out how it is going with you. If, for example, you are permitted only to deal with the vice-principal, and it is the principal who exclusively makes decisions on selection of replacement teachers, you might consider moving on to another school. (It is a useful idea to find out right away—but be very subtle—who makes those decisions.) If the administrators, or other staff, have no time for you, you might question how important and valuable you are considered to be.

Are you given only the undignified or non-professional jobs? While photocopying and cleaning paint pots are necessary tasks and it is reasonable to help with them, if that is all you are ever trusted to do, it does not look as good as it could for your being considered an equal! If you see others in your situation consistently being treated this way, it may be time to say goodbye before it happens to you.

If the teacher you are with has a style vastly different than your own, it may be time to go to another classroom or school. You probably won't be valued and reinforced for your strengths where you are.

If you are frequently made to feel uncomfortable or even subjected to harassment, including sexual harassment, it is probably time to move on.

"We don't like their sound, and guitar music is on the way out."
—*Decca Records executive, rejecting "The Beatles"*

USE JUDGEMENT

Since you are a qualified teacher, it is reasonable to expect that you will be given responsibilities and duties that are different than those for an untrained person.

Always remember that your time is valuable; use it where it is likely to reap most benefit. If you find that one person or school does not value it, you might be able to find someone who does.

ENEMY ACTION?

Although it is bound to happen occasionally, if there are opportunities for you to be offered paid work, and you are consistently overlooked, that is a fairly strong sign. As Bond, James Bond, said, "Once, it's accident; twice, it's coincidence; but three times ... it's enemy action."

Fair or unfair, you may feel disempowered in such a situation; you will have to decide whether to stand up for your legal and moral rights, or to move on quitely until you have the added security of a permanent position. Although there is absolutely no possible excuse for the person who is causing your discomfort, you may want to consider what a Director of Education told me many years ago when I was dealing with irrational parents in a very different but equally complex situation: "you may be dead right, but you may be still dead." There are good administrators and good teachers and good schools. Sometimes moving on is the best choice, and is not success the best revenge?

If you find that you are in a school where the person in charge of calling replacement teachers does not respect teacher requests, it might be time to move on to one with a different approach. Again, you and your time are valuable; give them only to those who show appreciation. If you are in a school where you are told that you cannot be hired (either in their school or another) if it will interfere with your volunteer schedule, you might re-evaluate your role there.

In conclusion, then, these are some of the "danger signs" of the "downside," the limitations, of volunteering. It can be, however, and increasingly is, one of the routes to an occasional, then a part-time and eventually a full-time position in exactly the school you want.

Each provincial and territorial teachers' union has guidelines, of which you should be aware, with respect to volunteering. (See APPENDIX 10 for details.) It is a fine line you have to walk between breaching Teachers' Association/Federation/Union/Society policy and wasting your time where there will be no potential for reward. It can, however, be just the ticket into the next staging area of your career.

Volunteering can put you onto the "inside track."

PART X

HOW YOUR TEACHERS' FEDERATION, UNION, SOCIETY, OR ASSOCIATION CAN HELP

As a teacher you will pay rather large sums in annual fees to your teachers' professional federation, association, society or union, as they are variously called. While admittedly some of them may seem to offer more for their members than do others, they all do a lot more than collective bargaining!

If you have ANY questions about particular boards or areas, or the contract you are offered, or salaries, or benefits, or P.D. or ANYTHING of a professional nature, a call to the *local president of your federation* should help. Try it! The Provincial or Territorial office, or any school, can give you the name and phone number of your local or district president. No matter where you go, the local federation/union/association/society president is someone who wants to welcome and help you as a colleague. It is a "guaranteed friend in a strange town." As professional teachers, we are all bound to help each other.

After you are hired, it is advisable to give very careful consideration to enrolling in some of the professional development programs and activities offered by the teachers' unions or federations. Not only will it look good on your next C.V., but they are designed to be **useful** to you, the **teacher**! They tend to be careful to blend the theoretical with the practical! Most teachers' associations also have kits, resources, books, workshops, etc., available to members. In the case of most federations and societies, "membership" can include replacement teachers as "voluntary" members (at reduced fees). Just ask!

Any time you have any questions or concerns about any issue relating to your contract or security, you absolutely must contact them; to fail to do so may be putting yourself at extreme risk. They have the expertise, including the legal specialists, to assist you with any employment-related issue. They can advise you how to handle the situation, whatever it is.

Following are the teachers' federations/associations/societies/unions, etc., in Canada. Do not hesitate to contact them. Their purpose is to serve education by serving teachers.

NEWFOUNDLAND
Newfoundland and Labrador Teachers' Association
3 Kenmount Road
St. John's, NF   A1B 1W1
Tel: (709) 726-3223
Fax: (709) 726-4302
www.stemnet.nf.ca/Organizations/NLTA/

"It's only a suggestion, and there's no need to do it—unless you want to keep your job."
—*Anon.*

"When eating bamboo sprouts, remember the one who planted them."
—*Chinese proverb*

NOVA SCOTIA
Nova Scotia Teachers' Union
3106 Dutch Village Road
Halifax, NS   B3L 4L7
Tel: (902) 477-5621
Fax: (902) 477-3517
www.nstu.ns.ca (This is a particularly good site.)

PRINCE EDWARD ISLAND
Prince Edward Island Teachers' Federation
24 Glen Steward Drive
P.O. Box 6000
Charlottetown, PE   C1A 8B4
Tel: (902) 569-4157
Fax: (902) 569-3682

NEW BRUNSWICK
If you are hired to teach in a school where English is the language of instruction, you will be a member of:

New Brunswick Teachers' Association
P.O. Box 752
650 Montgomery
Fredericton, NB   E3B 5R6
Tel: (506) 452-8921
Fax: (506) 453-9795

If you are hired to teach in a school where French is the language of instruction, you will be a member of:

Association des enseignantes et des enseignants francophones du Nouveau-Brunswick
650 Montgomery, C.P. 712
Fredericton, NB   E3B 5B4
Tel: (506) 452-8921
Fax: (506) 453-9795

Overseeing and uniting both these associations is the "union" voice of:

New Brunswick Teachers' Federation
Fédération des enseignants du Nouveau-Brunswick
P.O. Box/C.P. 1535
Fredericton, NB   E3B 5G2
Tel: (506) 452-8921
Fax: (506) 453-9795

QUEBEC
Quebec has recently acted upon legislation passed in 1995, and then put "on hold," changing the organization of schools away from religious division to linguistic division. If you will be teaching in schools, Kindergarten to Grade 11, where French is the language of instruction, you will be a member of the:

"It is not the employer who pays wages—he only handles the money. It is the product that pays wages."
—*Henry Ford*

Centrale de l'enseignement du Québec
9405, rue Sherbrooke est
Montréal, QC   H1L 6P3
Tel: (514) 356-8888
Fax: (514) 356-9999

If you will be teaching in schools, Kindergarten to Grade 11, where English is the language of instruction, you will be a member of the:

Quebec Provincial Association of Teachers
17035 Brunswick Boulevard
Kirkland, QC   H9H 5G6
Tel: (514) 694-9777
Fax: (514) 694-0189

"A teacher affects eternity; he can never tell where his influence stops."
—*Henry Adams*

These unions bargain together, so collective agreements are almost identical for members of both.

ONTARIO

As of September 1997, the role of teachers' federations in Ontario has been profoundly changed by the legislated establishment of, and enforced membership of all teachers in, the new College of Teachers. The College is mandated to assume many of the duties previously the purview of the Ministry of Education and Training (e.g., accreditation of pre-service training, qualifications and licensing) and the federations (e.g., discipline, professional development and maintenance of standards of performance). The one area the College will not be involved in is member protection.

Ontario Teachers' Federation
Suite 700
1260 Bay Street
Toronto, ON   M5R 2B5
Tel: (416) 966-3424
Fax: (416) 966-5450

In Ontario, Bylaw I of the Ontario Teachers' Federation requires you to join specific affiliate federations depending on variables such as; the level of school: elementary or secondary; language of instruction; and whether employed by a (Public) District School Board or a Roman Catholic Separate School Board.

Here they are, in alphabetical order:

1. Association des Enseignantes et des Enseignants Franco-Ontariens

If you will be teaching in a school where French is the language of instruction, whether for a public Board of Education, or for a Roman Catholic Separate School Board, you will be a member of **A.E.F.O.**

Association des Enseignantes et des Enseignants Franco-Ontariens
681 Chemin Belfast
Ottawa, ON   K1G 0Z4
1-800-267-4217
Tel: (613) 244-2336
Fax: (613) 563-7718

2. Elementary Teachers' Federation of Ontario

If you will be teaching in Public (i.e.: not Roman Catholic Separate) schools, at the elementary level (grades Junior Kindergarten to Grade 8), you will be a member of E.T.F.O.
480 University Avenue, Suite 1000
Toronto, ON   M5G 1V2
Tel: (416) 962-3836
1-888-838-3836

YOUR FEDERATION

Remember: you are, or are about to be, a member of a very proud and worthy profession. Your federation will reflect that. Make full use of their professional expertise.

This federation has also organized (unionized) many groups of Occasional Teachers, and, as well, they welcome voluntary members, including teachers in private schools, to many of the privileges associated with statutory membership.

IMPORTANT NOTE

If you want to receive an evaluation of your qualifications for salary category placement purposes from the Qualifications Evaluation Council of Ontario (Q.E.C.O.), you must be a member or voluntary member of one of the these federations.

Qualifications Evaluation Council of Ontario
1300 Yonge St., 2nd Floor,
Toronto, ON   M4T 1X3
Tel: 416-323-1969, or
        1-800-385-1030
Fax: 416-323-9589

3. Ontario English Catholic Teachers' Association

If you will be teaching for a Roman Catholic Separate School Board, in either secondary or elementary school, where English is the language of instruction, you will become a member of **O.E.C.T.A.**

Ontario English Catholic Teachers' Association
65 St. Clair Avenue East, Suite 400
Toronto, ON   M4T 2Y8
Local Calls: 416-925-2493
From area code 416: 1-800-268-7001
From area code 519, 613, 705: 1-800-268-7230
Fax: (416) 925-7764

4. Ontario Secondary School Teachers' Federation

If you will be teaching in a secondary school in the public (not private or Roman Catholic Separate) system, you will be a member of **O.S.S.T.F.**

Ontario Secondary School Teachers' Federation
60 Mobile Drive
Toronto, ON   M4A 2P3
Local Calls: 416-751-8300
From area code 416: 1-800-268-5725
From area code 519, 613, 705: 1-800-268-6515
From area code 807: 1-800-268-5730
Fax: (416) 751-3394

If you want your qualifications assessed for salary category purposes, and are a member of O.S.S.T.F., contact their Certification Department at the 60 Mobile Drive address above.

If you teach in a private school (not tax-funded), you can still apply to join one of the above as a voluntary member, with limited but valuable benefits. For details, contact the federation directly and ask for an application.

Together with the teachers' federations, **The Ontario College of Teachers** is a good source of information. They are located at:
121 Bloor Street East, 12th Floor
Toronto, ON   M4W 3M5

Their phone numbers: (416) 961-8800 or 1-888-534-2222

A tip: instead of trying to phone them, you might get through and get a response more quickly if you fax them at (416) 961-8822; or, much better, e-mail them. (In your message, ask them to call you, if your question cannot be asked simply and clearly nor answered by e-mail.) Their web site is <www.oct.on.ca> and has the necessary e-mail addresses for the various departments.

That's Ontario, though it is a little confusing.

"I'm a teacher. I touch the future."
—*Christine MacAuliff*

MANITOBA
The Manitoba Teachers' Society
191 Harcourt Street
Winnipeg, MB   R3J 3H2
Tel: (204) 888-7961
Fax: (204) 831-0877

SASKATCHEWAN
Saskatchewan Teachers' Federation
2317 Arlington Ave.
Saskatoon, SK   S7J 2H8
Tel: (306) 373-1660
Fax: (306) 374-1122
www.stf.sk.ca
Regina Office: (306) 525-0368

ALBERTA
The Alberta Teachers' Association
11010-142 Street
Edmonton, AB   T5N 2R1
Tel: (780) 447-9400
Fax: (780) 455-6481

BRITISH COLUMBIA
British Columbia Teachers' Federation
100-550 6th Avenue West
Vancouver, BC   V5Z 4P2
Tel: (604) 871-2283
Fax: (604) 871-2290

NORTHWEST TERRITORIES
Northwest Territories Teachers' Association
5018-48th Street
P.O. Box 2340
Yellowknife, NT   X1A 2P7
Tel: (403) 873-8501
Fax: (403) 873-2366

NUNAVUT
Information on the Teachers' Association for this new territory is not
determined at press time. Contact the Nunavut Department of Education at
(867) 975-5000 or the Canadian Teachers' Federation at (613) 232-1505 or visit
their web site at <www.ctf-fce.ca> or the NWT Teachers' Association (as
Nunavut was formerly a part of the NWT).

YUKON TERRITORY
Yukon Teachers' Association
2064 Second Avenue
Whitehorse, YT   Y1A 1A9
Tel: (867) 668-6777
Fax: (867) 667-4324

*The Canadian Teachers'
Federation* is located at:
110 Argyle Avenue
Ottawa, ON K2P 1B4
Tel: (613) 232-1505
FAX: (613) 232-1886
www.ctf-fce.ca

(This one has links to provincial
and territorial sites.)

"It was God who made me so
beautiful. If I weren't, then I'd
be a teacher."
—*Linda Evangelista,*
supermodel, *Newsweek
Magazine,* 1998

A NOTE ON NUNAVUT

In what is arguably a very Canadian way of doing business, but a move that is unusual in a world where political change is usually accompanied by war, April 1, 1999, saw the formation of a new political identity in Canada. The Northwest Territories divided peacefully, democratically, after years of negotiation, and following the rules of law. The three most eastern administrative regions of the N.W.T.: Qikiqtaaluk (formerly known as Baffin), Kivalliq (Keewatin) and Kitikmeot, became Nunavut. Although it remains a territory—rather than a province—it's official name does not include the word "territory." In Inuktitut, "Nunavut" means "our land," and among other objectives of the establishment of Nunavut was the drive to return to the Inuit people control of their land and their destiny in the area.

Nunavut is huge, over 1,994,000 square kilometres (about one-fifth the land mass of Canada), but with a population of under 25,000. For sake of comparison, this population density would translate to having 7.8 people reside in the geographic area of the City of Toronto. (Toronto's population is around 2.4 million.) Similarly, the area of the city of Vancouver would have a population of 1.4 persons. (Would that be one person visiting for part of the year while the other one stayed there year 'round?) Nunavut also includes four time zones, although only three of them—Eastern, Central and Mountain—are used, and the government has voiced its intention to change the whole territory to just one zone.

The government and people of Nunavut are determined to go slowly and get it right. This extends to their view of their education system, and what it should offer their children. What will it be like? They will call on their heritage, including many of the excellent practices of the N.W.T. education system, together with the "best practices" from all over Canada and around the world, and take advantage of this opportunity they have to create an excellent school system, unencumbered by regulations, procedures and policies that they may have found did not always serve them and their unique needs as well as might. Thus, while the target date for finalizing most of the plans around educational governance is June 1, 2000, officials are very open about the fact that many decisions will be made after that date. (Besides, when was the last time you remember any provincial education ministry adhering to its own schedule in anything they released?)

Revisions to the *Education Act* are almost complete. Nunavut will continue to use many of the procedures it enjoyed while it was a part of the N.W.T. (including the famous "three-legged polar bear" license plate for vehicles, the only non-rectangular vehicle plate in North America) but will not use the same teacher's contract. This is, at press time, going under revision, along with the hiring procedures for teachers in their 26 or so schools. Another change we may anticipate will be the eventual impact of the plan to have the population demographically reflected in the public service, which will mean about 85% of teachers will eventually be expected to be Inuit. No date has been given for the implementation of this guideline.

Iqaluit, on Baffin Island, is the seat of government, including for the Department of Education, but its Human Resources activities, including hiring, is to be handled out of Pond Inlet. (Pond Inlet is one of the other historic locations of educational governance.)

PART XI

FURTHER READINGS

Here are a few good resources. Those of a more subjective nature are included either: (a) to confirm what is said here—just so you know this is not, in the words of the late Dean of Education Al Johnson, some "lofty tome being thrust, proudly, into the void"—or else, (b) to provide another opinion than that provided here, to show that there is a diversity.

The more objective hard-data-related ones are listed here to provide clear and easy access to information related to teaching in Canada, but which is not directly a part of this document. All these are arranged, rather loosely, by category. Within the categories, books are listed—in order of my perception—starting with the very best.

"It is always a silly thing to give advice, but to give good advice is absolutely fatal."
—*Oscar Wilde*

1. Getting into a Faculty of Education in Canada

• *Admission to Faculties of Education in Canada: What You Need to Know.* A Report from the Canadian Education Association, Toronto, 1993. Available for the princely sum of twelve whole dollars, plus GST and shipping.

Some information is obsolete but still a MUST-GET if you need this data. Lists every faculty in Canada with details regarding admission requirements and procedures and specific programs offered. Their address is as follows: Suite 8-200, 252 Bloor Street West, Toronto, Ontario M5S 1V5; phone: (416) 924-7721; fax: (416) 924-3188; e-mail: cea-ace@acea.ca.

Before seeking admission into faculties or schools of education in countries other than Canada, you should check first with the ministry or department responsible for education in the province or territory in which you intend to teach to ensure that the program in the university you are inquiring about will be deemed acceptable by that ministry/department. In other words, make sure the certificate will be recognized before you get it!

Some provinces (Saskatchewan, Manitoba, Nova Scotia, New Brunswick, Prince Edward Island and Newfoundland) have an agreement to recognize certificates from each others' provinces for immediate certification in their own province. (If additional training or education is required, temporary certification is ascribed, pending completion of the required training.) Similarly, Ontario, Quebec and New Brunswick have agreements among themselves. For specifics, refer to the excellent booklet listed below and see APPENDIX 7 of this book. Be aware, though, that as indicated in APPENDIX 7, this whole area is about to become much more flexible for teachers. You will need to check authorative sources (listed) to keep current.

"The future of the earch is in our hands."
—*Pierre Teilhard de Chardin*

2. Requirements for Teaching Certificates in Canada

• Get a book entitled *Requirements for Teaching Certificates in Canada*. Toronto: Canadian Education Association, 1997. $12.00 (see above for their address).

This lists the many types of certificates and licenses required for teaching in the provinces and territories of Canada along with their required qualifications. It also outlines, in simple chart form, the grades for which each is valid, how to make them permanent and, where applicable, cross-qualification opportunities among provinces/territories and citizenship requirements. Very handy if you want an overview of possibilities, and more detail than in APPENDIX 7.

3. Résumé Preparation and "The Great Job Hunt" in General

• Bolles, Richard Nelson. *What Color is Your Parachute? A Practical Manual for Job Hunters and Career-Changers*. Berkley: Ten Speed Press, 1997. About $25.00.

Peter Drucker described it as "Excellent ... a distinguished public service." It is reasonable, readable, clear, down-to-earth, and simply good advice on the whole process of securing the job you want. It does not address the specific culture of education, unfortunately, but most of it applies. This book will give a lot of the generic extras this document has had to leave out. Especially if you are really having trouble getting a job, you must buy this book. Absolutely the best in its general field.

If you are a teacher who is re-doing your C.V. so you can for some reason fight for a promotion, all the while finding that you are already too busy to enjoy life, then read another book by Bolles: *The Three Boxes of Life* (same publisher.) Start by reading the Epilogue. That will motivate you to read the rest. **Warning**: you may end up not re-doing your C.V.!

• Cashman, Kevin J. and Sidney Reisberg. *Job Hunter's Guide to Career Fulfilment.* St. Paul, (Minnesota): Devine Multi-Media, 1996.

The book that goes with this multi-media computer package (3.5 DD disk) is almost worth the cost of the whole package. It also includes a video, a motivational tape, a filing system (to keep track of your job-hunt process), as well as the software.

This gives some good advice about being interviewed and gives a lot of good advice about cover letters and follow-up letters which, with appropriate modification, can apply to the teaching profession! There is also some other good general advice about the whole process. At $39.95, this is a good deal.

(Note: I would not recommend the majority of the other computer software "résumé programs," as they tend not to be worth the cardboard they are wrapped in. Many of them are not much more than a fill-in-the-blanks template, which does not usually come close to complying with the requirements of a professional teacher's C.V.)

• Cohen, Hiyaguha. *The No Pain Resume Workbook: A Complete Guide to Job-Winning Resumes.* Homewood (Illinois): Business One Irwin: 1992. $21.50.

Really quite good. Certainly the best (other than this one, of course) of the "how-to" books on the specific topic of C.V. preparation. Much of it does not relate to the teaching profession, but the general advice and guidelines are

NOTE

Some especially good material on analyzing past jobs to find experience related to the present field is included in PART III of *The Inside Track*.

"By working faithfully eight hours a day you might eventually get to be the boss and work twelve hours a day."
—*Robert Frost*

for the most part "right on." Contains some insights and suggestions which I have been sharing with clients for several years but which I had not seen in print anywhere before. This caused mixed feelings; I wanted to be unique in suggesting them; on the other hand, it's nice to see that I'm not totally "a voice crying in the wilderness."

- Murphy, Kevin J. **Surviving the Cut: An Executive's Guide to Successful Job Hunting in Today's Tough Market.** New York: Bantam, 1991.

  A good guide to the whole process. Applies fairly well to the teaching career as the book is directed toward the professional employee. Worth the $13.00, unless you can get a copy of Bolles' book and have time to read it. (Murphy's is shorter and, in some cases, more to the point, though less interesting reading, perhaps.)

4. The Cover Letter

- Yate, Martin. **Cover Letters that Knock 'Em Dead**. Holbrook: Adams Media, 1998. $16.95.

  A superb book, written in an easy, yet direct, style. Gives a lot of good examples, and a lot of commentary on how, when and why to use specific styles and methods. Analytical. A thick book on such a narrow topic, but packed with information and ideas. One bit of neat advice on measuring the impact of your application on a jaded reader in the H.R. department: without taking a break read thirty or so cover letters from their samples, and then read yours. Does yours have impact? Does it jump out as representing a person who you really want to interview? (And, they add, don't forget that the samples in the book which you have just read are good letters; imagine how weary you would feel if you had just wallowed through several that are, shall we say, less than exemplary.) It also gives a hint of what some of your competition will be like. And please remember, to be on the "Inside Track" we have to be just a bit better than the competition. Let the competition have the other jobs that are posted; you want exactly the one you want. And you can get it!

  Like most books, a lot of it does not apply directly to the teaching profession, but it is food for thought, and will stimulate your creative juices. Definitely worth the $16.95.

- Kennedy, Joyce L. **Cover Letters for Dummies.** Chicago: IDG Books, 1996. $17.99.

  Quite good; direct and clear, as most of their books are. Much of its advice applies well to the teaching profession. Gives a reasonable selection of "Do's and Don't's" and several examples, some of which are more-or-less transferable. The concept of "Red-Hot" cover letters is quite inspiring.

  Much of what it offers is similar to PART IV of this book (it's nice to know someone else agrees) but it is rather more general as it's aim is not specific to the professional educator. Overall, if the cover letter is a real area of difficulty for you, this book could help.

- Beatty, Richard H. **The Perfect Cover Letter.** Toronto: John Wiley and Sons, 1989. $10.95.

  Excellent. Much very specific advice on this important component of the winning application. A lot of it does not apply to the teaching profession, but it will make you realize how important it is to be different than the rest, brief and enthusiastic in your cover letter. Certainly worth a look! Gives

"There was a man who was so appalled by what he read about the dangers of smoking that he immediately gave up reading."
—Mark Twain

"Keep on going and the chances are you will stumble on something, perhaps when you are least expecting it. I have never heard of anyone stumbling on something sitting down."
—Charles F. Kettering

> "Teaching is the greatest act of optimism."
> —Coleen Wilcox

some interesting sample letters. Goes into a bit of detail on what not to include. Analyzes letters and C.V.'s to show why they work or don't, and identifies necessary characteristics for excellence.

- Reimold, Cheryl. *How to Write a Million Dollar Memo*. New York: Dell, 1984. $5.95.

Because it is just as important to make every word the exact word in writing a memo as in preparing a C.V. or cover letter, there are a lot of useful tips in this little book. Well worth the price: $5.95.

5. Where to Apply if You Don't Know Anything about the Area

Again, the Canadian Education Association is your best ally. See their *CEA Handbook* for a listing of every school board in Canada, together with data re: enrollments, personnel there, etc. It's $40.00, but contains a lot of hard data, all conveniently in one place.

If you want a listing of every school in Canada, they distribute *The MDR's Canadian School Directory.* This document (over 800 pages) provides the name, address, phone and fax numbers for every school system and every school and gives the names of principals, board administrators, their titles, etc. Unfortunately, the most recent edition is April 1995, so there will be inaccuracies, but if you need this information, this is one place to get it. ($94.95)

If you are specifically interested in teaching in religious or in private schools, their *Public Funding of Private Schools in Canada* ($5.00) will give you some information on whether it is reasonable to consider pursuing your objective in that province/territory (money talks!), and their *Requirements for Teaching Certificates in Canada*, mentioned above, gives specifics re: qualifications required for teaching in private schools in each province, with a little more detail than APPENDIX 5 hereinafter. Their address: Suite 8-200, 252 Bloor Street West, Toronto, Ontario M5S 1V5.

6. Being Interviewed

- Medley, H. Anthony. *Sweaty Palms, The Neglected Art of Being Interviewed.* Berkley: Ten Speed Press, 1993. $14.95.

A great guide to surviving the interview process. The best single book I have seen. If you have an early edition, (1984 era), however, while it has basically only one fault, it is a big one—Chapter 12 on "Sex." Now that I've mentioned it, it will probably be the first chapter you read, of course. But please do not pay attention to it; its advice is WRONG, WRONG, WRONG for the teaching profession. Otherwise, a Masterpeice! More than excellent!

If you have the 1993 edition, this very serious shortcoming has been corrected, and the contents of the book brought up to the present. This latter version won't advise you to do things which will get you fired. Even more of a masterpiece than it was before! An absolute "Must buy."

- Eigen, Barry. *How to Think Like a Boss & Get Ahead at Work.* New York: Avon, 1992. $5.50.

Simple, and simply excellent! Could be the best $5.50 you ever spend. Explains how to adjust your mind-set so you concentrate on presenting and providing what those offering the position are looking for. A simple example: they have a problem—a gap in staff. If you can help them fill it, and with an excellent person, you will have helped them, and they will be interested in that. They don't care about, and will not hire you because of,

> "A teacher must believe in the value and interest of his subject as a doctor believes in health."
> —Gilbert Highet

your pressing debts. People are not hired because they need a job; schools are not designed to provide employment to the needy. Staff are hired because the employer believes it is worth gambling that they will contribute significantly and substantially to the health of and work of the organization. How can you get into their mindspace? How can you focus on what matters to them? How can you make it easy for them to give you the job? That will put you on the "inside track!"

- *Teacher Recruitment and Retention*. Toronto: Canadian Education Association, 1992. $8.00.

This publication of the CEA gives a bit of interesting information "from the employers' viewpoint." It is, however, less than objective, as it is a compilation of survey results from over 100 boards across Canada and thus, perhaps, reflects the ideal more than the real, in some cases. At $8.00, it won't break the bank, though. Besides, we can learn a lot from what others want us to think about them, no?

- Half, Robert. *Robert Half on Interviewing.* New York: Crown, 1985.

Out of print, but the personnel section of a university library should have a copy. Written from the employer's viewpoint, and more aimed at industry than education, it is useful for providing the other "point of viewing;" i.e., that of the interviewer.

7. Occasional or Substitute Teaching

The resources in this section are listed because, perhaps more than all others, replacement teachers have to have "all the tricks" if they are to be successful. As a replacement teacher you don't have a week or two to get "into the groove"; it has to be instantaneous!

- Wong, Harry K. and Rosemary T. Wong. *The First Days of School: How to Be an Effective Teacher.* Sunnyvale, California: Harry K. Wong Publications, 1991. $45.00.

This is a very practical book. It is expensive, but will pay for itself many, many times by providing you with skills which make you more "saleable."

Also consider the audio tape series by Dr. Wong: "How You Can Be a Super Successful Teacher." Again, expensive at $42.95, but well worth it! Nothing destroys your opportunity for full-time employment as quickly as failing as a temporary teacher, just as nothing helps your application like success in this role! This is similar, but not identical, to the book above. The advantage of the audio tape format is you can listen to it over and over as you drive to school in the mornings!

- Coloroso, Barbara. *Kids are Worth It.* Toronto: Somerville House, 1995. $14.95.

An excellent resource, equally applicable to parenting and teaching. She has also released a tape cassette, "Winning at Parenting" ($20.00), and is well known for her workshops for teachers called, "Winning at Teaching Without Beating Your Kids." She is a teacher with a broad range of experience in classrooms of all types and levels, and her down-to-earth insights just make sense. I occasionally find myself quoting her when counselling moms and dads regarding general parenting skills and found some of her advice really useful with my own kids. Her descriptions of the various types of kid "con" artists, and how to deal with each type, is just excellent.

"The problem is not to get people to do what they are told, but to do what they are not told, or even what they can't be told ... You can command a man to turn a nut on an assembly line, but you cannot command him to be creative or concerned or resourceful."

—*Richard Cornuelle*

• Jardine, Lorraine and Jack Shallhorn. ***Sub Support: Survival Skills for Occasional Teachers.*** Toronto: Ontario Secondary School Teachers' Federation, 1988. About $10.00.

Aimed mostly at the Secondary scene, it has a lot of good advice for elementary teachers as well. Well worth the ten dollars or so. It has sections on getting hired, classroom management, establishing rapport with students, relationships with the regular classroom teacher and other school staff, and a section I really like, "What to Do If All Else Fails."

• Trimble, Doug, Bruce Cassie, et. al. ***Answering the Call: A Handbook for Occasional Teachers.*** Mississauga: Ontario Public School Teachers' Federation, 1995. $6.00.

This 56-page book almost pays for itself with its description of an emergency lesson which could save your day. It also gives some good tips on "Time-to-Spare" lessons and gives almost a dozen plans for impromptu lessons at various levels. It has some information on characteristics of students in the 11-15 age group and has some useful information on classroom management which could serve as a review for you before the students arrive. This book focuses on working with students under the age of 15. A good addition to the professional library of replacement teachers just starting out.

• Rosewine, Mary Frances. ***Substitute Teacher's Handbook.*** Carthage, Illinois: Fearon Teacher's Aids, 1970. $9.95.

It provides a few good general ideas about replacement and a lot of specific and easy ideas for teaching lessons from kindergarten through Grade 6. Very practical, easy reading and well organized. Its only fault is that it seems to assume that all substitute teachers are female and, more specifically, that they are mothers or grandmothers who just want something to fill in their time. It is worth the price, however.

8. Professional Development Reading on a Tight Budget

A collection of booklets which are specifically designed to provide information clearly and directly—almost like executive summaries—are available from the Canadian Education Association (address, fax and phone numbers are provided earlier in this chapter). They are very inexpensive. Of special note might be their ***Building Student Self-esteem***, a report on initiatives being used across Canada and their effects, and how they got started and are maintained. It's really practical and costs $8.00.

Another interesting one, in this era of financial cutbacks, is ***The Entrepreneurial School*** which addresses alternative sources of revenue. This whole topic may be especially relevant to issues such as the continuation of co-curricular activities, but some school districts are suggesting this is how they will pay for I.T. hardware! You may also find that grant monies are sometimes available only on a "matching funds" basis, in which case we need ways to come up with the first half. Ethics are discussed, along with some really good examples. It was published in 1996, and costs $8.00.

They have many other booklets, all published at cost. Just ask for their catalogue.

As mentioned earlier, in PART VI, another good source on current educational issues is the many teacher-oriented magazines on the market: ASCD, Union/Society publications, some of the more scholarly journals, etc. One method here, instead of subscribing to them all, is to find out which schools get them as part of their PD budget, and browse through them when you are in

"Learning is either a continuing thing, or it is nothing."
—*Frank Tyger*

next time, either as an replacement teacher or a volunteer. You might even ask if you can borrow them for a day or two, after everyone else has had a chance to read them, and, if you just ask where the back-issues are kept, you've hit the "mother-lode." Do, however, be respectful of copyright. You don't want to be seen as unprofessional.

If you know, personally, a principal or a superintendent, they often have subscriptions to more educational magazines and journals than they can get through and are often a good source of recommendation for specific articles they think are "must-reads." A few of them will also lend some of their books. Personally, I still find this a significant way to save money and trees. Then, after I have read the book, I can decide if I want to buy a copy for my own collection and future reference. (If you borrow them, just don't forget to return them, or you may find yourself, suddenly, <u>off</u> the "inside track!")

Check around. You might find that your teachers' organization has a library for members. If you live near a university, it will have access to current publications that you can browse at no cost. And don't forget the internet! There are all kinds of articles and teacher discussion groups to help keep us up to date.

Again, our creativity can help make up for our lack of money. Some of us are almost getting used to it.

9. The Humour Factor: Keeping It All in Perspective

• Barry, Dave. *Claw Your Way to the Top: How to Become the Head of a Major Corporation in Roughly a Week.* Emmaus: Rodale, 1986. $7.95.

Totally hilarious! Not at all useful except hyperbolic presentation of what not to do. It will, however, help you to laugh and gain some perspective on this whole stressful process.

"To hire a man because he needs a job, rather than because the job needs him, is to assure him that he is useless. On the other side of the coin, to help a man because it is in your own best interest to help him is to treat him as an equal."

—Henry Ford

NOTES

APPENDIX 1

PROVINCIAL AND TERRITORIAL MINISTRIES AND DEPARTMENTS RESPONSIBLE FOR EDUCATION

NEWFOUNDLAND
Department of Education
Government of Newfoundland and Labrador
3rd Fl, Confederation Building, West Block
St. John's, NF A1B 4J6
Tel: (709) 729-5097
Fax: (709) 729-5896
www.gov.nf.ca/edu

NOVA SCOTIA
Department of Education
Box 578
Halifax, NS 3J 2S9
Tel: (902) 424-5605
Fax: (902) 424-0511
www.ednet.ns.ca

PRINCE EDWARD ISLAND
Department of Education
2nd Floor, Sullivan Building
16 Fitzroy Street, Box 2000
Charlottetown, PE C1A 7N8
Tel: (902) 368-4600
Fax: (902) 368-4663
www.gov.pe.ca/educ

NEW BRUNSWICK
Department of Education
P.O. Box 6000
Fredericton, NB E3B 5H1
Tel: (506) 453-3678
Fax: (506) 453-3325
www.gov.nb.ca/education/index.htm

QUÉBEC
Ministere de L'Education
Edifice Marie-Guyart
28e étage, 1035, rue de la Chevrotière
Québec, QC G1R 5A5
Tel: (418) 643-7095
Fax: (418) 646-6561
www.meq.gouv.qc.ca

ONTARIO
Ministry of Education and Training
Mowat Block
900 Bay Street
Toronto, ON M7A 1L2
Tel: (416) 325-2929
or, 1-800-263-5514
Fax: (416) 325-2934
www.edu.gov.on.ca

MANITOBA
Department of Education and Training
Legislative Building
450 Broadway
Winnipeg, MB R3C 0V8
Tel: (204) 945-2211
Fax: (204) 945-8692
www.gov.mb.ca/educate

COUNCIL OF MINISTERS OF EDUCATION

With frequent changes in governments and education's constant re-organizations, URL's tend to change. If you can't find the Ministry or Department you are looking for, the Council of Ministers of Education will have the most current listing at:
www.cmec.ca

PLEASE HOLD THE LINE

When calling a government office, don't be discouraged by automated answering systems. With persistence, you can usually eventually get to a real person who can give a reasonably definitive answer. If all else fails, fax them your question and your phone number. As a last resort, have your Member of Parliament call on your behalf—then you should get your answer.

SASKATCHEWAN
Department of Education
Department of Post-Secondary
Education and Skills Training
2220 College Avenue
Regina, SK   S4P 3V7

Tel: (306) 787-6030
Fax: (306) 787-7392
wwww.sasked.gov.sk.ca

ALBERTA
Department of Learning
West Tower, Devonian Building
11160 Jasper Avenue
Edmonton, AB   T5K 0L2

Tel: (780) 427-7219
Fax: (780) 427-0591
www.ednet.edc.gov.ab.ca
www.aecd.gov.ab.ca

BRITISH COLUMBIA
Ministry of Education
P.O. Box 9156, Stn. Prov. Govt.
Victoria, BC V8W 9H2

Tel: (250) 387-4611
Fax: (250) 387-3200
www.bced.gov.bc.ca

Ministry of Advanced Education,
Training and Technology
P.O. Box 9884, Stn. Prov. Govt.
Victoria, BC V8W 9T6

Tel: (250) 356-6069
Fax: (250) 356-5468
www.aett.gov.bc.ca

NORTHWEST TERRITORIES
Department of Education,
Culture and Employment
P.O. Box 1320
4501 - 50 Avenue
Yellowknife, NT X1A 2L9

Tel: (867) 920-6240
Fax: (867) 873-0456
www.siksik.learnnet.nt.ca

NUNAVUT
Department of Education
P.O. Box 2410
Government of Nunavut
Building 1088E
Iqaluit, Nunavut   X0A 0H0

Tel: (867) 975-5000
Fax: (867) 975-5095
www.nunavut.com/basicfacts_4govtS.html

YUKON TERRITORY
Department of Education
P.O. Box 2703
Whitehorse, YT Y1A 2C6

Tel: (867) 667-5141
Fax: (867) 393-6339
www.gov.yk.ca/depts/education

APPENDIX 2a

CANADIAN FACULTIES OF EDUCATION

NEWFOUNDLAND

MEMORIAL UNIVERSITY OF NEWFOUNDLAND
Faculty of Education
Memorial University of Newfoundland
St. John's, NF   A1B 3X8

Tel: (709) 737-8588
Fax: (709) 737-8637
www.mun.ca

NOVA SCOTIA

ACADIA UNIVERSITY
School of Education
Acadia University
Wolfville, NS   B0P 1X0

Tel: (902) 585-1229
Fax: (902) 585-1071
www.acadiau.ca

MOUNT SAINT VINCENT UNIVERSITY
Department of Education
Mount Saint Vincent University
166 Bedford Highway
Halifax, NS   B3M 2J6

Tel: (902) 457-6128
Fax: (902) 457-6498
www.msvu.ca

ST. FRANCIS XAVIER UNIVERSITY
Department of Education
St. Francis Xavier University
P.O. Box 5000
Antigonish, NS   B2G 2W5

Tel: (902) 867-2219
Fax: (902) 867-2329
www.stfx.ca

UNIVERSITÉ SAINTE-ANNE
Bureau d'admission
Université Sainte-Anne
Pointe-de-l'Église Nouvelle-Écosse, NS B0W 1M0

Tel: (902) 769-2114
Fax: (902) 769-2930
www.ustanne.ednet.ns.ca

PRINCE EDWARD ISLAND

UNIVERSITY OF PRINCE EDWARD ISLAND
Faculty of Education
The University of Prince Edward Island
550 University Ave.
Charlottetown, PE   C1A 4P3

Tel: (902) 566-0330
Fax: (902) 566-0416
www.upei.ca

FOR ADDITIONAL INFORMATION

For precise details, including application deadlines which vary from university to university and year to year, contact the universities directly. A word of advice to save you money: most have a "1-800" toll-free number but they don't always publish it, so just ask for it the first time you call.

Alternatively, refer to an absolutely excellent and inexpensive book: *Admission to Faculties of Education in Canada*. See *Suggested Further Readings* in *PART XI*.

"To be long-lived, republics must invest in education."
—*Benjamin Rush*

"The greatest obstacle to growth and development, to learning and to improved function, or even to continued function on the level already reached, is discouragement, doubt in one's own ability."

—*R. Dreikurs*

NEW BRUNSWICK

ST. THOMAS UNIVERSITY
The Registrar
St. Thomas University
P.O. Box 4569
Fredericton, NB   E3B 5G3

Tel: (506) 452-0644
Fax: (506) 452-0609
www.stthomasu.ca

UNIVERSITÉ DE MONCTON
Service de l'admission
Centre universitaire de Moncton
Université de Moncton
165, rue Massey
Moncton, NB   E1A 3E9

Tel: (506) 858-4400
Fax: (506) 858-4317
www.umoncton.ca

UNIVERSITY OF NEW BRUNSWICK
Faculty of Education
University of New Brunswick
P.O. Box 4400
Fredericton, NB   E3B 5A3

Tel: (506) 453-4862
Fax: (506) 453-3569
www.unb.ca

QUEBEC

BISHOP'S UNIVERSITY
Graduate School of Education
Bishop's University
P.O. Box 5000, Station Lennoxville
Lennoxville, QC   J1M 1Z7

Tel: (819) 822-9600
(ext. 2462)
Fax: (819) 822-9661
www.ubishops.ca

CONCORDIA UNIVERSITY
Department of Education
Concordia University
LB-579, 1455 de Maisonneuve Blvd. West
Montreal, QC   H3G 1M8

Tel: (514) 848-2029
Fax: (514) 848-4520
www.concordia.ca

MCGILL UNIVERSITY
Faculty of Education
McGill University
3700 McTavish St.
Montreal, QC   H3A 1Y2

Tel: (514) 398-7037
Fax: (514) 398-1527
www.mcgill.ca

UNIVERSITÉ DE MONTRÉAL
Département des sciences de l'éducation
Université de Montréal
C.P. 6128, succursale Centre-ville
Montréal, QC   H3C 3J7

Tel: (514) 343-7622
Fax: (514) 343-2283
www.umontreal.ca

UNIVERSITÉ DE SHERBROOKE
For Educational Programs contact:
Faculté d'éducation
Université de Sherbrooke
2500, boulevard de l'université
Sherbrooke, QC J1K 2R1

Tel: (819) 821-7400
Fax: (819) 821-7950

For Admissions or Registration contact:
Bureau du registraire
Université de Sherbrooke
Sherbrooke, QC J1K 2R1

Tel: (819) 821-7000
Fax: (819) 821-7966
www.usherb.ca

"Knowledge has to be improved, challenged, and increased or it vanishes."
—*Peter Drucker*

UNIVERSITÉ DU QUÉBEC À CHICOUTIMI
Département des sciences de l'éducation
Université du Québec à Chicoutimi
555, boul. de l'université
Chicoutimi, QC   G7H 2B1

Tel: (418) 545-5011
(ext. 5368)
Fax: (418) 545-5012
www.uqac.uquebec.ca

UNIVERSITÉ DU QUÉBEC À HULL
Bureau du registraire
Université du Québec à Hull
C.P. 1250, succursale B
Hull, QC   J8X 3X7

Tel: (819) 595-4415
Fax: (819) 595-4459
www.uqah.uquebec.ca

UNIVERSITÉ DU QUÉBEC À RIMOUSKI
Bureau du reglstraire
Université du Québec à Rimouski
C.P. 3300, succursale Bureau-chef
300, Allée des Ursulines
Rimouski, QC   G5L 3A1

Tel: (418) 723-1986
Fax: (418) 724-1525
www.uquar.uquebec.ca

UNIVERSITÉ DU QUÉBEC À MONTRÉAL
Département des sciences de l'éducation
Université du Québec à Montréal
C.P. 8888, succursale Centre-ville
Montréal, QC   H3C 3P8

Tel: (514) 987-4123
Fax: (514) 987-4608
www.uqam.ca

UNIVERSITÉ DU QUÉBEC À TROIS-RIVIÈRES
Bureau du registraire
Université du Québec à Trois-Rivières
3351, boulevard des Forges
C.P. 500, succursale Bureau-chef
Trois-Rivières, QC   G9A 5H7

Tel: (819) 376-5093
Fax: (819) 376-5127
www.uqtr.uquebec.ca

UNIVERSITÉ DU QUÉBEC EN ABITIBI-TÉMISCAMINGUE
Bureau du registraire
Université du Québec en Abitibi-Témiscamingue
445, boul. de l'université
Rouyn-Noranda, QC   J9X 5E4

Tel: (819) 762-0971
Fax: (819) 797-4727
www.uqat.uquebec.ca

UNIVERSITÉ LAVAL
Faculté des sciences de l'éducation
Université Laval
Cité universitaire
C.P. 2208, succursale Terminus
Québec, QC   G1K 7P4

Tel: (418) 656-3062
Fax: (418) 656-7347
www.ulaval.ca

NOTE

It must be noted that each province and each university has specific requirements, specific timelines, specific procedures of admission and, in some cases, specific personal characteristics sought, all of which are subject to change. Some also offer special admission to mature students, those of aboriginal ancestry, physically challenged persons, etc. It is impossible to generalize.

ONTARIO

All students applying for admission to a Faculty of Education in Ontario must apply to the Teacher Education Application Service. The TEAS at the Ontario Universities' Application Centre (OUAC) provides the processing, but all documentation (letters, transcripts, etc.) go to the individual university. The necessary application forms may be obtained at secondary schools, university registrar's offices, and OUAC: 650 Woodlawn Road West, P.O. Box 1328, Guelph, Ontario N1H 7P4 (Tel: 519-823-1940).

"One must learn by doing the thing, for though you think you know it, you have no certainty until you try."
—R. Dreikurs

"The great end of education is to discipline rather than furnish the mind; to train it to use its own powers, rather than to fill it with the accumulation of others."
—*Tyron Edwards*

In the Ontario Ministry of Education, there are still rumblings about introduction of legislation permitting graduates of Community Colleges with diplomas in Early Childhood Education to teach Junior and Senior Kindergarten (SK) in schools. This appears to be largely a combination of the indisputable fact that the training is relevant to the job, coupled with the government's overpowering desire to cut funding to education and their suspicion that they could get non-university-educated personnel more cheaply. Ultimately, the Ontario College of Teachers is responsible for certification but they, of course, are subject to the legislature.

There are also questions about the future of Junior Kindergarten (JK) after funding has been decreased for it, in an interesting reversal that would have seen legislation mandating boards to provide it. SK will probably stay; in fact, the government has released a curriculum document for it.

It should also be noted that additional qualification courses and professional development courses offered by universities in Ontario are very much in a state of transition, largely as a result of changes in funding structures. Specific enquiries should be made to the universities.

BROCK UNIVERSITY
Faculty of Education
Brock University
500 Glenridge Ave.
St. Catharines, ON L2S 3A1

Tel: (416) 688-5550
Fax: (416) 688-0540
www.brocku.ca

LAKEHEAD UNIVERSITY
Faculty of Education
Lakehead University
955 Oliver Rd.
Thunder Bay, ON P7B 5E1

Tel: (807) 343-8520
Fax: (807) 344-6807
www.lakeheadu.ca

LAURENTIAN UNIVERSITY
Admissions Office
Laurentian University
935 Ramsey Lake Road
Sudbury, ON P3E 2C6

Tel: (705) 673-6592
Fax: (705) 675-4816
www.laurentian.ca

NIPISSING UNIVERSITY
Faculty of Education
Nipissing University
100 College Drive, Box 5002
North Bay, ON P1B 8L7

Tel: (705) 474-3461
or 1-800-461-1673
Fax: (705) 474-3264
www.unipissing.ca

QUEEN'S UNIVERSITY
For Post-degree program contact:
The Office of the Registrar
Faculty of Education
Duncan McArthur Hall
Queen's University
Kingston, ON K7L 3N6

Tel: (613) 533-6205
Fax: (613) 533-6203
www.queensu.ca

For concurrent program and other programs contact:
Assistant Registrar (Admissions)
Queen's University
Victoria School Building
110 Alfred Street
Kingston, ON K7L 3N6

Tel: (613) 533-2218
Fax: (613) 533-6810

"The first idea that the child must acquire, in order to be actively disciplined, is that of the difference between good and evil; and the task of the educator lies in seeing that the child does not confound good with immobility, and evil with activity."
—*Maria Montessori*

THE UNIVERSITY OF WESTERN ONTARIO
Office of Admissions
Faculty of Education
The University of Western Ontario
1137 Western Road
London, ON   N6G 1G7

Tel: (519) 661-2080
Fax: (519) 661-3833
www.uwo.ca

TRENT UNIVERSITY
Registrar's Office
Trent University
P.O. Box 4800, Station Main
Peterborough, ON   K9J 7B8

Tel: (705) 748-1464
Fax: (705) 748-1008
www.trentu.ca

UNIVERSITY OF OTTAWA
Faculty of Education
University of Ottawa
145 Jean-Jacques Lussier, P.O. Box 450, Stn. A
Ottawa, ON   K1N 6N5

Tel: (613) 562-5804
Fax: (613) 562-5146
www.uottawa.ca

UNIVERSITY OF TORONTO
Faculty of Education
University of Toronto
252 Bloor Street West
Toronto, ON   M5S 1V6

Tel: (416) 923-6641
(ext. 3223)
Fax: (416) 971-2293
www.utoronto.ca

UNIVERSITY OF WINDSOR
Faculty of Education
University of Windsor
401 Sunset Ave.
Windsor, ON   N9B 3P4

Tel: (519) 253-3000
(ext. 3800)
Fax: (519) 971-3612
www.uwindsor.ca

YORK UNIVERSITY
Faculty of Education
York University
Office of Student Programs
N801 Ross Building
4700 Keele Street
North York, ON   M3J 1P3

Tel: (416) 736-5002
Fax: (416) 736-5913
www.yorku.ca

MANITOBA

BRANDON UNIVERSITY
Faculty of Education
Brandon University
Brandon, MB   R7A 6A9

Tel: (204) 727-9656
Fax: (204) 728-3326
www.brandonu.ca

COLLÈGE UNIVERSITAIRE DE SAINT-BONIFACE
Bureau du registraire
200, avenue de la Cathédrale
Saint-Boniface, MB   R2H 0H7

Tel: (204) 233-0210
(ext. 302)
Fax: (204) 237-3240
www.ustboniface.mb.ca

UNIVERSITY OF MANITOBA
Faculty of Education
University of Manitoba
4th Floor, University Centre
Winnipeg, MB   R3T 2N2

Tel: (204) 474-9092
Fax: (204) 474-7551
www.umanitoba.ca

TEACHING LEVELS IN ONTARIO

Teaching certification levels in Ontario continue to reflect obsolete divisions: Primary (K-3). Junior (4-6), Intermediate (7-10) and Senior (11-O.A.C.). Certification is obtained in any two adjacent divisions: P-J, J-I, or I-S.

As a point of interest, current Ministry of Education and Training policy divides programs into the following divisions in Ontario, not yet reflected in the official licensing categories: Early Years (JK-3), Formative Years (4-6), Transition Years (7-9), Specialization Years (10-12) and Ontario Academic Credits (O.A.C.'s).

"The important thing is not so much that every child should be taught, as that every child should be given the wish to learn."

—*John Lubbock*

UNIVERSITY OF WINNIPEG
Admissions Office
The University of Winnipeg
515 Portage Avenue
Winnipeg, MB   R3B 2E9

Tel: (204) 786-9491
Fax: (204) 772-7980
www.uwinnipeg.ca

SASKATCHEWAN

UNIVERSITY OF REGINA
Faculty of Education
Education Building
University of Regina
Regina, SK   S4S 0A2

Tel: (306) 585-4500
Fax: (306) 585-4880
www.uregina.ca

UNIVERSITY OF SASKATCHEWAN
For programs other than those directed exclusively toward aboriginal persons contact:
College of Education
University of Saskatchewan
Saskatoon, SK   S7N 0X1

Tel: (306) 966-7647
Fax: (306) 966-7624
www.usask.ca

ALBERTA

CONCORDIA UNIVERSITY COLLEGE
Faculty of Education
7128 Ada Boulevard
Edmonton, AB   T6J 6G1

Tel: (780) 479-9277
Fax: (780) 474-1933
www.concordia.ab.ca/

FACULTÉ SAINT-JEAN, THE UNIVERSITY OF ALBERTA
Faculté Sainte-Jean
Bureau des admissions
8406-91 rue Marie-Anne Gaboury
Edmonton, AB T6C 4G9

Tel: (780) 465-8700
Fax: (780) 465-8760

THE KING'S UNIVERSITY COLLEGE
Teacher Education Program
9125 - 50 Street N.W.
Edmonton, AB   T6B 2H3

Tel: (780) 465-3500
Fax (780) 465-3534
www.kingsu.ab.ca

UNIVERSITY OF ALBERTA
For basic teacher certification programs contact:
Undergraduate Student Services
Faculty of Education
University of Alberta
Edmonton, AB T6G 2G5

Tel: (780) 492-3751
Fax: (780) 492-0236
www.ualberta.ca

UNIVERSITY OF CALGARY
Faculty of Education, University of Calgary
2500 University Drive N.W.
Calgary, AB T2N 1N4

Tel: (403) 220-5627
Fax: (403) 282-5849
www.ucalgary.ca

UNIVERSITY OF LETHBRIDGE
Faculty of Education
University of Lethbridge
4401 University Drive
Lethbridge, AB T1K 3M4

Tel: (403) 329-2251
Fax: (403) 329-2252
www.home.uleth.ca

"The aim of education is the knowledge not of fact, but of values."
—*William Inge*

BRITISH COLUMBIA

MALASPINA UNIVERSITY COLLEGE
Department of Education
900 Fifth Street
Nanaimo, BC V9R 5S5

Tel: (250) 741-2555
(ext. 2567)
Fax: (250) 741-2393
www.mala.bc.ca

NORTHERN LIGHTS COLLEGE
Alaska Highway Consortium on Teacher Education
(AHCOTE)
11401 - 8th Street
Dawson Creek, BC V1G 4G2

Tel: (250) 782-5251
(ext. 1334)
Fax: (250) 784-7610
www.nic.bc.ca

OKANAGAN UNIVERSITY COLLEGE
Department of Education
3333 College Way
Kelowna, BC V1V 1V7

Tel: (250) 762-5445
www.ouc.bc.ca/ed

SIMON FRASER UNIVERSITY
Assistant to the Associate Dean
Faculty of Education
Simon Fraser University
8888 University Drive
Burnaby, BC V5A 1S6

Tel: (604) 291-3620
(ext. 3149)
Fax: (604) 291-3203
www.sfu.ca

TRINITY WESTERN UNIVERSITY
Department of Teacher Education
7600 Glover Road
Langley, BC V2Y 1Y1

Tel: (604) 888-7511
Fax: (604) 513-2061
www.twu.ca/academics/default.htm

UNIVERSITY OF BRITISH COLUMBIA
Faculty of Education
UBC Teacher Education Office
Faculty of Education
2125 Main Mall
Vancouver, BC V6T 1Z4

Tel: (604) 822-5211
Fax: (604) 822-6501
www.ubc.ca

UNIVERSITY OF NORTHERN BRITISH COLUMBIA
Master's Program – Education
3333 University Way
Prince George, BC V2N 4Z9

Tel: (888) 419-5588
Fax: (250) 960-5536
www.unbc.ca

UNIVERSITY OF VICTORIA
Faculty of Education
University of Victoria
P.O. Box 3010, Stn. csc

Tel: (604) 721-7766
Fax: (604) 721-7767
www.uvic.ca

NUNAVUT

NUNAVUT ARCTIC COLLEGE (AFFILIATED WITH MCGILL UNIVERSITY)
Nunavut Campus
Iqaluit, Nunavut X0A 0H0

"We are increasingly being stripped of the comfortable notion that a bright mind will make its own way. Intellectual and creative talent cannot survive educational neglect and apathy."

—Sidney Marland

"If all students are helped to the full utilization of their intellectual powers, we will have a better chance of surviving as a democracy in an age of enormous technological and social complexity."

—Jerome S. Bruner

"A poor education is immensely expensive to the individual who achieves it, and to the country that must depend on him later."

—*Sarah Caldwell*

NORTHWEST TERRITORIES

The NWT has no teacher-training facilities of its own.

YUKON

The Yukon has no teacher-training facilities of its own.

APPENDIX 2b

AMERICAN FACULTIES OF EDUCATION OFFERING PROGRAMS WHICH CAN LEAD TO ONTARIO TEACHER CERTIFICATION

Each Province and Territory has its own requirements and procedures for certification of out-of-province/territory teachers, and out-of-Canada teachers. The following is, however, illustrative of the possibilities.

In Ontario, only faculties of education have authorization to recommend officially that, upon completion of their program, The Ontario College of Teachers grant to the candidate a Certificate of Qualification (the Ontario teacher's license together with official record of related qualifications). With the intense competition for places in Ontario's faculties, however, several colleges, especially in New York State, have started to expand to accommodate the demand. The Ontario College of Teachers offers, upon application, to graduates of specific teacher training programs which it approves, a "Letter of Eligibility" which permits the holder to seek employment as a teacher in the province of Ontario in the divisions for which the College deems she or he is qualified, depending upon the training received. Teachers in Ontario must be qualified in two of three divisions: Primary/ Junior (Kindergarten to 6) Junior/Intermediate (4 to 10) Intermediate/Senior (7 to 12). The program for Intermediate/ Senior must include a teaching subject listed in Schedule A, Ontario Regulation 297. (Contact the Ministry of Education and Training, Ontario, for specifics.) This is one of three areas of certification the College does not handle. (The other two are: approving and issuing Letters of Permission—to unqualified persons when no qualified candidate is available—and issuing Supervisory Officer certificates.)

To be approved, the teacher training program: (a) must lead to teaching certification in the jurisdiction where it is earned—unless there is a citizenship requirement or restriction in which case the university can confirm that all requirements for certification have been met except the immigration/citizenship requirement, (b) must be the equivalent of at least one year of specific teacher training beyond an undergraduate degree, (c) must include at least one full course in curriculum development and teaching methods, one full course in educational foundations (educational psychology, history of education, learning and development), and include forty days of supervised practice teaching, and the program must be preparation for certification to teach in regular classes, i.e., not Special Education. For specifics, and to ensure that the program satisfies Ontario Certification requirements, contact:

The Ontario College of Teachers
121 Bloor Street East, 6th Floor
Toronto, ON M4W 3M5

Tel: (416) 961-8800
Fax:(416) 961-8822
www.oct.on.ca

CIRCUMVENTING ENROLLMENT CAPS

There are ways around the enrollment cap in Canadian Faculties and Schools of Education. It takes some work but, if you are determined, the example here of Ontario shows how you can use the global economy to your advantage.

If you want, you can even get certified for Ontario this way (or similarly for another province), and then apply for cross-certification for your own province or territory (see APPENDIX 7).

IMPORTANT

Before enrolling in an out-of-province or out-of-Canada teacher training program, confirm in writing with the Department or Ministry of Education or College of Teachers *in the province in which you intend to teach* that the professional program you are considering is acceptable to them for certification.

Letter of Eligibility and Temporary Letter of Standing

The "Letter of Eligibility" is valid for three years and may be renewed if the requirements for qualification have not changed. If they have, the applicant would then have to obtain the additional qualifications. Application forms for the Letter of Eligibility are available from The Ontario College of Teachers.

The Letter of Eligibility permits a candidate to seek employment as a teacher in Ontario. When the fact that a candidate has been hired to teach in Ontario is certified by a supervisory officer, the candidate is granted a "Temporary Letter of Standing" which is good for six years. After only one year of certified successful teaching, however, the candidate can apply for a Certificate of Qualification, which is permanent upon issue. (One year of teaching is: 10 months (not necessarily consecutive) of full-time teaching; or 200 occasional/supply teaching days (may be with more than one school board/private school/education authority and may be accumulated over several years); or five (or equivalent) credit courses taught in night school, summer school or a school board's continuing education program. Any teaching experience prior to the issue date of your Temporary Letter of Standing will not be accepted toward the requirements for a Certificate of Qualification. Experience in post-secondary institutions or at the pre-school level is not acceptable as experience either.

The really neat thing is: the year of teaching does not have to be full-time. As stated above, it can be part-time, or even occasional/replacement teaching. In fact, being offered occasional teaching, or even being accepted onto an "Approved Occasional Teacher List," is considered an offer of employment, and is enough to get the wheels in motion; it will get you a Temporary Letter of Standing! This offer of employment can be from a board, a private school, the Provincial Schools Authority, the Department of Indian Affairs and Northern Development or a band council for First Nations persons.

Tuition for Canadian Students

Be aware that non-resident's tuition for some of these programs can be quite expensive: around the $8,000.00 to $11,000.00 U.S. mark. On the other hand, some offer tuition in Canadian dollars at par and others offer Canadian students tuition which is less expensive than that charged to out-of-state American students. A few examples are specified below.

With that in mind, if this is the way you want to go, following are some of the programs which have in recent past met with "ministerial approval" in Ontario. Some other provinces have similar acceptance of certification from American universities. You need to check carefully with the relevant provincial ministry or department to determine the acceptance status of an off-shore program before enrolling. By contacting the Certifications Branch of the education authority in the province or territory you are interested in (see the final section of APPENDIX 7), you can also get the names of universities offering out-of-province/territory programs which have been accepted in the recent past by them.

CANISIUS COLLEGE
2001 Main Street
Buffalo, New York 14208-1098
Tuition: $325.00 U.S. per credit hour (1994)

Tel: (716) 888-2545
1-800-950-2505
Fax: (716) 888-2525
www.canisius.edu

D'YOUVILLE COLLEGE
One D'Youville Square
320 Porter Avenue, Rm HSB 103
Buffalo, New York 14201-9985

Tel: (716) 881-7676
or 1-800-777-3921
Fax: (716) 881-7760
www.dyc.edu

Tuition: $8,920.00 for the two semester program (1994). This is the Canadian Student tuition; out-of-state Americans pay more.

MEDAILLE COLLEGE
Agassiz Circle
Buffalo, New York 14214

Tel: (716) 884-3281
Fax: (716) 884-0291
www.medaille.edu

Tuition: for the 42 credit hours over 11 months: $10,672.00 U.S. (1994).

NIAGARA UNIVERSITY
New York, New York 14109
Tuition: $9540.00 U.S. (1994)

Tel: (716) 285-1212
Fax: (716) 286-8733
www.niagara.edu

ROBERTS WESLEYAN COLLEGE
2301 Westside Drive
Rochester, New York 14624
Tuition: $8,254.00 (1994)

Tel: (716) 594-9471
Fax: (716) 594-6371
rwc.edu/index.htm

The good news is: they accept Canadian money at par! You should also be aware that because they are a "religious" university, they have a specific standard of moral and behavioural conduct which they require of all students.

ST. BONAVENTURE UNIVERSITY
Graduate School
St. Bonaventure, New York 14778

Tel: (716) 375-2086
www.sbu.edu

UNIVERSITY OF MAINE
181 Main Street
Presque Isle, Maine 04769

Tel: (207) 764-0311
Fax: (207) 768-9608
www.umcs.maine.edu

Tuition: The program requires three or four semesters depending upon number of liberal arts courses in your undergraduate degree (it must meet Maine requirements). If three semesters are required, tuition would be $6075.00 total; if four semesters, $8,100.00 (1994). This is the Canadian Student tuition; out-of-state Americans pay more.

CROSS-CERTIFICATION

You might also want to see APPENDIX 7 for information on cross-certification—having credentials transferred from one province or territory to another. Could you, for example, get Ontario certification from an American university and then have it recognized by, shall we say, New Brunswick? APPENDIX 7 will tell you.

"Kites rise against the wind—not with it."
—*Sir Winston Churchill*

NOTES

APPENDIX 3

OCCASIONAL TEACHER INFORMATION RECORD SHEET

School: _____ Date(s) _____ to _____

Class/Subject(s) taught: _____

Name(s) of teacher(s) replaced:_____

Lessons taught: _____

_____

_____

Exceptionalities or peculiarities of the class or school:_____

_____

_____

Unusual or unlisted school routines: _____

_____

_____

_____

Potential network persons, and their areas of expertise:

_____

_____

_____

Does the school have a copy of your résumé?   ❏ YES   ❏ NO

Has Principal or Vice-Principal observed teaching?   ❏ YES   ❏ NO

From: *The Inside Track: Getting Hired to Teach in a Canadian School* (Toronto: ON:
Thompson Educational Publishing, Inc., 2000).
Original purchaser may make unlimited copies for personal use.

APPENDIX 4

OCCASIONAL TEACHER READINESS CHECKLIST

Night Before:

— map of area schools near phone

— pencil and paper for messages near phone

— family instructed not to answer phone in morning unless you are in shower

— clothes selected and ready for next day, including those suitable if on outdoor yard duty

— car filled with gas and ready to go (if it is winter, be sure driveway is shoveled)

When Called:

— record name of school, be certain you already know route to it, and name of teacher you are replacing, and subjects (if applicable) _____

— load appropriate emergency lesson plan, materials, etc., into box and *into the car*

— are you on yard duty?   ❑ YES   ❑ NO
If yes, when?_____

When You Arrive:

— arrive at least 30 minutes before start of classes

— check in at office with
  _ Principal/Vice Principal, and
  _ Secretary
  _ Department Head (if appropriate)

— get school routines

— any special events today? If Yes:_____Time: _____

— confirm duty schedule if any: _____

When You Enter the Classroom:

— check day-plan book

— check for a list of special instructions for an occasional teacher

— organize, into order required, the work left by teacher

— in absence of above, get own plans and materials ready

— gather any necessary materials or equipment

— duplicate any required materials

— find seating plan

— print your name on board or chart-paper, if unknown to class

— introduce yourself to teachers in adjoining rooms

When Pupils Arrive:

— greet them in the hall with a smile (By standing very close to the doorway, you can supervise both hall and classroom)

— follow opening exercises routine

— spend a few minutes confirming classroom routines (washroom, pencils, monitors, "special person of the day," etc.)

— confirm names as on seating plan, or make name tags for each desk

— take attendance, record it in day-plan book and send copy to office if required

Throughout the Day:

— record *in detail* all work accomplished and assigned from teacher's day-plan

— get to know the rest of the staff, and be willing to ask for suggestions or to accept and record offers of help in your career

— check bulletin boards for job postings!

— demonstrate willingness to be flexible, without being exploited

— constantly recall to memory significant behavioural strategies you are intending to use, and use them as required

— find out about extra-curricular programs, or other program areas, in which you could contribute to the school and make yourself indispensable

— be alert for a classroom you could gain volunteer experience in, if you will benefit and/or learn from it

After Final Dismissal:

— do all marking

— finish recording what was or was not completed of teacher's day-plan

— finish recording in detail what else was taught

— make specific comments about how the day went, including any concerns or issues which might need to be addressed when the teacher returns

— if you enjoyed the class and would like to be called back, say so in your note to the teacher

— make certain room is clean (keep the custodians from black-listing you) and the teacher's desk is neat, but don't move their stuff!

— leave your name and phone number for the teacher when he/she returns

— write up a "contingency" day-plan for the next day

— say "goodbye" to the principal or vice-principal, and the secretary, and let them know you are available again tomorrow, "if needed"

When You Get Home:

— fill out your *OCCASIONAL TEACHER INFORMATION RECORD SHEET* (Appendix 3)

— record names of colleagues you met who might be able to offer assistance in future

— pack another lunch

— replenish your box of lessons

From: *The Inside Track: Getting Hired to Teach in a Canadian School* (Toronto: ON: Thompson Educational Publishing, Inc., 2000). Original purchaser may make copies for personal use.

APPENDIX 5

PROVINCIAL AND TERRITORIAL FUNDING OF PRIVATE SCHOOLS AND CERTIFICATION REQUIRED OF PRIVATE-SCHOOL TEACHERS

"We never reflect how pleasant it is to ask for nothing."

—*Lucius Annaeus Seneca*

Private schools in Canada are designed to offer children admitted to them one of the following distinguishing features:

- education within a specific religious milieu,
- a specific pedagogic methodological process,
- residential schooling,
- an atmosphere of traditional British "public" school,
- programming for special needs,
- education in a specific language, or
- training to ready non-Canadian students for North American universities.

In exchange for that freedom, they may have to forfeit all or part of the usual provincial funding of schools. While total school enrollment in Canada declined approximately 15% in the two decades of the 1970s and 80s, private school enrollment increased over that time by about 65%.

While there is not a 1:1 correlation between the degree of government funding and the scale of pay for teachers, candidates are advised to decide whether they are willing to teach for the remuneration available in the particular school to which they are applying. In some non-tax-funded schools, especially those operated by religious groups, staff sometimes are expected to offer their services as a contribution to the "mission" effort, receiving minimal financial reward. In some other private schools the pay is competitive with tax-funded schools, and there may be other very significant advantages to working in such an environment: they can, for example, select the students they will accept! Think of dear old Lucius Seneca and check it out first!

Candidates for teaching positions in these schools may require regular teaching certification and usually require additional qualifications or personal qualities depending upon the nature of the school: facility in the language taught, adherence to specific religious dogma, etc.

NEWFOUNDLAND

Newfoundland has, perhaps, the most interesting history of any province or territory in Canada with regard to funding of schools. It is now also, arguably, the least discriminatory.

There is a long tradition of denominational schools in Newfoundland. Written into its constitution at the time of confederation (1949) was the provision for control of their schools by the Anglican, Pentecostal, Roman Catholic, Salvation Army, Seventh-Day Adventist and United churches. This resulted in some interesting anomalies, whereby there could be an isolated outpost with five elementary schools, each with only a handful of pupils. Another "feature" of this— which, to a lesser extent is still repeated in some other provinces—was that the buses carrying one group of children 65 kilometers to study in a school of one denomination would meet the buses of the other denomination heading the other way, just as far. Then, at night, they would all return to, hopefully, live happily side by side.

"The foundation of every state is the education of its youth."

—*Diogenes*

To address this duplication, in the early 1990s, some of these churches joined to form "Integrated" school boards, with the Roman and Pentecostal churches remaining the hold-outs, insisting, it would appear, that the specific virtues of their faith could not survive uncloistered (my apologies to the late Rev. John Milton). Then, religious conflict around the issues of school closures and religious designation of some of the very small schools made the "inter-denominational" concept unworkable, and in the referendum of September 2, 1997, the people of Newfoundland voted to remove church control of education and to move to a rather unique situation where "all children, regardless of religious affiliation, attend the same schools, where opportunities for religious education and observances are provided." The legislation confirming this plan was unanimously passed in the Newfoundland House of Assembly (provincial legislature).

Of course, families who still want their children to have a denominational education are free to operate a denominational school, so long as the staff hold valid Newfoundland teaching certifications and follow the prescribed provincial curriculum, or one approved by the Minister of Education, and adhere to the safety laws, etc. Unlike most other provinces which provide state funding for schools operated by only one or two select religions, Newfoundland treats all church-controlled schools equally by providing none of them with funding, but allows for all children to practice their own religion in the public schools, if they wish to do so.

Nor does Newfoundland fund private schools, although they are permitted to operate under the same requirements as denominational schools regarding curriculum, teacher certification, and other laws related to public buildings.

Newfoundland also permits home schooling, but in a slightly different way. All children must first be enrolled in a school, then the parents apply for permission to have their attendance excused while they are under alternate instruction. This way, the child gets free textbooks to use while being taught at home. There is, of course, no requirement regarding certification of instructors of home-schooled children, but the law requires that the instruction must be demonstrably "efficient."

NOVA SCOTIA

Nova Scotia does not fund private schools. It has a non-sectarian education system which it does fund. Private schools which follow the provincial curricula, however, receive the same per pupil "grant" credit for purchasing books from the Nova Scotia School Book Bureau as is given to "public" schools. There are no requirements regarding qualifications of teachers in private schools.

PRINCE EDWARD ISLAND

Like Nova Scotia, Prince Edward Island has a non-sectarian publicly funded system of schools and does not fund private schools or religious schools. Again like Nova Scotia, private schools which follow the provincial curricula receive free textbooks. All teachers and administrators employed in private schools in the province must be "eligible for a P.E.I. teaching certificate." That means you would need to prove that you have all the training necessary to get one, i.e., you have certification from another province.

NEW BRUNSWICK

Like N.S. and P.E.I., New Brunswick's schools are non-sectarian. Private (independent) schools are not funded or financially supported, although they are inspected. Pupils require annual exemption from public schools to attend private schools. There are no requirements regarding qualifications of teachers in private schools.

QUEBEC

Quebec has recently seen major changes in this area. This may be a belated effect of the "quiet revolution" which started in the 1960s and marked a decrease in control by the church of everyday life, or a reflection of the post-Levesque division between French and English in the province, or both. Whatever the case, rather than the religious division found in the past—and still in existence

RELIGIOUS REQUIREMENTS

It might be useful to be aware that in church schools that are not tax-funded (i.e., private), you may well find that they expect a higher standard of piety and θρησκεια (*threskeia*, the outward, ceremonial observance of the religious requirements). This expectation tends to be somewhat more diluted in tax-funded religious schools.

Perhaps this reflects the additional effort, determination and dedication necessary on the part of the supporters to maintain a non-tax-funded operation.

"The intelligent anticipation of consequences is a vital goal of education."
—*John Dewey*

PRIVATE SCHOOL PAY SCALES

Remember to check: some private schools pay <u>very</u> poorly.

in some provinces—schools are now divided between those where French is the language of instruction and those where English is the language of instruction. (There are very stringent rules governing who can attend the English-language schools.)

There are at least two schools in small Quebec communities which accommodate both, two separate identities within the same building. One is located on the Ontario border at Temiscaming and another in the Montreal area.

Quebec fully funds both systems, and pupils of all religions, or none, enroll depending upon language. While—as a result of 15th century history—French schools are predominantly Roman Catholic, and the English schools are mostly a mixture of Protestant and other religions, pupils in each school take compulsory education in Roman Catholicism (R.C.) or "Moral Instruction" (M.I.). Members of the clergy are permitted, upon approval, and at their own expense, to enter the schools to offer religion-based activities as part of these R.C. or M.I. curricula.

In addition, private schools which already have a permit to operate may apply for accreditation which makes them eligible to receive grants, though the grants are less per pupil than that given to public religious schools.

Most private schools in Quebec serve minority religions or are boarding schools. All teaching staff in private schools in Quebec must hold teacher certification.

ONTARIO

Private schools in Ontario are mostly of a religious nature (Jewish, Fundamentalist Christian, etc.), although special education schools, residential schools, college preparatory schools and Waldorf and Montessori schools exist. (The British Prince Andrew attended one of Ontario's preparatory schools when he was younger.)

Except for the very small, historic Protestant Separate School Board of the Town of Penetanguishene—which has been, uniquely, prevented by law from expanding its geographic borders beyond the town limits—the only religion to receive state funding for education in Ontario is Roman Catholicism. Like the non-sectarian public schools, Roman Catholic Separate Schools in Ontario are tax funded from Kindergarten to Ontario Academic Credits (Grade 13).

Will this change? On November 5, 1999, the United Nations ruled this policy as "discriminatory" and ordered Canada to indicate within 90 days how it intended to end this education funding policy. While such a UN ruling is not binding, treaties such as that with the United Nations do obligate Canada and cannot, usually, be ignored. They can, however, be side-stepped, and Canada, of course, indicated immediately that education is a provincial matter, and the provincial response was equally terse. There is a lot of history involved. As a condition of confederation The *British North America Act* (1867) guaranteed Roman Catholic education for the 17% of Ontario residents who were Catholic at that time and Protestant education for the very few Protestants in Quebec. Then, as in Ontario, the "Protestant" schools quickly became "public" schools, welcoming pupils of all backgrounds. Will Ontario follow the Newfoundland example or the litigation events in Ontario in the early 1990s which confirmed state funding to support one religion only? With around 50% of Ontario's residents now being Roman Catholic, it is difficult to say.

Schools operated by all other religions are deemed to be private schools and like any other private schools receive no financial support.

"When you're through changing, you're through."
—*Bruce Barton*

In Ontario there are no requirements regarding qualifications of teachers in private schools.

MANITOBA

In addition to its non-sectarian publicly funded school system, Manitoba funds private schools which meet specific criteria outlined in regulations. It's Instruction and Services grant totals almost 60% of the grant available to pupils in public schools. The Ministry also offers an additional grant for special needs pupils in private schools, depending upon the severity of their needs. Curriculum materials receive a grant, and financial support is available to public schools if they offer support to private schools for transportation, clinical services and facilities and resources.

Teachers in funded private schools must hold valid teaching certificates. Those teaching in unfunded private schools are not regulated with regard to certification.

SASKATCHEWAN

Most independent (private) schools in Saskatchewan are religion based, though one is a French-language high school. Only Historical High Schools and Alternative Schools receive government funding.

The Historical High Schools are those which were established in the early 1900s in areas where there was no "public" high schools. They are required to meet specific criteria including the requirement that the teachers hold valid Saskatchewan teacher's certification. Alternative schools are for special needs pupils and are funded by the Department of Education and sometimes partially by the Social Services department as well.

Saskatchewan funds equally its public and separate schools. Until recently, all separate schools were Roman Catholic, but as the law specifies that the "religious minority" can be funded the same, there is now one Protestant Separate school in the province. Will there be more?

There are also "Associate Schools" in Saskatchewan. In these, members of a religious minority enter an agreement with a public school system to work together with them, sharing resources such as busing, and funding is then granted to them "through" the public board.

ALBERTA

Alberta is the "province of parental choice." The government has intentionally opted to maximize the spectrum of options for its students and their families.

"Registered Private Schools" in Alberta do not receive any government funding, although they are required to meet standards acceptable to the Minister of Education, who may approve or prohibit the use of any courses.

Note the difference between "Registered" and "Accredited" private schools in Alberta.

"Accredited Private Schools" do receive funding. One of the criteria for funding is that "individuals whose qualifications are approved by the minister are employed to teach at the school." (The other requirements are that it meet the standards of safety, etc., required of a non-funded private school, and that "seven or more students from two or more families are enrolled....")

Alberta has publicly-funded public and separate (Roman Catholic and Protestant) school systems. In addition to religious private schools (most of which are Seventh-Day Adventist or associated with the Association of Christian Schools International or the Association of Independent Church Schools), they have Montessori, Waldorf, special schools for children with learning disabilities, schools for children who are identified as "gifted," and a visa school for foreign students.

Alberta also funds "Charter Schools" at the same rate as other publicly-funded schools. Most charter schools are under the jurisdiction of "public" schools, although some are more independent and are deemed to be directly under the jurisdiction of the Minister.

"Children are our most valuable natural resource."
—*Herbert Hoover*

All teachers in all types of schools are required to be Alberta certified.

As part of its parental choice vision, Alberta also funds "home education," although not to the same level as other schools. (In fact, it is about ¼ the rate.) Of this, the "supervising board" which is responsible for testing and quality assurance can take half for their expenses. Families can also opt for a "blend": part of the time in a school and part-time being taught at home.

All students in all types of schooling (including home education) are required to take the same tests to assure competency of the pupils and the education provider.

BRITISH COLUMBIA

Independent schools in British Columbia must have a certificate of group classification which, in turn, determines the amount of government funding the school receives, if any.

Group 1 schools (mostly Roman Catholic schools) receive 50% of the funding per pupil given to non-private schools. Teachers in these schools must be certified. Group 2 schools (mostly low pupil-teacher ratio settings: special education schools or British style "exclusive" schools) receive 35% of regular grant. Teachers in these schools must be certified. Group 3 schools receive 10% of regular per-pupil grants. They are not required to meet government requirements for curriculum, nor are their teachers required to possess any certification. Group 4 schools receive no government funding or grants, though 80% of their teachers must be certified, and they must comply with time requirements and are evaluated to ensure student progress is satisfactory. These schools are mostly for foreign and out-of-province students. Group 5 schools do not receive any government funding. They address the needs mostly of minority religious groups. After one year, and satisfactory evaluation/inspection results, they may apply for a funded classification.

All private or independent schools in British Columbia are classified in Group 4 or Group 5 for the first year of their operation. Their requirements for certification of teachers will, then, be a factor in the category they intend to attain.

NORTHWEST TERRITORIES

The Northwest Territories have tax-funded public and separate (Protestant and Roman Catholic) school systems. (There is only one Roman Catholic Separate Board, it being in Yellowknife.) There are, as of June 1994, no private schools in the N.W.T., although regulations permit their establishment. The requirement relevant to certification in these schools is that "the work of every teacher [be] inspected in order to ensure that a satisfactory standard of instruction is maintained." There is no reference to credentials required of teachers. With further revisions of the *Education Act* may come provisions for funding of private schools, should they be established.

NUNAVUT

There are no provisions in the *Education Act* for funding of private schools or parochial schools in Nunavut. All schools are non-denominational.

YUKON TERRITORY

The Yukon Territory funds public schools and Roman Catholic separate schools, although schools of other faiths are expressly prohibited from receiving direct or indirect funding or contributions from government, school boards or school councils. Private schools seeking accreditation must employ "persons who meet the qualifications required by the regulations," i.e., must be certified teachers. Private schools registered but not seeking accreditation are not required to employ certified teachers. Private schools in the Yukon are operated by minority religious groups.

"Whatever you do, do it passionately well."
—*St. Francis of Sales*

APPENDIX 6

CITIZENSHIP OR LANDED IMMIGRANT STATUS REQUIREMENTS FOR CERTIFICATION OR EMPLOYMENT FOR THOSE APPLYING FROM OUT OF PROVINCE/TERRITORY/COUNTRY

QUEBEC

Canadian citizenship is required for permanent certification.

ONTARIO

Persons born outside Canada must indicate the "basis upon which the candidate is present in Canada" (i.e., acquired citizenship, landed immigrant status, work visa) to be permitted to teach.

MANITOBA

Citizenship, landed immigrant status or work visa is required for certification.

ALBERTA

Canadian citizenship or landed immigrant status is required for interim certification; citizenship is required for permanent certification.

NUNAVUT

Candidates must be "eligible to work in Canada." Applications from those whose eligibility is pending are not considered.

NORTHWEST TERRITORIES

Canadian citizenship or permanent resident status is required even for interim certification.

YUKON TERRITORY

Canadian citizenship, landed immigrant status or other qualification to meet work requirements of the Yukon are required to obtain a teaching contract or certificate.

OTHER

Other provinces have no specific requirement, except that candidates be legally able to work in Canada.

"A nation that has schools has a future."
—*Otto von Bismarck*

APPENDIX 7

CROSS-CERTIFICATION—PROVINCES AND TERRITORIES WITH AGREEMENTS RE: CERTIFICATION OF TEACHERS FROM EACH OTHER'S PROVINCE OR TERRITORY

"Imagination is more important than knowledge."
—*Albert Einstein*

As the *Chapter of the Agreement on Internal Trade/Teaching Profession* in the *Agreement-in-Principle on Labour Mobility* states, "Teacher education/teacher certification in Canada is an evolving, not static, landscape." This is an area which is undergoing fundamental change in Canada as a result of the Agreement on Internal Trade (AIT) which all provincial and territorial governments have, as of October 29, 1999, approved (this means they have given a commitment to work toward implementing it).

The objective of this agreement parallels the thrust to reduce trade barriers among provinces and territories. In this case, as the agreement also states, it "aims to reduce barriers to teacher mobility. It is intended to allow any teacher who holds a teaching credential in one province or territory to have access to teacher certification in any other province or territory in order to be eligible for employment opportunities in the teaching professions."

One of the significant changes is the agreement to have their respective Registrars for Teacher Certification "continue to work on the reconciliation of the standards for teacher certification and on accommodation mechanisms to facilitate the mobility of teachers between the provinces and territories." While they will not be making every province and territory's expectations or requirements the same (in Canada education is a provincial—not federal—responsibility), they are moving towards an inclusive policy which will ensure that every candidate who is certified in any Canadian jurisdiction can obtain a certificate for another jurisdiction, whether permanent or temporary, while the candidate has opportunity to obtain the required bridging qualifications. Another significant commitment is to post on the government's education web site of each province and territory specifics regarding their certification requirements. They have also agreed to develop vehicles whereby they can keep the governmental licensing agencies, as well as private schools, aware of any cases of suspension or cancellation of teaching certificates of individuals where that would be "in the best interest of children, the public, and the teaching profession."

This is good news for those wanting to relocate. While we wait, however (and it is evolving while you read this), the following gives some indication of circumstances you may find as you attempt your cross-certification. Please note that the following is a guide only. For greater detail, refer to *Requirements for Teaching Certificates in Canada* listed in Part XI, or for authoritative information, check their web site or contact directly the appropriate education ministry or department or college of teachers at the locations listed at the end of this appendix.

"Go out on a limb—that's where the fruit is."
—*Will Rogers*

NEWFOUNDLAND

Newfoundland is getting a jump on the other provinces and territories and is already implement the *Agreement-in-Principle on Labour Mobility* (*Teaching Profession*).

All certificates are valid for all grades.

All certificates are interim until two years of successful teaching have been completed; then they may become permanent.

NOVA SCOTIA

Nova Scotia has a reciprocal agreement with Newfoundland, New Brunswick, Prince Edward Island and Manitoba that candidates qualified in one province are immediately recognized as qualified in the others. Level of certification depends upon extent of education and professional training.

All certificates are valid for all grades.

Except for a vocational certificate, all are permanent when issued.

PRINCE EDWARD ISLAND

Prince Edward Island seems especially eager to implement the *Agreement-in-Principle on Labour Mobility* and has made a commitment, not only to implement it by July 1, 2001, like all the other provinces and territories, but is determined to recognize other provinces as soon as they indicate an intention to reciprocate.

All certificates are valid for all grades.

All certificates are interim until two years of successful teaching have been completed; then they may become permanent after approval of the Office of the Registrar.

NEW BRUNSWICK

New Brunswick has a reciprocal agreement with Newfoundland, Nova Scotia, Prince Edward Island and Manitoba that candidates qualified in one province are immediately recognized as qualified in the others. Level of certification depends upon extent of education and professional training.

New Brunswick also has agreements with Ontario and Quebec, provided that candidates have an undergraduate degree, basic teacher training and are certified in the province where trained.

All teachers coming from outside New Brunswick are issued a Letter of Standing, valid for three years. After two years of successful teaching, a permanent certificate is issued. If there are any outstanding qualification requirements, they must be fulfilled before the permanent certificate is issued.

All, except the Vocational Certificate, are valid for Grades 1-12. A vocational Letter of Standing is valid for four years and can become permanent only if the candidate has a degree.

QUEBEC

Quebec has agreements with Ontario and New Brunswick that teachers may be certified from one province to another. If there is a lack of qualified personnel (with Quebec certification), teachers from these other provinces will be issued a Provisional Teacher Authorization, valid for two years. It may be renewed. After two years of successful teaching, a permanent Teaching Certificate may be granted. Quebec's rules are complex. For specifics, it is vital that the Ministry of Education there be contacted regarding granting of Provisional Authorization Certificates.

"Cultivation of the mind is as necessary as food to the body."
—*Cicero*

"Nothing in the world can take the place of persistence."
—*Calvin Coolidge*

"Schools need not preach political doctrine to defend democracy. If they shape men capable of critical thought and trained in social attitudes, that is all that is necessary."

—*Albert Einstein*

ONTARIO

Ontario has an agreement with Quebec and New Brunswick as indicated above.

Those trained in other provinces, whose qualifications are deemed acceptable, are granted a Temporary Letter of Standing which, after one year of teaching, qualifies the holder for a Certificate of Qualification that is permanent upon issue. As indicated in Appendix 2b, this teaching may be part-time or even occasional.

Teachers in Ontario are certified by divisions: Primary (Junior Kindergarten-3), Junior (4-6), Intermediate (7-10) and Senior (11-O.A.C.—Ontario Academic Credits, which were formerly called Grade 13, and in other provinces qualify as first-year undergraduate university). Teachers are initially certified in two adjacent divisions. Additional Basic certification is taken as additional training (Additional Qualification courses) and like areas of Basic Certification and all AQ's the additional areas of certification are recorded on the Certificate of Qualification.

MANITOBA

Manitoba has a reciprocal agreement with Newfoundland, New Brunswick, Nova Scotia and Prince Edward Island that candidates qualified in one province are immediately recognized as qualified in the others. Level of certification depends upon extent of education and training.

Provisional certificates are issued to those teachers who do not have enough undergraduate training to be granted the Professional Certificate. The Provisional one may be made permanent by taking an additional 30 hours of education course work or a pre-master's year or equivalent. Those who qualify for the Professional level receive a permanent certificate.

All certificates are valid Kindergarten to Grade 12.

SASKATCHEWAN

Like all other provinces and territories, Saskatchewan has agreed to the *Agreement in Principle* and has committed to work towards its implementation. All its previous reciprocal agreements have lapsed. Thus, pending full implementation of the *Agreement*, applications from teachers will be considered on an individual basis, and level of certification will depend upon extent of education and professional training.

Teachers from outside the province receive a "Provisional" certificate and receive permanent certification after one year of successful teaching.

All certificates except Professional A are limited to endorsed subject areas and related curriculum areas.

Probationary B Certificates and Letters of Eligibility (granted to uncertified persons when no certified candidate is available) are for one year only and are never made permanent.

ALBERTA

Canadian Citizenship is required for permanent certification and, at least, landed immigrant status for interim certification.

So far, Alberta has no standing agreements with any other province. All applications are considered independently with approval given if the Minister is satisfied that the institution and its training are acceptable.

"Don't be afraid to take a big step if one is indicated. You can't cross a chasm in two small jumps."

—*David Lloyd George*

If acceptable, the interim certificate is valid for one year, renewable 3 times, and can be made permanent following two years of successful teaching.

The Provisional Certificate for teaching in vocational fields is valid for three years and is made permanent only upon completion of the B.Ed degree.

BRITISH COLUMBIA

Certificate type depends upon educational qualifications. All certificates are valid for all grades.

Those trained out of B.C. receive Interim credentials which are valid for 48 months. After 1½ years of full-time satisfactory teaching (or equivalent in part-time teaching) in an acceptable school with a principal who is a member of the BC College of Teachers, teachers may qualify for permanent certification.

NORTHWEST TERRITORIES

To be acceptable to the Minister (for granting of an Interim Certificate), the basic teacher training from another province must include a minimum of five full courses (6 semester hours each) in education, a supervised teaching practicum and must lead to certification in the province in which it was obtained. The interim certificate is valid for three years. The exception is for Vocational and Aboriginal Languages Specialist certificates which require journeyman certification and a specialized training program, respectively.

N.W.T. also recognizes the 2-year program at Arctic College. To achieve certification in other provinces, graduates of this program would have to meet the requirements of the other provinces.

Canadian citizenship or permanent resident status is required for interim certification in N.W.T.

After two years of successful teaching an interim certificate can be made permanent.

NUNAVUT

Nunavut recognizes the certification of teachers from all other provinces and territories. While no degree is necessary for admission to the teacher-training program for teaching in Grades K to 9, a Bachelor of Education degree is necessary to become certified to teach all grades from K to 12.

YUKON TERRITORY

Teachers entering the Yukon with a valid certificate from another province but who have inadequate academic qualifications are issued a Basic-Transitional certificate, valid for three years. Upon acquiring satisfactory qualifications, a Yukon Professional Teaching Certificate will be issued.

Those with adequate university training, but lacking adequate concentration or additional studies in Yukon or Northern Canadian or First Nations studies, are eligible to receive a Provisional Professional Certificate which is valid for two years pending completion of the required studies, and this may be renewed once for one year.

Certificates are valid until they expire, are cancelled or suspended or become invalid. They become invalid if the holder is not actively employed in an educational capacity for ten consecutive years. They may be re-validated by taking one academic and one pedagogical course acceptable to the minister.

"Man ultimately decides for himself. And in the end, education must be education toward the ability to decide."
—*Victor E. Frankl*

OFFICIAL AND AUTHORITATIVE INFORMATION RE: CERTIFICATION REQUIREMENTS OR EQUIVALENT STANDINGS IS AVAILABLE FROM THE FOLLOWING:

NEWFOUNDLAND
Registrar, Teacher Certification
Division of School Services
Newfoundland and Labrador Department of Education
Confederation Building, West Block
P.O. Box 8700   Tel: (709) 729-3020
St. John's, NF   A1B 4J6   Fax: (709) 729-5026

NOVA SCOTIA
Registrar – Teacher's Certification
Planning and Research Division, Policy Branch
Nova Scotia Department of Education
P.O. Box 578   Tel: (902) 424-6620
Halifax, NS   B3J 2S9   Fax: (902) 424-0519

PRINCE EDWARD ISLAND
Office of the Registrar
Administration and Corporate Services Dept.
Prince Edward Island Department of Education
2nd Floor, Sullivan Building
16 Fitzroy Street   Tel: (902) 368-4651
Charlottetown, PE   C1A 7N8   Fax: (902) 368-4663

NEW BRUNSWICK
Teacher Certification
New Brunswick Department of Education
P.O. Box 6000   Tel: (506) 453-2785
Fredericton, NB   E3B 5H1   Fax: (506) 444-4761

QUEBEC
Directrice, Direction de la Formation et de la Titularisation du
Personnel Scholaire
Ministère de l'Éducation
150, boul. René-Lévesque est   Tel: (418) 643-8610
Québec, QC   G1R 5W8   Fax: (418) 643-2149

ONTARIO
The Ontario College of Teachers   Tel: (416) 961-8800
121 Bloor Street East, 6th Floor   1-888-534-2222
Toronto, ON   M4W 3M5   Fax: (416) 961-8822

MANITOBA
Professional Certification Unit   Tel: (204) 773-2998
Manitoba Education and Training   Fax: (204) 773-2411
450 Broadway
Winnipeg, MB   R3C 0V8

"Wholly wrong are those
masters who expect their little   **SASKATCHEWAN**
pupils to act as though they   Teacher Services   Tel: (306) 787-6085
were diminutive adults."   Saskatchewan Education   Fax: (306) 787-0035
—*Erasmus*   1500 4th Avenue
                                    Regina, SK   S4P 3V7

ALBERTA
Teacher Certification and Development
Alberta Education
West Tower, Devonian Building
11160 Jasper Avenue
Edmonton, AB   T5K 0L2

Tel: (780) 427-2045
Fax: (780) 422-4199

BRITISH COLUMBIA
Registrar
British Columbia College of Teachers
405-1385 West 8th Avenue
Vancouver, BC   V6H 3V9

Tel: (604) 731-8170
1-800-555-3684
Fax: (604) 731-9142

NORTHWEST TERRITORIES
Office of the Registrar
Teacher Certification
Northwest Territories Department of Education, Culture and Employment
3rd Floor, Lahm Ridge Tower
P.O. Box 1320
Yellowknife, NT   X1A 2L9

Tel: (403) 873-7392
Fax: (403) 873-0338

NUNAVUT
While details of organization are being worked out within the government,
contact the Nunavut Department of Education at their head office:
P.O. Box 2410
Iqaluit, Nunavut X0A 0H0

Tel: (867) 975-5600
Fax: (867) 975-5605
www.nunavut.com/education

YUKON TERRITORY
Director of Personnel
Yukon Department of Education
P.O. Box 2703
Whitehorse, YT   Y1A 2C6

Tel: (403) 667-8631
Fax: (403) 393-6254

"We can do anything we want to do if we stick at it long enough."
—*Helen Keller*

APPENDIX 8

DATES, DETAILS AND DEADLINES FOR TERMINATION OF A CONTRACT; TYPES OF CONTRACTS AND THEIR DURATIONS

EXTREMELY IMPORTANT

Any time potential termination arises, contact your union, society, association, or federation!

NEWFOUNDLAND AND LABRADOR

Teachers with no previous experience in Newfoundland and/or Labrador and teachers who have never attained tenure (the equivalent of permanent contract status) are hired on probationary contract until they have completed two years of successful teaching with the same school board. Service in a permanent part-time position applies (occasional teaching does not) but the teacher cannot be away or on leave for more than 94 days in either year or the year may have to be repeated.

In Newfoundland and Labrador, if you complete the probationary period and then are allowed to continue to teach for the board, you are deemed to have tenure (permanence) and, unless the teacher is officially notified that they are hired on a temporary basis, they are deemed to have tenure.

A teacher with tenure who leaves to teach for another board has immediate tenure with the new board. A teacher with tenure who leaves teaching for more than four years may be required to serve a one-year probationary period when again hired. Boards have the right to waive any probationary periods.

To terminate a contract, a board must give three months' notice (or pay in lieu of notice) if it is being terminated during the school year and two months' notice if it is to be terminated at the end of the school year, if the termination is not for incompetence, gross misconduct or other serious cause. If the contract is a permanent (continuous) one, the reasons for the termination must be given in writing; if probationary, the reasons may be given verbally.

If the termination is for incompetence, 30 calendar days' notice must be given; if termination is for gross misconduct, insubordination, neglect of duty or similar just cause, or if the teacher's certificate has been suspended, cancelled or is no longer recognized, no notice period is required. The termination takes effect immediately.

As is the case for the board, to terminate a contract, a teacher must give three months' notice if the contract is being terminated during the school year, and two months' notice if it is to be terminated at the end of the school year.

NOVA SCOTIA

All contracts in Nova Scotia begin with a two-year probationary period, becoming permanent on the first teaching day of the third year.

Nova Scotia also has Term contracts, used when hiring a teacher to replace another who is on leave or has gone to a new position from which they retain the right to return, etc. These are time-definite. These are usually for a full year and are for at least a full term or semester; shorter periods are filled by substitute teachers.

Boards intending to notify a teacher of their intent to terminate the contract are required to do so by May 15, to take effect July 1, while teachers intending to resign must notify the board by April 15.

"Either we are fired with enthusiasm, or we are fired, with enthusiasm."
—*Frank Manley*

PRINCE EDWARD ISLAND

Prince Edward Island starts new teachers on a two-year probationary contract. If, however, a teacher has had two years of successful teaching in a recognized school in P.E.I., even with another board, they are hired on a permanent contract; probation has been served.

Both teachers and boards wishing to give notification of intent to terminate a contract must give notice by April 30, to take effect the following August 31.

NEW BRUNSWICK

New Brunswick has a variety of contract types, referred to as Schedule B to Schedule E, each to address a different situation, but all with the same security provisions. In all cases, technically, there is a three-year probationary term, but with all of them, layoffs must be by seniority; so, in some ways, can be considered to have similar benefits to a permanent contract. Like all other provinces and territories in Canada, terminations of even probationary contracts must be with at least some (though arguably less) burden of proof of just cause and due process; termination cannot be capricious.

Schedule B is a regular teacher's contract (see sample in APPENDIX 9), permanent until the teacher chooses to resign or is terminated for just cause. Thus the concept of the "probationary" term is largely illusionary. If, however, you have questions or concerns regarding this issue, contact the New Brunswick Teachers' Federation immediately! (phone 506-452-8921; See PART X for their address and fax.)

A Schedule C contract is for non-licensed persons fulfilling the duties of a teacher; for example, where no certified teacher is available. It is for one term or one semester only but can be renewed. It is time-definite and expires at its pre-determined date.

Schedule D is also time-definite. It is used when hiring a teacher to replace another who is away—ill, seconded, or on any other type of leave—but is expected to return to his or her duties. This contract can be for up to two years but is not permanent and expires at its pre-determined date.

A Schedule E contract is used to hire teachers for special projects, time-definite, short-term, not expected to continue past their set duration. These are usually positions which are financed by short-term moneys, usually federal grants related to specific work-force training or re-training. When the money runs out, so do they.

All term-definite contracts terminate at their specified date. Schedule B contracts can be terminated by the board only for just cause. Teachers wishing to resign may do so effective July 1 in any year by giving notice by the preceding April 30.

NOTE: Schedules B to E, inclusive, in the Agreement between the NB Board of Management and the NB Teachers' Federation are teaching contracts. Schedule A is the Grievance Form.

FOR MORE INFORMATION

This information is for general guidance only. For definitive information, contact your teachers' union, society, association or federation (or the ministry or department of education) in your province or territory.

At all other times, terminations must be by mutual consent.

QUEBEC

In Quebec, there is a rather interesting technicality. After teachers have started teaching in a position which will continue (not temporarily replacing a teacher who is ill, for example—see B.C. for contrast), they are offered a probationary contract. After two years of successful teaching, they are given a permanent contract. In both cases, termination for cause (not down-sizing, for example) must be demonstrably for "just cause." Thus, for all intents and purposes, both can be considered permanent. However, teachers whose work is less than full time do not qualify for permanence, no matter how long they teach. They can be terminated at the end of a session (end of year, for example) with no cause being given. This is an important technicality.

Quebec also has temporary contracts, which are time definite.

Their dealing with teachers on permanent contract in the event of surplus situation (more teachers than they need), deserves mentioning as it is somewhat unusual. When a teacher who has been on full-time contract with a board for a minimum of two years is declared surplus, that teacher remains with the board, on "availability," and is paid 80% of her/his wages while the board attempts to locate for them a new position, or a position with another board within 50 km.

In the case of a teacher who has been with a board for less than two years full-time and who is declared surplus, the board has no further obligation to them, but their name is kept on a recall list at provincial level.

Boards are required to give notice of their intent to terminate a contract by May 30, to take effect August 31 following. Teachers intending to terminate a contract are required to do so by April 30, to take effect August 31 following.

ONTARIO

There has been significant change in Ontario since 1998. Teachers are no longer under contract with a board; instead, they are employees governed by the provincial *Employment Standards Act*. Unless you are hired on a daily basis (Short-term Occasional), or for a time-definite period (Long-term Occasional), you are considered a "permanent employee."

The issue of a probationary period is now handled in the collective agreements between the federations and the boards. In most cases, it is between ten months and two years. Probationary status, however, has very little impact except that you will have your performance formally appraised more frequently. Even probationary teachers cannot be dismissed without cause.

Details of termination (for down-sizing, etc.) or resignation are also addressed in collective agreements. Many agreements in Ontario have stuck with the long-established dates: to be terminated or resign, December 31st of any year, notice must be given by one party to the other before the preceding November 30th, or by April 30th to take effect the following August 31st. This supersedes the *Employment Standards Act* requirement of two weeks' notice.

In cases of termination "for cause," such as incompetence (the legal terminology is: "where a matter arises that in the opinion of the Minister adversely affects the welfare of the school"), termination is usually immediate, and, if appealed, it will be left to a court to determine what pay in lieu of notice—if any—shall be provided.

Teachers who are offered employment in Ontario are given that offer "subject to approval by the board," as it is boards and not principals who actually hire (the principal and/or committee "make recommendation"). Usually you will be asked to sign an Acceptance of Position Form (see sample in APPENDIX 9) which indicates that you accept the offer subject, of course, to Board approval. Your employment will also be conditional upon your being a member in good standing with the Ontario College of Teachers, and providing evidence of health, a CRC, and other documentation—the H.R. department will give you a list of what they need.

MANITOBA

Manitoba addresses permanence as a tenure issue. Teachers new to the province or the profession have no tenure for one year; that is, until their first teaching day of the second year. Upon commencing teaching in their second year they get a "Form 2" contract which indicates tenure. This tenure is transferable from board to board, thus a teacher with tenure in one board must be given tenure immediately upon being hired by another board.

Manitoba has a "Temporary" contract called a Form 2A. This permits a board to hire a teacher without giving him or her tenure and to replace another teacher who is on leave or ill or who for another reason is not filling their position but is expected to return to their position. These contracts are worded so that they are "until return or until June 30." They are for short-term employment only.

Except for those terminations by mutual consent, either teacher or board must give notice by November 30 for the contract to terminate effective December 31, or by May 30 to be effective at the end of June.

SASKATCHEWAN

Saskatchewan has no term contracts for periods of a year or more. Temporary contracts are used to fill a position left vacant by a person expected to return; for example, after a long-term illness.

A board may terminate a contract upon thirty days' notice, but only for just cause. This could include criminal conduct or downsizing, etc.

A teacher may terminate a contract by giving 30 days' notice to the Board. Terminations by mutual consent are also recognized.

Teachers in their first or second year of a contract do not have the right to appear before a Board of Reference to dispute a termination if such termination becomes effective June 30 unless it is strictly a claim of incorrect application of seniority. Instead, their only route of appeal is a "show cause" hearing with the board.

ALBERTA

Alberta is interesting in that, by law, contracts must be in writing; i.e., there is not provision for verbal agreements being binding. It also has, arguably, the most complex regulations or provisions in Canada with regard to contract types and conditions. Note: in any area of doubt, contact the Alberta Teachers' Association! Their number: (780) 447-9400; see PART X for address and fax number.

There are five types of teaching contracts in Alberta:

1. Probationary Contracts are issued to teachers who were not employed in the year previous by that board except as an occasional/replacement or who were employed on a temporary contract.

RESOURCES

The Executive Firing Line: Wrongful Dismissal and the Law, by Brian A. Grossman, gives good background information on this stress-filled topic.

"I owe all my success in life to having been always a quarter of an hour beforehand."
—Horatio, Lord Nelson

185

CONTRACTS

APPENDIX 9 has samples of several contract types. Check it out.

- If the total amount of time that the teacher teaches for the board under a part-time contract is at least equal to the amount of time the teacher would have been required to teach in a year of full-time teaching, this will fulfil the requirements of a probationary year.
- All probationary contracts terminate June 30 following their commencement.
- If evaluations of the teacher indicate that a further probationary period is required, and the teacher agrees, the probationary contract may be extended until the next June 30.

2. A Continuing Contract continues from year to year.

3. A Temporary Contract may be issued to replace a teacher expected to be absent for more than twenty consecutive teaching days. All temporary contracts expire June 30 if not specified to do so earlier. A temporary contract may be terminated by either party upon giving thirty days notice to the other party.

4. An Interim Contract may be offered to a teacher who did not teach for that board in the year previous except as a substitute teacher or on a temporary contract. An interim contract cannot be for more than 360 teaching days. If the teacher has taught on a part-time contract for the amount of time equalling those he/she would have taught in a full-time position, they are deemed to have been employed under an interim contract. Unless otherwise specified, an interim contract terminates the June 30 following its commencement.

5. A Part-time Contract may be offered to a teacher to teach every day on a part-time basis, being paid only for the time they teach. The board may, unless the contract specifies otherwise, vary the amount of time the teacher is to teach in the subsequent semester or school year and, if the teacher does not agree to the variance, the board may terminate the contract.

Substitute teachers are hired day to day or for vacancies expected to be less than twenty consecutive teaching days. Substitute teachers may not appeal to a Board of Reference upon termination.

A teacher may terminate a contract (resign) by giving thirty days' notice. (If this notice is because a teacher refuses a transfer, the board may terminate immediately after the teacher gives notice, by paying the moneys to the teacher that they would have earned during thirty days from the date of the giving of the notice of resignation. Theoretically, therefore, if the teacher gives sixty days' notice and the reason given is the refusal of a transfer, the board could reduce it to thirty days. Again, contact your federation and be sure before you do anything you may regret!)

A board may terminate a contract by giving thirty days' notice, together with reasons for the termination. The board is bound by regulation to "act reasonably." A board may suspend immediately (with pay) for cause (e.g., gross misconduct) and terminate after a hearing.

Any contract may be terminated at any time by mutual consent.

Do not enter into a contract with a board lightly! An interesting little technicality, and I quote: "If a teacher has terminated his contract of employment with a board before rendering any service under the contract, the teacher shall not be employed by another board unless the board with which the teacher's contract was terminated gives its prior approval to the teacher's employment with the other board." (Chap. S-3.1 89(2)) You could be forced to start teaching, then give

"Fortune is not on the side of the fainthearted."
—*Sophocles*

your thirty days' notice, by which time the next board probably will have filled the position with someone else able to start right away.

Note: Neither a board nor a teacher may give notice of termination during or in the thirty days preceding a vacation period of 14 days or more.

BRITISH COLUMBIA

There are now only two types of contracts for teachers in B.C.: Continuing and Temporary, but specifics of their applicability are determined in the collective agreement negotiated between the BCTF local for the area and the area board. You will need to check with the federation office for specifics.

Continuing contracts (in some other provinces known as "permanent") are just that, and can be terminated by the board only for just cause: incompetence, abuse, other serious criminality, etc. In the event of down-sizing, in most districts the board must give 60 days' notice, and seniority applies, with recall rights. (Usually a teacher is required to give 30 days' notice to terminate a contract, unless there is mutual agreement to vary the requirement of notice.)

Temporary contracts are offered to teachers hired to replace those who are on a leave and expected to return: illness, maternity leave, secondment, sabbatical, etc., or in some cases, where the position is not continuing (it is funded through special non-renewable grant or is a pilot project). Some local collective agreements have done away with temporary contracts, and any teacher hired is given a continuing contract so that at the end of the maternity leave for the person they are replacing, for example, they are laid off with recall rights.

The concept of a probationary period is not covered by contract in B.C. but is in the collective agreement for some areas. In all cases, there must be demonstrable "cause." Termination cannot be capricious.

NORTHWEST TERRITORIES

You need at least a N.W.T. Interim Teaching Certificate to get a contract in the Territories. When hired, you are on contract with the board, the contract is not considered probationary, and you cannot be terminated without just cause. If, however, you are on a probationary (temporary) teaching certificate (you have fewer than two years teaching in N.W.T.), then they have more leeway in determination of cause—the onus of proof is less demanding.

If you come from another province where you had permanent certification, they have the option of granting you a permanent certificate after one successful year but are not required to do so.

The issue of termination dates is rather complex in the N.W.T. This is determined by each school board, rather than by the Department of Education. Some Boards have one date—April 30 to take effect August 31; while some have two—usually November 30 as well to take effect December 31. Note, however, boards in the N.W.T. have—what to the rest of us seems to be—incredible autonomy in setting dates including those of the school year; so generalizations are not as meaningful as they might be. Again, contact the Northwest Territories Teachers' Association (403-873-8501) for specifics regarding the particular board involved.

Of course, any contract may be terminated at any time by mutual consent.

NUNAVUT

Canada's newest territory is still undergoing some radical change and adjustment as it works out the details of how it will do business. Previously three Divisional Educational Councils (similar to school boards) handled education in their various

> "It is the duty of the human understanding to understand that there are things which it cannot understand."
> —Søren Kierkegaard

"Though knowledge is one chief aim of intellectual education, there is another ingredient ... more dominating in its importance. The ancients call it 'wisdom'. You cannot be wise without some basis of knowledge, but you may easily acquire knowledge and remain bare of wisdom."

—*Alfred N. Whitehead*

regions, but part of the new governance model (to take effect July 1, 2000—with some parts to evolve after that date) will see them dissolved and integrated into the new Department of Education. The headquarters of the territorial Department is expected to remain in Iqaluit, but it is expected that one of the former Divisional offices, in Pond Inlet, will take over hiring for the twenty-two schools throughout the territory. (For current status on the process, contact the Nunavut Department of Education, P.O. Box 2410, Iqaluit, Nunavut X0A 0H0.)

It is anticipated that teachers will not work under contract but will be employees of the government under a negotiated collective agreement. There are two types of positions: indeterminate and term. Those hired to term positions are hired to replace a teacher on leave or who is expected to return to his/her teaching duties. Indeterminate hirings are for permanent positions.

Indeterminate positions commence with a two-year probationary period, but dismissal can be instituted only "with cause."

Should the employer wish to terminate an employee without cause (for example, in cases of down-sizing) they must give three months' notice to the employee. Should the employee want to terminate the agreement, they must give the employer two months' notice, and the termination shall usually take effect at the end of the school year. A teacher who quits at other times may find his/her request accepted "with prejudice" (which isn't really good on one's professional record) unless it is by mutual agreement. As replacing staff in Nunavut is usually not only not simple, but involves significant expenses in moving the employees, "mutual agreement" is not common. Of course, this is one area where competence may work against you—if you are good, they may not want to let you go.

Dates for notice of intent to terminate a contract, whether by the employer or the teacher, vary from area to area, as the beginning and ending dates of the school year are not consistent and vary significantly among regions. You really need to check with the area in which you hope to teach or with the Nunavut Department of Education (Tel: (867) 975-5000, Fax: (867) 975-5095, Web site www.nunavut.com).

YUKON TERRITORY

There are no school boards, as such, in the Yukon Territory; all teachers are hired (appointed) by the Department of Education. (Appointments to Roman Catholic schools are subject to veto by the Bishop.) New teachers to the Yukon are put on a two-year "probationary appointment"; after successful conclusion of these two years' teaching, they are on a "continuing appointment."

Termination of a contract by the Department is upon three months' notice. Teachers wishing to terminate a contract must also give three months' notice. However, during the last three months of a school year in that area of the territory (the school year varies according to geography), a teacher may not resign; they must wait until the beginning of the new term, then give their 3 months' notice.

The exception to this would be if there was mutual consent.

EXTREMELY IMPORTANT!

Remember: All this is a guide only! In <u>any</u> issues involving a contract, before you do anything else, contact your teachers' union/society/federation/association! They can guide you so that you don't do something you will later regret! ***This is extremely important!***

SAMPLE CONTRACTS FROM VARIOUS REGIONS OF CANADA

Types, styles and designs of contracts vary extensively across Canada. (See also APPENDIX 8: **Dates, Details and Deadlines for Termination of a Contract**; **Types of Contracts and Their Duration**.) To illustrate some of the variety, examples from several of the provinces and territories of Canada follow. As you can see, generalizations would be so tenuous to be meaningless, **except a reminder to contact your teachers' society or union for help whenever you venture into the realm of contracts!** These are not organized in the precise east-to-west order used in the other appendices; instead, there is some re-grouping within this section to illustrate a few similarities and differences.

Whatever area you are interested in, remember that—as stated elsewhere in this book—**if you verbally accept an offered contract you are bound by your acceptance even if the required documents are not yet signed. If you then accept another, you are in breach of contract. This is considered un-professional conduct and you will, in all likelihood, find both offers withdrawn.** (Exceptions to the above include Alberta's requirement that all contracts be in writing before they are binding and the technicalities in some provinces having to do with the number of hours you have to give formal "notice" of acceptance of another, superseding, contract. **This whole issue of contracts is intensely serious; do be very careful, and work closely with your teachers' association.**)

The first sample below is from **Newfoundland**. Here individual boards develop their own contract; there is no provincially-mandated one. Note in this one the extensive detail regarding termination. It is not as long as might seem; they use a larger print font than most. Unlike Manitoba, for example, they don't get into a detailed discussion of "sick leave" in the actual contract.

The following three examples are from **Prince Edward Island**. In addition to the Form 7A – Probationary Contract, they also use Form 7B – Permanent Contract and Form 7C – Fixed Term Contract. All three are included to demonstrate the similarities often to be found among the various types of contracts: permanent, probationary, and those for a fixed term or short-term, such as when replacing a teacher "until the return of X." As you can see, the only differences are that Form 7B also injects a fourth "whereas"—between the first and second—reading "AND WHEREAS the Teacher has completed the probationary period required by the Act;" and form 7B section 2 states instead "This contract commences on _____ and continues from school year to school year until terminated." Form 7C, section 2, in turn, reads "This contract commences on _____ and ends on _____ ." Note that, while these variations among types are addressed in only a few words, they are profound.

Next are copies of the probationary contract and permanent contract from **Nova Scotia.** As in most cases, there is very little variation between the two, except the section dealing with duration, in this case, Article One.

"Education should make people competent not only 'to do' but 'to be'."
—*Mark Van Doren*

GET ADVICE FIRST

Remember: Any time there is any question about any part of your contract, contact your teachers union immediately. Get their advice before committing to anything!

In **Ontario**, since 1998, teachers are no longer under contract; they are employees governed by the *Employment Standards Act* and any other conditions which are specified in the negotiated collective agreement covering their employer-employee relationship.

Instead of a contract, teachers sign an "Acceptance of Position Form," which confirms the agreement to offer and accept employment. There is, however, a technicality that you should be aware of—in Ontario, as in most provinces and territories, even if you have not signed anything, a verbal agreement to accept a position is considered binding. Because of historical process, Ontario tends to take verbal employment agreements very seriously. Both parties are expected to follow through unless there is mutual consent to set aside the verbal agreement. Don't get caught in breech of agreement.

There is no longer a provincially mandated form; boards now use one they design for their own purposes. A sample, from one board, is found later in this appendix.

Simpler, and still more brief, is the sample from **Quebec,** next. Their "Full-Time," "Part-Time" and "Teacher-By-The-Lesson" contracts are all similar except for three things: their title, the section I–A specifying the contract type, and the section III–A, giving the respective starting and expiry dates for each. Please remember, though, the little technicality in Quebec: only a full-time position can become "permanent." Part-time positions can be terminated even after many years of service.

A **Manitoba** contract follows that, combining some of Newfoundland's concern with termination procedures along with extensive description of pay procedures. This "Form 2" is a permanent or continuing contract.

Another province using the "letter-style" contract, but a much abbreviated form of it, is **Saskatchewan**. In recent years, Saskatchewan has gone from each board using their own forms, to provincially-standardized ones. In the samples included, Form Y is the contract for a temporary offer, Form Z is the teacher's scripted acceptance letter, and Form AA is the Board's letter confirming the contract. Saskatchewan is somewhat different in having a separate form of confirmation; most other Canadian provinces deem the other documentation when signed and counter-signed to be binding.

Please check to see how much time you have to sign the contract before it becomes null and void. Saskatchewan was known for its four-day grace period, which gave a teacher some nice thinking time, but after which the offer was withdrawn. Check to see that that window is still available to you, before you decide to "get back to them." Most provinces expect your response right away.

Following that is a sample of Saskatchewan's "Mutual Agreement to Amend Contract of Employment for a Specified Term" form. This is used when a teacher on permanent full-time contract wishes to revise her/his teaching assignment to part-time, for a fixed period only, thereafter to revert to their full-time duties. In some other provinces this issue is addressed in the collective agreement instead. This example illustrates, once again, the importance of contacting your Federation /Union/Association or Society any time there is a question about your contract. Every province and territory is significantly different in contractual procedures.

Unlike Saskatchewan, **Alberta** allows each Board to develop its own format. Note that, as indicated in APPENDIX 8, Alberta contract law is very complex. They also have contracts for "Full-Time Temporary," "Part-Time Probationary with FTE as assigned by the Board from time to time in its sole discretion," "Full-Time Continuing" (permanent), "Part-Time Continuing with FTE as assigned by

"For peace of mind, resign as general manager of the universe."
—*Larry Eisenberg*

the Board from time to time in its sole discretion," "Part-Time Temporary," and "Part-Time Temporary with FTE as assigned by the Board from time to time in its sole discretion." In each, the second sub-section provides specifics on start and end dates. It is usually printed on 8 ½ X 14 paper and ends with a section for the candidate to fill in attesting to the fact that they have read, understand and agree to be bound by the provisions of the offer of employment.

Remember that little technicality in Alberta: all agreements are required to be in writing before they are considered binding—no value is given to verbal agreement. This is an important technicality. See also APPENDIX 8 and contact your provincial or territorial teachers' association, society or union for further details or clarification! If you don't, you may well regret it!

The **British Columbia** sample is interesting in that it is made up of a letter to the teacher together with their scripted responding letter. Again, the format differences between a "Temporary" and "Continuing" contract are reflective of their duration; all other sections are the same, except that the "Continuing" one leaves out the second sentence of the third paragraph. Individual school boards here establish the wording of their own contracts. Note in the "Temporary" one following, the specifics regarding the exact teacher being replaced. Notice, too, that you might want to be sure to get your proof of qualifications in to them on time!

The format of contracts, and much of the specifics around the issues of employment policy and procedures for **Nunavut** was still in development when this book went to press. For specifics, please contact the Department of Education, Nunavut, or the Nunavut Teachers' Association. Barring that, you might want to contact the Northwest Territories Teachers' Association as, until it became a separate territory, the teachers in Nunavut (NTA) were all members of the NWTTA. There may well be parallels which continue, as Nunavut works to research "best-practices" and to develop its own procedures.

The final example is another "letter" format, this one from **Yukon Territory**. Even though it is a formal contract, and follows an established pattern, isn't it rather pleasant the way they end the letter with "best wishes for a successful year?"

Of course with any of these samples, as with any other documents, if you have questions about what you are being offered, **call your federation/association/society or union!** See "PART X earlier in this book for addresses, phone numbers, fax numbers and membership criteria by province and territory.

AVALON EAST SCHOOL BOARD
EMPLOYMENT CONTRACT

THIS EMPLOYMENT CONTRACT made in duplicate the 3rd day of November, 1999.

BETWEEN   **AVALON EAST SCHOOL BOARD,** a school board organized and existing under The Schools Act of Newfoundland and any successor legislation,

         (hereinafter called the 'Board')

         of the one part

AND   in the Province of Newfoundland,

         (hereinafter called the 'Teacher')

         of the other part

The Board and the Teacher hereby agree as follows:

1. The Board agrees to employ the Teacher on a **Probationary Contract** as a.

2. Unless a specific term is inapplicable because of the nature of the contract, this employment contract shall be for a duration commencing on September 7, 1999 to June 22, 2001.

3. The Board and the Teacher agree that this contract shall at all times be subject to the Schools Act and Education Act of Newfoundland, any regulations made thereunder, any amendments thereto and any and all successor legislation thereto together with the terms and conditions outlined in any subsisting collective agreement between the Board as represented by the Newfoundland and Labrador School Boards Association or its successor, her Majesty the Queen in Right of Newfoundland as represented by Treasury board and the Newfoundland and Labrador Teachers' Association. In addition, this contract shall be governed by the Constitution and By-Laws of the Board and all rules, regulations and policies passed by the Board relating to terms and conditions of employment and duties and responsibilities of teachers employed by the Board.

- 2 -

e Teacher agrees to perform the duties prescribed by the hools Act and the Education Act and all regulations issued ereunder including any amendments thereto together with all cessarily incidental duties and responsibilities expressly implicitly required to be performed by teachers in order to scharge their functions in accordance with the Schools Act, e Education Act, the collective agreement and the nstitution, By-Laws, rules, regulations and policies of the ard.

e remuneration of the Teacher who is party to this contract all be governed by the provisions of the subsisting llective agreement between the Board as represented by the wfoundland and Labrador School Boards Association, Her ...jesty the Queen in Right of Newfoundland as represented by Treasury Board and the Newfoundland and Labrador Teachers' Association.

This contract may be terminated pursuant to the provisions of the collective agreement or pursuant to the Schools Act and any regulations issued thereunder or otherwise according to law including, without limiting the generality of the foregoing:

(a)   at any time by mutual agreement in writing of the Board and the Teacher;

(b)   at any other time during the term of the contract by either party giving to the other at least three (3) months notice in writing;

(c)   with thirty (30) calendar days notice in writing by the Board when the Teacher is incompetent;

(d)   without notice, by the Board, when the certificates of trade or license of the Teacher has been suspended, cancelled, or are no longer recognized under the regulations;

(e)   without notice, by the Board, where there is gross misconduct, insubordination, neglect of duty or other similar just cause arising from the conduct of the Teacher;

- 3 -

(f)   without notice, by the Board, when the Teacher fails to make a reasonable effort to obtain a medical examination as required by the Board under Section 76 of the Schools Act or where the certificate submitted to a board pursuant to Section 76 of the Schools Act shows that the physical or mental health of the Teacher would be injurious to an employee of the Board or the students entrusted to the Board.

7.   The Teacher agrees to undergo such medical examinations, including X-rays, as may be required from time to time by the Board in the administration and conduct of schools in addition to any requirements regarding medical examinations otherwise required by the Schools Act or regulations issued thereunder. The Teacher also acknowledges that any serious deviation from the Constitution, By-Laws, rules, regulations and policies of the Board may also constitute grounds for termination of employment.

8.   The Board and the Teacher also acknowledge that the contract shall be subject to any and all provincial legislation, regulation or policies dealing with teacher training and certification as may exist from time to time affecting the eligibility of the Teacher to carry out the duties and responsibilities contemplated by this contract.

AVALON EAST SCHOOL BOARD

_____   _____
Witness   Director of Personnel

_____   _____
Witness   Teacher

                                                            _____
                                                            School(s)

Sample Contract—PRINCE EDWARD ISLAND (Probationary)

Province of Prince Edward Island
Form 7A – Probationary Contract
(Instructional Personnel)

THIS AGREEMENT made this _____ day of _____ , 19__

BETWEEN: _____ School Board, a body corporate pursuant to *the School Act* R.S.P.E.I. 1988, Cap. S-2.1 (hereinafter referred to as the "School Board")

AND _____ , of

_____

being a teacher who holds a valid instructional license (hereinafter referred to as the "Teacher")

WHEREAS the School Board wishes to hire the Teacher;

AND WHEREAS the Teacher has agreed to work for the School Board on the terms and conditions herein contained;

AND WHEREAS the School Board and its employees are subject to the provisions of the *School Act* and the regulations;

In CONSIDERATION of these premises and of the agreed salary to be paid to the Teacher pursuant to this agreement, the parties hereto agree as follows:

1. The School Board hereby employs the Teacher and the Teacher agrees to perform the duties of a teacher for the School Board, as follows:

   _____ percentage of full-time

2. This contract commences on _____ and terminates on June 30 of the school year in
   which the teacher was hired or on _____ , whichever is earlier.

3. The salary rate payable and benefits for the Teacher shall be the salary rate and benefits for instructional personnel determined by the collective agreement for instructional personnel made pursuant to the *Act*.

4. This contract is subject at all times to the Teacher obtaining and continuing to hold an instructional license and further, this contract becomes void if the Teacher's instructional license is revoked under the *Act*.

5. The Teacher agrees to be diligent and faithful in the performance of the Teacher's duties during the period of employment, to abide by the *Act* and the regulations and to teach such subjects and to perform such duties as may be assigned by the School Board or the principal.

6. The Teacher agrees further that this contract is subject to the collective agreement.

7. Notwithstanding anything herein to the contrary, this contract may be terminated as provided in section 88 of the *Act*.

Signed, sealed and delivered by the Teacher and by the School Board as of the date above written

School Board

_____   _____
Witness

_____   _____
Witness   Teacher

Distribution: Copy 1 – School Board Office
                       Copy 2 - Employee

Sample Contract—PRINCE EDWARD ISLAND (Permanent)

Province of Prince Edward Island
Form 7B – Permanent Contract
(Instructional Personnel)

THIS AGREEMENT made this _____ day of _____ , 19__

BETWEEN: _____ School Board, a body corporate pursuant to *the School Act* R.S.P.E.I. 1988, Cap. S-2.1 (hereinafter referred to as the "School Board")

AND _____ , of

_____
being a teacher who holds a valid instructional license (hereinafter referred to as the "Teacher")

WHEREAS the School Board wishes to hire the Teacher;

AND WHEREAS the Teacher has completed the probationary period required by the *Act*;

AND WHEREAS the Teacher has agreed to work for the School Board on the terms and conditions herein contained;

AND WHEREAS the School Board and its employees are subject to the provisions of the *School Act* and the regulations;

In CONSIDERATION of these premises and of the agreed salary to be paid to the Teacher pursuant to this agreement, the parties hereto agree as follows:

1.   The School Board hereby employs the Teacher and the Teacher agrees to perform the duties of a teacher for the School Board, as follows:

_____ percentage of full-time

2.   This contract commences on _____ and continues from school year to school year until terminated.

3.   The salary rate payable and benefits for the Teacher shall be the salary rate and benefits for Instructional personnel determined by the collective agreement for instructional personnel made pursuant to the *Act*.

4.   This contract is subject at all times to the Teacher obtaining and continuing to hold an instructional license and further, this contract becomes void if the Teacher's instructional license is revoked under the *Act*.

5.   The Teacher agrees to be diligent and faithful in the performance of the Teacher's duties during the period of employment, to abide by the *Act* and the regulations and to teach such subjects and to perform such duties as may be assigned by the School Board or the principal.

6.   The Teacher agrees further that this contract is subject to the collective agreement.

7.   Notwithstanding anything herein to the contrary, this contract may be terminated as provided in section 88 of the *Act*.

Signed, sealed and delivered by the Teacher and by the School Board as of the date above written

School Board

_____   _____
Witness

_____   _____
Witness   Teacher

Distribution: Copy 1 – School Board Office
                                     Copy 2 - Employee

Sample Contract—PRINCE EDWARD ISLAND (Fixed-Term)

Province of Prince Edward Island
Form 7C – Fixed Term Contract
(Instructional Personnel)

THIS AGREEMENT made this _____ day of _____, 19__

BETWEEN: _____ School Board, a body corporate pursuant to *the School
Act* R.S.P.E.I. 1988, Cap. S-2.1 (hereinafter referred to as the "School Board")

AND _____, of

_____
being a teacher who holds a valid instructional license (hereinafter referred to as the
"Teacher")

WHEREAS the School Board wishes to hire the Teacher;

AND WHEREAS the Teacher has agreed to work for the School Board on the terms and conditions
herein contained;

AND WHEREAS the School Board and its employees are subject to the provisions of the *School
Act* and the regulations;

In CONSIDERATION of these premises and of the agreed salary to be paid to the Teacher
pursuant to this agreement, the parties hereto agree as follows:

1. The School Board hereby employs the Teacher and the Teacher agrees to perform the duties
    of a teacher for the School Board, as follows:

    _____ percentage of full-time

2. This contract commences on _____ and ends on _____.

3. The salary rate payable and benefits for the Teacher shall be the salary rate and benefits for
    instructional personnel determined by the collective agreement for instructional personnel
    made pursuant to the *Act*.

4. This contract is subject at all times to the Teacher obtaining and continuing to hold an
    instructional license and further, this contract becomes void if the Teacher's instructional
    license is revoked under the *Act*.

5. The Teacher agrees to be diligent and faithful in the performance of the Teacher's duties
    during the period of employment, to abide by the *Act* and the regulations and to teach such
    subjects and to perform such duties as may be assigned by the School Board or the
    principal.

6. The Teacher agrees further that this contract is subject to the collective agreement.

7. Notwithstanding anything herein to the contrary, this contract may be terminated as provided
    in section 88 of the *Act*.

Signed, sealed and delivered by the Teacher and by the School Board as of the date above written

School Board

_____   _____
Witness

_____   _____
Witness   Teacher

Distribution: Copy 1 – School Board Office
                              Copy 2 - Employee

Sample Contract—NOVA SCOTIA (Probationary)

PROBATIONARY CONTRACT

APPROVED BY THE MINISTER OF EDUCATION AND CULTURE UNDER THE EDUCATION ACT, S.N.S. 1995-96, c.1.

MEMORANDUM OF AGREEMENT made in duplicate and entered into the   day of   , 19   , A.D.

B E T W E E N :

.... of
....

Professional Number ....

hereinafter referred to as "the Teacher"

OF THE ONE PART

— and —

The .... of
....

hereinafter referred to as "the Board"

OF THE OTHER PART

The parties hereto have agreed as follows, that is to say:

ARTICLE ONE
Agreement to Teach

1.01   The Teacher agrees with the Board to teach, supervise or administer in a public school administered by the Board.

1.02   The term of this Agreement shall be during the two (2) academic school years commencing on the first day of August, 19   , and ending on the thirty-first day of July, 19   , unless this Agreement is terminated in the manner set out in Article Three hereof.

ARTICLE TWO
Remuneration of Teachers

2.01   The Board agrees with the Teacher to pay the teacher such proportion of the yearly salary in accordance with the provisions of the Teachers' Provincial Agreement, as amended or replaced from time to time, applicable to the class of teacher's certificate or permit, experience and position held by the teacher, as the number of days taught, or reckoned as days taught, by the teacher, bears to the total number of teaching days in the school year.

2.02   For the purpose of determining the remuneration or salary of a teacher, "days taught" shall include:

(a)   any days which may be reckoned as days taught under any regulation made pursuant to the Education Act;
(b)   any days agreed upon as days taught between the Minister or the Board and the Nova Scotia Teachers Union;
(c)   such other days as are allowed by the Board as days taught.

ARTICLE THREE
Termination of Agreement, Suspension, and Discharge

3.01   Where the parties hereto are in mutual agreement, this Agreement may be terminated at any time.

3.02   The Teacher may, by notice in writing, given to the Board on or before the fifteenth day of April, terminate this Agreement at the end of any school year.

3.03   The Board may, by notice in writing given to the teacher, on or before the fifteenth day of May, terminate this Agreement in accordance with the provisions of the Education Act and the Teachers' Provincial Agreement, as amended or replaced from time to time.

3.04   The Board may, by notice in writing, suspend or discharge the Teacher at any time during the school year in accordance with the provisions of the Education Act and the Teachers' Provincial Agreement, as amended or replaced from time to time.

ARTICLE FOUR
Miscellaneous Provisions

4.01   The Board and the Teacher mutually agree that the parties to this Agreement and the Agreement shall be in all respects subject to the provisions of the Education Act, the regulations made under authority of the Education Act, and the Teachers' Provincial Agreement, as amended or replaced from time to time.

4.02   The Board and the Teacher mutually agree that this Agreement is subject to the teacher holding a valid Nova Scotia Teachers' Certificate or Permit.

IN WITNESS WHEREOF the parties to this Agreement have hereunto set their hands this   day of   , 19   A.D.

....
Witness   Teacher
....
Witness   Secretary of Board

PERMANENT CONTRACT

APPROVED BY THE MINISTER OF EDUCATION AND CULTURE UNDER THE EDUCATION ACT, S.N.S. 1995-96, c.1.

MEMORANDUM OF AGREEMENT made in duplicate and entered into the . . . . day of . . . . , 19 . . . , A.D.

B E T W E E N :

. . . . of
. . . .

Professional Number . . . .

hereinafter referred to as "the Teacher"

OF THE ONE PART

— and —

The . . . . of
. . . .

hereinafter referred to as "the Board"

OF THE OTHER PART

The parties hereto have agreed as follows, that is to say:

ARTICLE ONE
Agreement to Teach

1.01   The Teacher agrees with the Board to teach, supervise or administer in a public school administered by the Board.

1.02   The term of this Agreement shall be during the school year commencing on the first day of August 19 , and ending on the thirty-first day of July 19 , both dates inclusive and thereafter from year to year until such time as the Agreement is terminated by one or both of the parties hereto in the manner set out in Article Three hereof.

ARTICLE TWO
Remuneration of Teachers

2.01   The Board agrees with the Teacher to pay the teacher such proportion of the yearly salary in accordance with the provisions of the Teachers' Provincial Agreement, as amended or replaced from time to time, applicable to the class of teacher's certificate or permit, experience and position held by the teacher, as the number of days taught, or reckoned as days taught, by the teacher, bears to the total number of teaching days in the school year.

2.02   For the purpose of determining the remuneration or salary of a teacher, "days taught" shall include:

(a)   any days which may be reckoned as days taught under any regulation made pursuant to the Education Act;
(b)   any days agreed upon as days taught between the Minister or the Board and the Nova Scotia Teachers Union;
(c)   such other days as are allowed by the Board as days taught.

ARTICLE THREE
Termination of Agreement, Suspension, and Discharge

3.01   Where the parties hereto are in mutual agreement, this Agreement may be terminated at any time.

3.02   The Teacher may, by notice in writing, given to the Board on or before the fifteenth day of April, terminate this Agreement at the end of any school year.

3.03   The Board may, by notice in writing given to the teacher, on or before the fifteenth day of May, terminate this Agreement in accordance with the provisions of the Education Act and the Teachers' Provincial Agreement, as amended or replaced from time to time.

3.04   The Board may, by notice in writing, suspend or discharge the Teacher at any time during the school year in accordance with the provisions of the Education Act and the Teachers' Provincial Agreement, as amended or replaced from time to time.

ARTICLE FOUR
Miscellaneous Provisions

4.01   The Board and the Teacher mutually agree that the parties to this Agreement and the Agreement shall be in all respects subject to the provisions of the Education Act, the regulations made under authority of the Education Act, and the Teachers' Provincial Agreement, as amended or replaced from time to time.

4.02   The Board and the Teacher mutually agree that this Agreement is subject to the teacher holding a valid Nova Scotia Teachers' Certificate or Permit.

IN WITNESS WHEREOF the parties to this Agreement have hereunto set their hands this . . . . day of . . . . , 19 A.D.

. . . .
Witness   Teacher

. . . .
Witness   Secretary of Board

ACCEPTANCE OF POSITION FORM

Teacher's name _____

Address _____   _____
                      Permanent   Other

Telephone _(_____)_____   Social Insurance Number _____

_____

AGREEMENT

I hereby accept appointment to the teaching staff of _____
                                                                                      (name of school)

_____ as a probationary/long term occasional teacher, at a salary
                    (name of board)

to be determined per the current collective agreement subject to confirmation of Ontario Teaching Certification,

QECO or OSSTF category placement and submission of proof of experience. My duties are to commence

_____. It is understood that this placement is dependent upon the submission of the

documents listed below:

1.   Ontario College of Teachers Certificate of Registration

2.   Ontario College of Teachers Certificate of Qualification

3.   Proof of Member in Good Standing with the Ontario College of Teachers

4.   Current Criminal Reference Check

5.   Medical Certificate of Good Health

Date _____, 19_____

Signature _____   Signed _____
                  (Teacher's Signature)   (Officer of the Board)

CONTRACT OF ENGAGEMENT OF THE FULL-TIME TEACHER

CONTRACT OF ENGAGEMENT

between

....SCHOOL BOARD

hereinafter called the BOARD

and

SURNAME: .... GIVEN NAME: ....

SEX: F ☐   M ☐

hereinafter called the TEACHER.

The Board and the Teacher agree as follows:

I-   **OBLIGATIONS OF THE TEACHER**

A)   The Teacher hereby undertakes, for all legal purposes, to teach as a full-time teacher in the schools of the Board for the school year beginning July 1, 19... or to complete the said school year.

B)   The Teacher declares that he or she was born

at ....
            (place)

on the ....
            (day, month, year)

C)   The Teacher agrees to comply with the law, with the regulations applicable to teachers in the employ of school boards, with the resolutions and regulations of the Board not contrary to the provisions of the collective agreement, as well as with the collective agreement.

D)   The Teacher undertakes to provide the Board, without delay, with the information and documents necessary to establish his or her qualifications and his or her experience.

E)   The Teacher undertakes to provide the Board, without delay, with all other information and certificates required by the Board before the date of this contract.

F)   It is the Teacher's duty to comply with the regulations applicable to teachers in the employ of school boards and to carry out the duties and responsibilities stipulated therein.

II-   **OBLIGATIONS OF THE BOARD**

The Board undertakes to pay the salary and to grant the Teacher all the benefits and privileg provided for in the collective agreement.

III-   **GENERAL PROVISIONS**

A)   This contract of engagement shall take effect on .... 19... and shall expire on .... 19...

B)   The provisions of the collective agreement shall forma an integral part of this contra

IN WITNESS WHEREOF, the parties have signed,

for the Board: ....

....

Teacher: ....

....

Dated at ....   Witness:...

                                    (name)

this ....19...   ....

                                    (address)

FORM 2

(Section 92)

THIS AGREEMENT made in duplicate this _____ day of _____ A.D. 19____.

BETWEEN:

The _____ School Division Number _____, or

The School District of _____ Number _____

(hereinafter called "the school board")

OF THE FIRST PART

AND

_____

Of _____ (home address)

The holder of Principal's _____ Certificate Number _____

Teacher's _____ Certificate Number _____

of a licence to teach in the Province of Manitoba, (hereinafter called "the teacher")

OF THE SECOND PART

1. The school board hereby employs the teacher, and the teacher hereby accepts employment with the school board at the yearly salary of _____ dollars, such employment to commence on the ____ day of _____, 19___.

2. The school board agrees that it will pay the said salary to the teacher in _____ equal consecutive monthly payments of $_____ each, on or before the last teaching day of each month beginning with the _____ day of _____, 19___, in each year during the continuance of this contract:

   Provided that if a salary schedule is in force, the school board shall pay the teacher at the rate prevailing form time to time in said schedule or any temporary modification of it.

3. If any salary is payable during July and August, it shall be paid on the last day of each month.

4. The teacher agrees with the school board to teach diligently and faithfully and to conduct the work assigned by and under the Authority of the said school board during the period of this employment, according to the law and regulations in that behalf in effect in the Province of Manitoba, and to perform such duties and to teach such subjects as may from time to time be assigned in accordance with the statutes and the regulations of the Department of Education and Training of the said Province.

5. This agreement is subject to the following conditions:

   (a) The teacher shall not be required to teach on holidays and vacations prescribed by the law and the regulations.
   (b) Subject to the regulations, the days on which the teacher has attended the meetings convened by the superintendent or the field representative (which attendance shall, if required, be evidenced by the certificate of the said superintendent or field representative), shall be allowed him or her as if he or she had actually taught for the school board during those days.
   (c) In the case of sickness, the teacher shall be entitled to receive his or her salary without deduction for such period as may be authorized under the statutes in that behalf.

6. This agreement shall be deemed to continue in force, and to be renewed from year to year, with such variations as to the time of payment and the amount of salary as may be provided under the by-laws, resolutions, or schedules of the school board from time to time in force (of which variations the teacher must be notified forthwith, and concerning which he or she shall have the right of conference with the school board, provided that no variations of salary shall take place before October 1, unless notice be given the teacher on or before June 30 of the same year) unless and until terminated by one of the following methods:

(a)   By mutual consent of the teacher and the school board.

(b)   By written notice given at least one month prior to December 31 or June 30, terminating the contract on December 31 or June 30, as the case may be, but the party giving notice of termination shall, on request, give to the other party the reason or reasons for terminating this agreement.

(c)   By one month's previous notice in writing given by either party to the other in writing given by either party to the other in case of emergency affecting the welfare of the school division school district or of the teacher, provided that in the event the school board may, in lieu of one month's notice, as aforesaid, pay the teacher one month's salary at the said rate.

(d)   By one month's notice in writing by the teacher in case of variation of salary, which notice hall be given, at the discretion of the teacher, at any time after notification of the variation, and shall take effect one month after the date it is given.

7.   Sections 41, 48 and 96 of The Public Schools Act shall form part of this agreement.

8.   If this agreement is terminated by notice as provided in clause 6 hereof, the final payment shall be so adjusted that the teacher shall receive, for the part of the year taught, such fraction of the salary for the whole year as the total number of days taught is of the number of days in the current school year as prescribed by the Minister.

As witness the corporate seal of the school division or school district attested by the signature of its chairman and secretary-treasurer, in virtue of a resolution or by-law passed by the school board at a meeting held on the _____ day of _____, 19___, ad the hand and seal of the teacher on the day and year first above mentioned.

_____
Chairman

_____
Secretary-Treasurer

_____ (SEAL)
Teacher

_____
Witness

_____
Teacher's Address

To be executed in duplicate, one copy to be retained by the school board, and the other by the teacher.

1999-2   EDUCATION, 1986   E-0.1 REG 1

FORM Y
[Section 200 of the Act]
[Subsection 57(3) of the Regulations]

[OFFER OF TEMPORARY CONTRACT]

This letter constitutes an offer of a temporary contract of employment to you by The Board of Education of the _____ School Division No. _____ of a:

☐ full time teaching position; or

(check)

☐ part-time teaching position.

(percentage)

This offer is conditional on your holding a valid Saskatchewan teacher's certificate.

The purpose of the temporary contract is:

☐ to fill an unexpected vacancy during the school year; or

☐ to replace a teacher who will be absent for the period set out below.

Your duties, as set out in *The Education Act, 1995*, commence on
_____ , _____ , _____ and expire on _____ _____ , _____ .
(month) *(day)* *(year)*   *(month)* *(day)* *(year)*

The Board of Education of the _____ School Division No. ___ .

_____
(address of Board of Education)

_____
Per: Director of Education

_____
(date)

2 Jan 98 SR 107/97 s8.

E-0.1 REG 1　　　　　EDUCATION, 1986　　　　　1999-2

FORM Z
[*Section 200 of the Act*]
[*Subsection 57(3) of the Regulations*]

[TEACHER ACCEPTANCE OF TEMPORARY CONTRACT]

To: The Board of Education of the _____ School DivisionNo. _____ .

I accept the offer of a _____ full time or _____ part-time temporary
　　　　　　　　　　　　　(check)　　　　　　　　*(percentage)*
contract of employment in the _____ School Division No. _____
commencing on _____　_____ , _____
　　　　　　　　　(month)　　　　　*(day)*　　　　　　*(year)*
and expiring on _____　_____ , _____ .
　　　　　　　　(month)　　　　　*(day)*　　　　　　*(year)*

I certify that:

☐　I hold a _____ Saskatchewan teacher's certificate Number _____ ; or

☐　my eligibility for a Saskatchewan teacher's certificate has been confirmed.

I have_____ years of teaching experience in Saskatchewan and _____
years of teaching experience outside Saskatchewan.

I understand that I am responsible for providing evidence that is satisfactory to the
Board of my years of teaching experience that are set out above.

My social insurance number is:_____ .

_____
(signature)

_____
(date)

_____
(address)

_____
(telephone number)

2 Jan 98 SR 107/97 s8.

1999-2 EDUCATION, 1986 **E-0.1 REG 1**

FORM AA
[Section 200 of the Act]
[Subsection 57(3) of the Regulations]

[BOARD CONFIRMATION OF TEMPORARY CONTRACT]

The Board of Education of the _____ School Division No. _____ confirms your acceptance of the offer of the Board of Education of a temporary contract of employment on a:

☐ full time basis; or
(check)

☐ part-time basis.
(percentage)

The purpose of the temporary contract is:

☐ to fill an unexpected vacancy during the school year; or

☐ to replace a teacher who will be absent for the period set out below.

Your duties, as set out in *The Education Act, 1995*, commence on
_____ , _____ , _____ and expire on _____ _____ , _____ .
(month)   *(day)*   *(year)*   *(month)*   *(day)*   *(year)*

The Board of Education of the _____ School DivisionNo.____ .

_____
(address of Board of Education)

_____
Per: Director of Education

_____
(date)

2 Jan 98 SR 107/97 s8.

MUTUAL AGREEMENT OF AMEND CONTRACT OF EMPLOYMENT FOR A SPECIFIED TERM

This agreement made in duplicate

BETWEEN:

(hereinafter referred to as "the teacher")

and

THE BOARD OF EDUCATION OF THE MOOSE JAW SCHOOL DIVISION NO. 1 OF SASKATCHEWAN
(hereinafter referred to as "the Board")

WHEREAS the teacher is presently employed by the Board on a full-time basis,

AND WHEREAS the parties wish to amend the contract of the teacher for the 19__ school year,

THEREFORE, THE TEACHER AND THE BOARD AGREE AS FOLLOWS:

1. THAT the teacher's contract of employment with the Board is amended to provide that the teacher shall be assigned __ percent of full-time duties for the ____ school year only.

2. THAT the amendment of the said contract of employment shall be effective for the ____ school year only.

3. THAT effective July 1, 19__, the within amendment of the said contract of employment shall cease to operate. The teacher's contract of employment with the Board will revert to a full-time basis commencing July 1, 19__.

DATED this ____ day of ____, 19__ at Moose Jaw, Saskatchewan.

_____   _____
(Witness)   (Teacher)

DATED this ____ day of ____, 19__ at Moose Jaw, Saskatchewan.

THE BOARD OF EDUCATION OF THE MOOSE JAW
SCHOOL DIVISION NO. I OF SASKATCHEWAN

Per:

_____
(Director of Education)

OFFER OF EMPLOYMENT

TO: _____ ("The Teacher")

1. **TYPE OF CONTRACT: Full-time Probationary**

2. **FROM:** *(date starting and ending probationary period)*

3. **PLACEMENT:** to be confirmed by the Board in writing

4. **ASSIGNMENT:** to be determined by the principal of the school of placement

5. **ACCEPTANCE:** In order to accept this Offer, the Teacher must:
   a) complete the "Acceptance of Employment" section below; and
   b) return this form to Personnel Services at the Centre for Education, Xxxxxxx, Xxxxxxxxxxx, Xxxxxxxxxxxxx, Alberta, X0X 0X0, within fourteen (14) days from the date written below.

6. **PROVISIONS OF INFORMATION:** After acceptance of this Offer, the teacher must:
   a) before the date of commencement of employment, satisfy the Board that the Teacher is a holder of a certificate of qualification as a teacher issued under the Department of Education Act, and
   b) comply with such further direction as the Board may give to the Teacher.

7. **RULES AND REGULATIONS:** The Teacher agrees to be bound by and comply with all policies, regulations, rules and operational guidelines of the Board in force from time to time.

8. **NOTICES:** Any notice required or permitted to be given by the Board to the Teacher, pursuant to the provisions of the *School Act*, may be given either by delivering the notice to the teacher or by mailing the notice in a prepaid envelope addressed to the Teacher at the last known mailing address of the Teacher and in the latter case, notice shall have been deemed to have been given on the date on which it was mailed.

9. **OVERPAYMENT:** The Teacher agrees that if at any time the Board has paid wages to the Teacher in excess of the amount due to the Teacher at the time of payment, the Board may deduct an amount equal to the overpayment from any money owing to the Teacher by the Board, and the Teacher hereby irrevocably authorizes the Board to deduct such amounts.

10. **NO UNTRUTHS:** The Teacher expressly promises that the Teacher's application form is truthful in all respects, and the Teacher has not intentionally omitted to provide the Board with any information pertinent to the Board's decision to make this offer of employment.

11. **CRIMINAL RECORDS:** The Teacher expressly promises that the Teacher has never been convicted under the *Criminal Code of Canada*, or similar legislation of any jurisdiction, of an offence relating to sexual misconduct, fraud, theft, or physical violence.

12. **DUTY OF FIDELITY:** The Teacher agrees that by accepting employment with the Board, the Teacher assumes a responsibility to at all times display conduct that is appropriate to the role of a teacher, and does not harm in any way the reputation of the Board, and that serves as an appropriate role model for students.

13. **EFFECT OF NON-COMPLIANCE:** This offer of Employment is conditional. If the Teacher does not strictly comply with all terms and conditions, the Offer is null and void and the Teacher's acceptance is of no force or effect.

Sample Contract—ALBERTA (cont'd)

Dated this _____ day of _____, 19___

THE BOARD OF TRUSTEES OF THE XXXXXXX SCHOOL DISTRICT NO. 7

Per: _____
Supervisor of Personnel Services

Acceptance of Employment

I have read, understand and agree to be bound by all of the provisions of this Offer of Employment

Dated this _____ day of _____, 19___

_____   _____
(Witness)   (Teacher)

(School District Letterhead)

OFFER OF TEMPORARY APPOINTMENT – NEW

1997 April 12

(inside address of recipient)

Dear _____ :

I am pleased to offer you a temporary appointment to the teaching staff of (name of school), effective from (start date) to (end date). You will be replacing (name of teacher) who is currently on leave of absence from his/her teaching duties. Please note that your contract may be lengthened or decreased subject to (name of teacher)'s approved date of return.

Your placement on the teachers' salary scale is determined in accordance with your qualifications and experience. Your beginning annual salary is based on a salary category of (level) with (number) years of experience and for (per-cent of) full-time. Placement shall be confirmed and salary adjusted retroactively, where necessary, when you present proof of qualifications and/or experience within 60 days. Otherwise, your salary adjustments will commence immediately following submission of proof.

All teaching appointments are subject to the regulations contained in the School Act. The conditions referred to in the Act are set out in summary form on the accompanying sheets entitled "Conditions of Temporary Contract" and "Acceptance of Temporary Contract". Particular emphasis should be placed on # 2 under "Conditions:, immediate proof of membership in the B.C. College of Teachers, and the production of a valid B.C. Teacher's certificate. Accordingly, top priority should be given to this item and compliance therewith make as soon as possible.

If you accept the appointment, I would appreciate your cooperation in completing the enclosed documents and providing, as soon as possible, the information outlined on the instruction sheet.

I look forward to receiving your replay.

Yours sincerely

_____
Personnel Manager

Enclosure

cc: Principal
Teacher's Federation
Data Entry

(Name and Address of School Board)

ACCEPTANCE OF OFFER OF TEMPORARY APPOINTMENT

Please complete and return this acceptance form to the Human Resources Division as soon as possible.

Date: _____

Dear Sir/Madam:

I accept the Temporary Appointment to the staff of _____ *School,*

in accordance with your offer dated _____ .

Yours truly

_____
Signature

_____
Name (please print)

_____
Address

_____   *Postal Code*

_____
Telephone Number

(Yukon Letterhead)

Dear Xxxxxxxxxx

I am pleased to confirm our offer and your verbal acceptance of an appointment as a full-time (probationary l) teacher at Xxxxxxxx School effective Xxxxxx XX, 19XX.

Your salary will be calculated in accordance with the salary schedule in force and will be based on your academic and professional qualifications and your teaching experience.

This appointment is made pursuant to Section 173 of the Education Act. If you do not receive notice in writing from the Superintendent of Education at least 30 days prior to the end of the probationary period, your appointment shall then become a continuing engagement until terminated pursuant to the Education Act.

All employees appointed under the Education Act who will be working directly with children now require that a security check be completed by the R.C.M.P. upon initial hire or transfer. To this end, please complete and return the enclosed "Consent to Release of Information" form along with a signed copy of this letter to the Superintendent of Education indicating your formal acceptance of this position at your earliest convenience.

Best wishes for a successful year.

Yours sincerely,   I UNDERSTAND AND AGREE TO THE
                                           OFFER AND CONDITIONS OUTLINED
                                           ABOVE:

                                           _____
Xxxxx Xxxxxxx   Signature
Superintendent of Education   _____
                                           Date

Encl. (copy of this letter)
        (Consent to Release of Information Form)

c.c.   Public Service Commission
         Yukon Teachers' Association
         Xxxxxx Xxxxxxxxxx, Director of Human Resources
         Xxxxxx Xxxxxxxx, Director of French Programs
         Xxxx Xxxxxxxxx, Principal, Xxxxxx School
         Xxxxxx Xxxxxxxxx, School Council Chairperson

TEACHERS' UNION/SOCIETY/ ASSOCIATION OR FEDERATION REGULATIONS/POLICY RE: VOLUNTEERING

"We must use time creatively."
—*Martin Luther King Jr.*

The following is an encapsulation for guidance only. For details in this very important area, it is advisable to contact the local president of your teachers' federation or union or association or society. Many of the provincial and territorial teachers' unions have booklets on volunteering. Ask for one! It is important that you not breach their policy! It may also be helpful to be aware of subtle messages you might be receiving from teachers or administrators. You don't want to get bumped off the "inside track." If in doubt, ask.

NEWFOUNDLAND AND LABRADOR

The Newfoundland and Labrador Teachers' Association's definition of volunteers is worth noting: "Volunteers in the school are responsible persons who provide a service to the school to fulfil specific needs, as determined by the principal and the teaching staff directly involved, without reimbursement or contractual commitments of any kind" (NLTA Policy III A 4). They specify that "Volunteers are usually part-time teacher assistants who offer their services without pay" (III A 2 c).

Unlike most districts, their policy (III A 6 a)) states that a teacher assistant's duties "may include the assessment of individual needs of pupils; the selection of materials to meet pupil needs; and the evaluation of pupil progress." This could suggest a role for a not-yet-hired teacher! It goes on, however, to state that "a teacher assistant shall not assume or be assigned duties reserved for teachers" and "shall not function in a classroom role if a certified teacher is not available for direction and guidance" (III A 6 b)).

NOVA SCOTIA

The issue of school volunteers is covered in the policies of individual boards. Reasonably typical is the Halifax County-Bedford District School Board requirement that volunteers work to "support" teaching staff, and that they "not conflict with or replace any regularly authorized personnel" (Halifax County-Bedford District School Board policy IIG).

Volunteers are required to be under the "immediate" supervision of a teacher. Section 1 of their *Handbook* states that "Teacher assistants can assist, <u>but they should not be assigned to the program</u>; rather, <u>they should be assigned to a student or teacher</u>" [their underlining].

Nova Scotia recognizes the role of volunteerism in building "an understanding of school programs among interested members of the community, thus stimulating widespread involvement in lifelong learning and the total educational process" and recognizes its ability to "strengthen school-community relations."

Section 2 of their *Handbook for Teachers on Teacher Assistants* states that "Persons with teacher's qualifications and/or license should not be hired for a teacher assistant position, so that it is understood by all [sic] that the teacher assistant is clearly under the direction of the licensed teacher and/or principal. This will avoid a role definition conflict." Note the word "hired"; this does not exclude licensed volunteers but you might want to consult with the NS Teachers' Union or with the board in which you are interested, just to be on the safe side.

PRINCE EDWARD ISLAND

Prince Edward Island does not address the issue of volunteers *per se* in its agreement with the P.E.I. Teachers' Federation, except to say that the term "Auxiliary Personnel" "is not limited to" the list they give such as teacher assistants, tutors, monitors, markers, and so on; so presumably volunteers are included. Section 36 of the agreement specifies that they are "to assist the teacher," teaching duties "shall not be delegated" to them, they must be "supervised by a certified teacher," and shall not be used as "replacements;" however, "supervision duties may be carried out by auxiliary personnel."

NEW BRUNSWICK

New Brunswick's Collective Agreement addresses the issue of Auxiliary Personnel, and in absence of other guidelines, might possibly be seen as applicable, *mutatis mutandis*, to volunteers as well.

Article 25.01 states that these auxiliary personnel "could, for example, provide assistance in classrooms, libraries, shops, labouratories ... " and so on. It further states "however, at no time shall they perform any professional function such as: Planning, diagnosing, prescribing, instructing and evaluating."

Article 25.05 is very specific: "Qualified teachers acting as auxiliary personnel shall at all times be restricted to the provisions of Clauses 25.01, 25.02, 25.03, and 25.04." Thus you, even though a certified teacher, cannot, while volunteering, "perform any professional function," or replace licensed teachers (25.02), and the teachers involved have to agree to your assignment working with them (25.03 and 25.04).

Where it states that you "may under no circumstances be used as replacement for licensed teachers" (25.02), you need to note, however, that NBTF Policy 31 emphasizes that those carrying out teaching functions must be "employed;" i.e., paid. Thus, if you are paid for a day to replace a temporarily absent teacher, you are arguably on that day not auxiliary personnel. You should be able to volunteer one day and be paid the next and volunteer again the third day, but your responsibilities would change dramatically between days!

Again, this can be a complex area of overlapping authorities. Check with your local NBTF representative and be on the safe side!

QUEBEC

There is no policy of the Teachers' Associations or regulation of the Ministry of Education regarding the use or duties of volunteers in Quebec schools. Quebec is unique in this, but you would be well advised to adhere to the general guidelines of other provinces and territories to prevent misunderstandings or problems.

ONTARIO

Ontario Teachers' Federation's policy specifies that "teaching functions which involve decisions regarding diagnosis of student difficulties, prescription of learning experiences, and evaluation of student programs [are] the exclusive responsibility of teaching staff" (XI A 4).

"Treat people as if they are what they ought to be and you help them to become what they are capable of being."
—Johann Wolfgang von Goethe

"Men, I want you to fight vigorously and then run. And, as I am a little bit lame, I'm going to start running now."
—*General George Stedman*, U.S. Civil War

"Ingratitude is always a kind of weakness. I have never known men of ability to be ungrateful."
—*Johann Wolfgang von Goethe*

It is interesting that their definition of "auxiliary personnel" (which includes volunteers) is "those persons other than teachers as defined in the *Teaching Profession Act* who function in a supportive role to principals and teachers in the school" (*OTF Policy on Auxiliary Personnel* A.). The *Teaching Profession Act* says "'teacher' means a person who is legally qualified to teach in an elementary or secondary school <u>and is under contract</u> in accordance with Part X of the Education Act but does not include a supervisory officer, an instructor in a teacher-training institution or a person employed to teach in a school for a period not exceeding one month" [underlining added] (*T.P.Act* 1). Thus it would seem that because you are not under contract you are free to be in the school as a volunteer, or as an "auxiliary personnel" member. You must be aware, however, that "Certified teachers who are employed as auxiliary personnel and are not, therefore, on a teaching contract, shall not perform tasks which are the responsibility of a teacher" (Auxiliary Personnel in the Schools of Ontario: General Statements: 8). The same would apply, *mutatis mutandis*, to volunteers (i.e., auxiliary personnel) who are not paid; thus, not employed.

Further to that, they simply require that "school volunteers who work with children shall work at all times under the supervision of a teacher" (XI C 1). As long as you are under the supervision of a teacher, and are willing to do the work without reward or commitment of any kind, and don't replace paid staff by doing the types of work specifically reserved for teachers (the big 4 in the first paragraph), you're basically on your own to do your thing as a volunteer member of the school's "auxiliary personnel." So go ahead. Show them that you are good at what you do and that you could contribute a whole lot to their school. That demonstration will do a great deal to get you onto the "inside track!"

The definition formerly used by OTF, before paid para-professionals in schools became more common, was a little more directive; although it is no longer official policy, it can provide useful guidance to anyone considering volunteering. It said, essentially, that a volunteer was a responsible person who provides a service to the school to fulfil specific needs, as determined by the principal and the teaching staff directly involved, without reimbursement or contractual commitments of any kind. It then went on to say that volunteers were to work at all times under the supervision of a designated teacher, and that the teacher was responsible for all diagnosis, prescription, planning, selection and implementing of program and evaluation of the pupil and program.

One important thing to remember, though, is that you cannot demand preferential treatment because you volunteer, but if you are not recognized for your contribution, why not go where you will be? (See PART IX).

MANITOBA

Manitoba has a good booklet for teachers called "Help at Last." Get a copy from the Manitoba Teachers' Society. It defines a volunteer as a "para-professional" and further as "part-time teacher aides or school aides who offer their services without pay." It would appear that volunteering certified teachers fit that category. It is important to note that MTS policy specifically states that "paraprofessionals" "shall not perform teaching tasks ... planning, diagnosing, prescribing, evaluating and selecting learning resources to meet pupil needs." It also states that "Paraprofessionals shall not be scheduled for supervision responsibilities in classroom environments including libraries." However, "Noon-hour supervision is permissible."

Manitoba Regulation 464/88R specifically includes volunteers as persons "having care and charge of pupils," and states (3.(2) that they "shall not assume or be assigned the duties set out in subsection (1) [i.e., "such duties as the principal assigns to him or her, subject to the instructions of the school board and the superintendent"] if a certified teacher is not available for direction and guidance." It further states that "volunteers shall not be used as substitute teachers," but it does not say that you cannot volunteer one day and be a paid substitute teacher the next; you just can't replace a teacher without being paid.

"It's not whether you get knocked down; it's whether you get up."
—*Vince Lombardi*

SASKATCHEWAN

Saskatchewan Teachers' Federation's policy requires careful reading and seems by implication only to address the specifics of non-hired certified teachers volunteering in schools. Section 18.1 says "Teacher associates include in-school employees of school boards who have not been hired as certified teachers and are responsible to and work under the direction of the principal and/or a designated teacher or teachers." Volunteers are not "employees" so do not specifically fit, however, the definition "not been hired as certified teachers" might be seen to allow out-of-work teachers both to volunteer and even to accept employment as a "Teacher Associate." It would be prudent to contact the federation for clarification before accepting such a position. Even though the policy states (18.3) that "Teachers may delegate to or share with others some of the tasks involved in the instruction of a student ... ," most federations discourage certified teachers working in paid positions as para-professionals. The policy clearly states that "Where a position requires and uses the skills of a certified teacher, the position must be filled by a person employed as a certified teacher. Teacher associates shall not displace teachers" (18.4).

ALBERTA

The Alberta Teachers' Association's pamphlet "Parent Volunteers" outlines their philosophy on volunteerism and could, probably, be extrapolated to include any volunteer. They specify that volunteers "do not take the place of teachers. Rather, their duties involve relieving teachers of many necessary non-teaching duties; thus teachers have more time for students."

They also specify the duties of volunteers as follows: "To ensure that there is no confusion between the roles of teacher and volunteer, all the volunteer's duties are performed under the direction of a teacher. The volunteer's duties may include:

- giving instructional support
- assisting with clerical tasks, audio-visual material and special projects
- contributing your own special talents, such as offering information on your hobby or area of special knowledge which may interest students."

Alberta also quite nicely pairs parent and community rights with responsibilities, including in the area of volunteerism. They specify, not surprisingly, that volunteers "must observe all school policies and regulations and be aware that teachers have the ultimate responsibility in the classroom ... must hold all matters connected with the school in confidence ... should respect the professional role and judgment of the teachers and school administration ... should try to meet their commitment on a regular basis ... if teachers are depending on the volunteer's help when planning activities."

"A child regards your cheery smile as an evidence that you are on his side."
—*George W. Crane*

THINK POSITIVELY

At first look this may seem forbidding, and you may wonder if it is possible to use volunteering to get yourself: (a) into schools working with kids, and (b) known and recognized.

There is, however, still a lot you can do in schools without putting someone out of work. Policy says you "should not be a substitute for adequate staffing by professional and non-teaching support personnel" (4.L.25(f)), but as long as you are not replacing a paid person, you may well find yourself welcomed to augment what the school can offer.

Just be certain to stay on the right side of the rules and ask when in doubt!

Their *School Act* also is clear in s. 21: "No person shall disturb or interrupt the proceedings of a school."

BRITISH COLUMBIA

The policy book *Members' Guide to the BCTF* addresses both the roles of volunteers and auxiliary personnel (paid non-professionals who assist the teacher) and gives what might be the Canadian Teachers Federation's most detailed description of the role of auxiliary personnel.

BCTF policy also states: "As a general rule, volunteers should be used on a by-need, special occasion basis in the co-curricular and extra-curricular activities of the school" and goes on to re-emphasize that "Teachers will respect the provisions of any collective agreements between boards and non-teaching employees regarding the use of volunteers in the schools" (4.L.25). It goes on to say: "Volunteers should not be used in schools to replace teachers, teacher aides or other school personnel who have been laid off or had their hours of work cut" (4.L25(e)).

Be sure you are not doing so, or you can guarantee that you will very quickly become embroiled in a dispute with one or more unions, and that is a pretty good way to ensure (unofficially, of course) that you will never, ever, be hired. Your best defence in a situation like this is to be certain that no paid person has been displaced in that classroom or school before you volunteer in it. The local BCTF president, or in-school federation representative or union representative can give you definitive information on this. (You can get their names from the school secretary.)

Policy 4.L.25 does recognize that "volunteers can bring their special talents to schools" but requires that policies should be "developed" (4.L.25(a)) and "monitored" (4.L.25(b)) regarding the use of volunteers. Check the local policy with the local BCTF president or representative. In order to stay on the "inside track" you really must avoid being in breach of policy!

THE NORTHWEST TERRITORIES

The NWT Teachers' Association says little about volunteerism except that By-law 16—Code of Ethics, 6.1. says: "A member should deal with other members of the profession in the same manner as he our she wishes to be treated." Not really specific or new, but certainly a good guide.

The NWT document *Learning, Tradition and Change* addresses the unique position and duties of the "classroom assistant" and some of the areas for care in maintaining the relationship between teacher and assistant. (These assistants are persons of aboriginal origin hired to assist in the inclusion of traditional culture and values in the classroom.) Take a look at it; much of it applies to any teacher/assistant relationship, including their statement that one identified problem facing southern teachers going to the NWT is that often they are "unable to make proper use of a classroom assistant." They give further advice for the relationship: "you [the teacher] will need your assistant—make up for their lower pay and perceived lower status with a <u>lot</u> of respect and courtesy!" A bit of good advice for all relationships.

YUKON TERRITORY

This is covered in the Collective Agreement. Section 53 specifies "THAT auxiliary school personnel include[s] adults who serve in a volunteer or paid capacity ..." The Agreement further states:

"We have committed the Golden Rule to memory; let us now commit it to life."
—*Edwin Markham*

[Section] "46 THAT auxiliary school personnel may be used effectively to perform:

(a) routine clerical duties, such as checking pupil attendance, distributing supplies and books, collecting and recording money, marking workbooks and exercises that may be checked by use of an answer key, recording marks as directed;

(b) general housekeeping, such as maintaining bulletin boards, setting up equipment;

(c) preparing teacher aids, such as charts, flash cards, transparencies, stencils, tapes and pictures;

(d) supervising in school buildings, on playgrounds[,] in study halls and on field trips;

(e) preparing and maintaining science and shop supplies and equipment;

(f) supervising pupils and performing clerical duties in the library."

The agreement then goes on to specify that auxiliary school personnel in a classroom must work "under the direction and supervision of a qualified classroom teacher," or if not under an individual teacher, "under the direction of the school staff" (section 47).

Section 48 specifies that they "shall not:

(a) infringe in any way on the responsibilities of a teacher;

(b) assume any instructional responsibilities in the absence of a teacher;

(c) provide any form of direct or independent remedial instruction, except under the direction of a teacher."

The Yukon is somewhat unusual in that they define clearly what the descriptors mean, viz:

Note: "Direction" means teaching and learning activities will be designed, initiated and evaluated by teachers; "supervision" means the activity will be carried out in such a place and manner that the teacher can readily conduct ongoing evaluation. Auxiliary school personnel include such persons as remedial tutors, education assistants, school aides, library aides, supervision aides, lab assistants, markers and child-care workers; excluded are school secretaries, janitorial maintenance and transportation staff.

AGAIN, REMEMBER

This is only a guide; consult the appropriate teachers' group for definitive information, analysis or decisions.

PERSONAL AND PROFESSIONAL CHARACTERISTICS OF EFFECTIVE TEACHERS

YOU'RE HIRED!

By the way, if you possess all of these characteristics all of the time, I want you on my staff.

Call me!

These succinct lists might be of benefit to you in establishing an even clearer picture of what you might want to emphasize in your C.V. and at the interview. These are some of the "general characteristics" which the details you provide might be designed to demonstrate.

In the realm of **personal characteristics**, it could be argued that the effective teacher:

- is respectful toward students,
- is respectful to other staff,
- is respectful to parents,
- is co-operative,
- is receptive to advice from colleagues and parents,
- is approachable,
- is moderately humble,
- is kind,
- is up-beat,
- is friendly,
- is flexible,
- is ready to make sudden changes for the benefit of the school or pupils,
- has a really good attitude,
- has a good sense of humour, and
- feels good about herself/himself, the profession, and the school.

In the realm of **professional characteristics**, again it could be argued that the effective teacher:

- is fair in assessment and all areas of classroom management involving authority,
- is aware of individual student needs,
- is capable of recognizing students in need,
- is capable of providing for exceptional needs,
- is discreet,
- is knowledgeable and skillful in teaching,
- is an excellent communicator,
- is assiduous in keeping pupils involved in meaningful, or "on-task," behaviours,
- is ready for each class,
- is a supportive and dependable member of the staff team,

"In the last analysis, what we are communicates far more eloquently than anything we say or do."
—*Steven Covey*

- is available, approachable and receptive to pupils and parents,
- is generous with positive reinforcement for work well done or good attitudes demonstrated,
- is careful to vary teaching styles and activities, both to avoid boredom, and to address different learning styles,
- is skillful in questioning,
- is open to pupil involvement in determining some aspects of the program, including some "rules of the classroom," and
- is aware of and sensitive to changes in society and their effect upon effective programming.

"I have found that the principal characteristic of genuine happiness is peace, inner peace.... I attribute my sense of peace to the effort to develop concern for others."
—His Holiness, the 14th Dalai Lama

On a related topic, an Environics Research Group poll regarding "Youth Unemployment and Entry Level Jobs" done in the early 90s, listed the following as some of the characteristics desired by current employers. It may be useful to you as it may reflect what and how you will teach your pupils—the world's future "workers"—those who will take over responsibility for society's continuation. I do suggest, however, that it reflects the importance society puts on many of the things we do, and need to do, as teachers.

It showed the percent of employers viewing various characteristics as very important for entry level jobs, to be:

Attitude	96%	That topped the list!
Punctuality	93%	
Maturity	66%	
Good grooming	56%	
Ability to speak with customers	56%	
Good grammar or language	41%	Do we recognize the importance of this?
Spelling accuracy	30%	Or this?
High School diploma	30%	
Writing skills	27%	
Trade skills	25%	
Previous job experience	24%	
Typing and office skills	23%	
Mathematics	22%	I would have expected this to be higher!
Computer skills	14%	Perhaps this one is now, almost a decade later!
Community College diploma	14%	
University degree	8%	Think how much effort we put toward getting our students ready to pursue this! What percent do? What about the others?
Working knowledge of French	3%	

Interesting! How can we be certain we value what the consumers and customers of our product value? How can we show them that what we are providing has consistent quality, or significantly enhanced value, or is distinguishable from (and superior to) what others are offering? If it isn't, why should they entrust their children's education to us instead of to the competition?

"Tomorrow's education will include placing greater emphasis on character development."
—Ralph Tyler

SOMETHING TO KEEP IN MIND

If we don't help our customers understand what they need and give them what they want, someone else will.

A book which has some really good ideas about getting down to what is important and what really works (in industry and in education) is *Fad Surfing in the Boardroom: Reclaiming the Courage to Manage in the Age of Instant Answers*, by Eileen C. Shapiro (Reading, Mass.: Addison-Wesley, 1995). If you have been teaching for more than two years I very strongly encourage you to read it! It's not just for principals; each of us is a manager in our classroom.

Again, with my sincere thanks to him, colleague Jack Jones put together a rather succinct outline for the "Teacher of Tomorrow" which I borrow here, with his permission. He says the teacher of tomorrow (that means now) must:

- empower students as learners by giving them ownership of their learning from an early age,
- help students to seek out information and develop the thinking skills necessary to use it effectively,
- encourage collaborative as well as independent learning,
- use a variety of approaches and aids to learning to accommodate differing styles and needs,
- build on the knowledge base of each student, and
- use a wide variety of assessment strategies to provide feedback to the learner.

Do you agree that he has captured the spirit of where teaching is going? Our pupils are different than any which have ever gone to school before. They are the Nintendo™ generation. They were raised on Sesame Street™, with its millions-of-dollars-per-half-hour-show budget. They process information differently than any group in history. It has been pointed out that we are no longer "the sage on the stage" expected to dole out information. We are, instead, helpers in the pupil's development of learning skills which will, with additions and refinement, have to last him or her for the rest of their life. This, too, may be of help in guiding you as you prepare yourself for getting hired to teach in a Canadian school. I hope it is.

Finally, coming at it from yet another slightly different point of viewing, when putting together your application package from cover letter and C.V. to preparing hypothetical answers to potential interview questions, you might want to consider the categories identified by Robert Tannenbaum and how you will illustrate your capabilities in light of them. He identified the characteristics of successful employees as fitting into three categories: Conceptual, Technical and Inter-Personal. Conceptual, according to him, is an understanding of the big picture: how does what we do fit into the grand scheme of things, and why is it important. Technical skills, of course, is reflected in our skill as everyday good teachers. The category inter-personal skills is self-explanatory, especially in a "communications profession" such as ours.

You might want to give thought to how you can phrase your answers to show that you are capable in all three. It will really help you sound assured and will confirm your "conceptual" awareness!

"Facing it, always facing it,
that's the way to get through.
Face it."
—*Joseph Conrad*

APPENDIX 12

RELATED CAREER OPPORTUNITIES AND ALTERNATIVE OPPORTUNITIES IN TEACHING

There is more than one way to succeed and more than one field of teaching. You don't have to start your career working in a narrowly-defined, traditional school. I didn't. I started in a hospital, teaching for the Ministry of Education. Instead of holding me back, though, that specialized experience—along with the additional intensive and focused training I took while there—helped to fast-track my career; I moved from there directly into a principalship in a highly specialized field of education! That may not, necessarily, be your career path, but let's not close any doors even before we get to them!

If you are in a non-typical setting, that does not mean you are not teaching. You can still be developing and refining your teaching skills and becoming better prepared for the next opening that comes up (in a regular school or elsewhere)! Look at your personality and skills set and see where you could be successful. Remember: any work requiring the skills of persuasion, group management, inter-personal relations, sequencing and/or analysis (of both task and concept), synthesis and evaluation is just what a teacher is trained to do! You are trained in diagnosis, decision-making, conceptualizing, mentoring and much more! Please don't sell yourself, and our profession, short.

You are also trained to be skilled in relating to people while effectively establishing frameworks for processes and sharing ideas whether or not you have personal experience applying them. Those are saleable qualities!

This could be either until you get hired in the type of school you were planning on, or until you are so successful you don't want to give it up and go where you originally intended. Don't worry if your life-path goes in an unusual direction, as long as you are successful. As Robert Frost said in his poem "The Road Not Taken":

> I shall be telling this with a sigh
> Somewhere ages and ages hence:
> Two roads diverged in a wood and I—
> Took the one less travelled by,
> And that has made all the difference.

Yes, there are many non-typical opportunities for teachers to put their teaching skills to use, either as a rewarding career in itself, or to gain further experience to add to the C.V. The opportunities are limited only by your imagination; in fact, the less likely that others have thought of it, the more likely there will be an opening for you! And remember, just because you are not in a regular run-of-the-mill school (the future of which is becoming more questionable every day), it doesn't mean you can't or won't experience the fulfillment you are looking for, guiding and helping others to learn and to become life-long self-directed learners.

You might also want to consider that there are benefits to some of the careers

"If your ship doesn't come in, swim out to it."
—*Jonathan Winters*

"Potential just means you ain't done it yet."
—*Darrel Royal*, football coach, U. of Texas

> "Vitality shows not only in the ability to persist, but in the ability to start over."
> —*F. Scott Fitzgerald*

listed below, and those which these may lead you to discover, which far exceed those to be found in a typical teaching setting. For your particular interests, which of the following is better: (a) two months off in the summer (of which you spend the first week "closing up" the classroom and getting stuff sorted away, the next three weeks recovering emotionally and psychologically so that you can be a normal person, and the last two weeks back at the school putting up bulletin boards and cutting out thirty little ducks that say "Quack, Quack, My name is _____") or (b) complete freedom to select the times of your own vacation. Or, perhaps you need to work on a typical reaction: in the words of one teacher, if you find you come back exhausted from your holidays, it means you need more practice at taking holidays.

A regular paycheque is nice (as long as that continues to be a reasonable likelihood in institutionalized education), but do you know many teachers who are really financially secure, not to mention wealthy? Have you any idea how much more income tax teachers pay than someone who runs their own business, can deduct more expenses so pays significantly less tax, and yet enjoys a much higher standard of living than teachers? Remember: when people suggest that a teacher's remuneration represents old fashioned value, they simply mean that teachers earn the same salary as they did several years ago!

What will limit your success, both in traditional teaching roles and in jobs where your teaching skills are applied in a less conventional manner, is your ambition, your perseverance, your interpersonal skills, your willingness to continue to learn and your willingness to commit effort toward your success, however you may choose to measure that. In life, one sage has said, "we take what we want and pay the price." Someone else said, "we tend to get what we want." What do you really, really want? Now figure out if you are willing to pay the price. You might pleasantly surprise yourself!

Here, then, are a few ideas, just to get the feelings of flexibility flowing freely. How about trying one of the following, or perhaps a combination or spin-off of one of these ideas?

Post-secondary Teaching Opportunities

Teaching at a university can be a rewarding opening. While teaching skills are (as you may know from bitter experience) not always valued as highly as scholarship, a master's level degree is often all that is required to get a foot in the door, at least part-time. If you have a reasonable list of publications in scholarly journals in your field, you will have a decided advantage and you may be able to get a tenure-track position with the understanding that you will commence doctoral studies (a nice way to do both at the same time).

Some universities allow even those with only honours level degrees to lecture in some first-year courses. The pay is good, and it looks great on a résumé!

Teaching in a Community College or College of Applied Arts and Technology is also a viable alternative. Colleges tend to look for experts in the field of study, above those with a teacher's license, but your teacher's training will strengthen your application. Again, it can be financially and emotionally rewarding, looks good on a C.V., and the instructional hours per week tend to be significantly fewer than in an elementary or secondary school, perhaps leaving time for you to continue studies to improve your qualifications.

> "Money is what you'd get on beautifully without, if only other people weren't so crazy about it."
> —*Margaret Chase Harriman*

There is another advantage to teaching in a post-secondary setting. W.C. Sellar's observation that "For every person wishing to teach there are thirty not wanting to be taught" applies somewhat less. Students who are paying tuition tend to be somewhat more inclined to participate in the teaching-learning process.

Although it is a personal opinion I cannot, in good faith, recommend pre-school teaching opportunities, though I will join you in proclaiming, to all who will listen, its absolute importance for society. Despite what our society says about valuing children, those who train or keep a boarding kennel for pets tend to be much more highly paid than those who teach in a pre-school or provide day-care for children. If, however, your idea of success is doing unappreciated work while attempting to support yourself in abject poverty, and you don't want to go to a third-world country to join Mother Theresa's Sisters of Charity, what can I say? That too will look good on your C.V. (either the pre-school teaching part or working with the nuns of the order founded by the late Mother Theresa).

"If you would be wealthy, think of saving as well as getting."
—*Benjamin Franklin*

Private Schools

Have you considered a private school? Depending upon the exclusivity of the school, you may find their requirements range up to doctoral degrees or as low as a regular bachelor's degree. You will also find the pay varies widely. One advantage: there tend to be fewer behaviour problems—when parents are pre-paying tuition, they tend not to want their child expelled part way through a term, so there is usually some additional home support. Also, private schools can get away with more stringent and intrusive codes of conduct than can a tax-supported school, which is supposed to meet the needs or whims of all, and thus can find itself pulled so many ways that its policies lose all direction. Often there is, and their customers demand, a very intense emphasis on academic achievement and/or "basic" skills acquisition, and they are less willing to tolerate anything which unnecessarily disrupts or detracts from this. That sort of support can be pleasant.

Have you thought about starting your own private school? If so, be aware that you can make a lot of money, but there are also a lot of regulations you need to be aware of, both to avoid being shut down and to avoid litigation: fire regulations, public building code, etc.

Tutoring

Tutoring may be a way to avoid much of the legalities of running a private school, although perhaps with the potential for lesser financial gain. It can also be a good option for you. It is a little bit unbelievable how much money you can make, and the opportunities are there to expand as much as you want. Another significant factor—you can choose your own caseload: (a) how many pupils you want to work with, and (b) you don't have to work with any that you find do not fit into your bounds of tolerance. Something to consider, whether advantageous or disadvantageous: most of this is evening and weekend work. Will it fit family obligations? While I know that money and the opportunity to be self-directed may not appeal to everyone, some find those to be factors they want to consider.

Skills Training

Perhaps you would enjoy driver training, either working for an established company or starting and building your own business. You will need extra certification, of course, from your province's or territory's Department or Ministry responsible for public transportation. I tried it for a while to supplement my beginning teacher's wage and, while it's not exactly relaxing, some people are really made for it, and enjoy it, and it requires excellent teaching skills!

Alternative Education and Training Systems

With the rise in "commercially available education packages," you might check to see if you can teach in a Kumon™-type school, or something like an Oxford

"I skate to where I think the puck will be."
—*Wayne Gretzky*

"There are obviously two educations. One should teach us how to make a living and the other how to live."

—*James Truslow Adams*

Learning Centre™ or work as a "consultant" for their clients.

Some "Learning Centres" do not require teaching qualifications of their instructors: it is attitude and willingness to learn that are the chief requirements. If you have those characteristics, however, and don't make them think you value your certificate so highly that you won't be willing to learn, you could have a chance there. You may, however, be paid substantially less than in positions which require teaching credentials.

How about working as a consultant to, or on-line help for, the clients of a satellite education supplier. These are becoming more plentiful and will take an increasing market share from conventional schools in the near future. Do you want to get into that field early?

There has been an exponential growth in "micro schools" in the past couple of years. These are where half a dozen or more (or fewer) parents who want something different than that available in regular public or separate schools join together to start a school to meet their expectations. You might be able to get a job as an educational consultant or a full-time or part-time instructor, assuming you fit their criteria, be it teaching style, religion, lifestyle, etc. There may also be opportunities to teach for specific cultural groups: cultural and language classes, for example.

Opportunities in a Field Related to the Education Field

Some educational publishers and suppliers like to have certified teachers as their sales representatives. Why not check that out. They do, however, tend to pay by commission. How confident do you feel?

How about teaching computer classes for one of the computer stores in your area. They are often pleased to find someone who has both the technical expertise and the ability to teach, if you have the knowledge to survive in that "knowledge society." This opportunity will open up as provincial governments continue to cut, or eliminate, funding of "Adult and Continuing Education."

Teaching Outside a School

Many boards provide home instruction for ill pupils—those who are unable to attend school because of injury or chronic illness. Check it out with your local school principal(s). Frequently, the principal is asked for recommendations, and if you are on the Occasional Teacher list, that is also an advantage.

You might like to work in a hospital. Some hospitals have a resident teacher to provide schooling to patients there. Some jails hire teachers to work with the inmates on upgrading or school completion. Again, this is usually organized through the local school authority; so check it out. It's something different!

Is there a company in your area which contracts with Employment Canada to provide upgrading or skills training? They may be hiring.

If you have a background in history, sometimes historical sites and theme parks want teachers to act as tour guides. Science Centres usually have teachers on permanent staff. Outdoor Education centres, programs and camps all like to hire teachers. Most Conservation Authorities and groups use the expertise of teachers.

"Instead of worrying about the future, let us labour to create it."

—*Hubert Humphrey*

I know one teacher who took early retirement and got a job "teaching" in the Human Resources Development department of a major manufacturing company. He loves it! Might this work for you, too?

Off-Shore Opportunities: Mixing Travel with Teaching

How about teaching out of Canada? Many countries, especially in the Pacific rim, welcome Canadian teachers for two reasons: they are well-trained, and they speak and can teach English. There is a lot of demand in some countries, notably Japan and even more especially Korea, right now. Also, some Middle East countries are very receptive to Canadian teachers. Although there are still some opportunities, the demand has decreased dramatically in China. It may resurrect, as the memory of Tiananmen Square continues to fade and even more open diplomatic relations are re-established.

Be aware, please, that sometimes other countries have cultural expectations regarding lifestyle very different than that to which we are accustomed. Such restrictions can Include what you wear, opportunity for sexual expression, what books or publications you can import into your home (including a ban on, and imprisonment or expulsion for possessing, those which they believe offer an insult to their religion or government), restrictions on alcohol consumption, etc. In some countries women, especially, are restricted in their activities and what they can do, what they can wear and where they can go, with or without a male escort. You may, for example, find it unusual to discover that in some countries, while your husband may hold another man's hand as he walks down the street, he cannot hold his wife's!

You may also want to determine how much or little impact your Canadian citizenship and embassy personnel might be able to have on a justice system very different than that to which you are accustomed and which you might deem to be somewhat arbitrary or summary in comparison to that of Canada. You may, however, find that their rather more direct justice systems provide an environment in which you are in many ways quite safe. Just check the murder statistics of Singapore, for example. One of my former staff taught there for a while and said she never felt in danger, no matter where she was and no matter the time of night. I read a piece on the web by one teacher in Korea who claims he could park his motorcycle and leave his helmet sitting on the seat, and it would be still there when he came back to it two days later!

You may want to decide whether you are prepared to live in an area where you will live on the seventh floor in a building with no elevator, or one elevator which you share with a thousand other people. If a "Stair-Climber" is your exercise machine of choice, then you might be right at home.

Perhaps in spite of, or perhaps because of, these differences in civilizations, there are wonderful opportunities to experience different cultures if you really like that. If getting "out and dirty" is not your idea of experience, however, you will miss much of what other areas have to offer. As James A. Michener said: "If you reject the food, ignore the customs, fear the religion and avoid the people, you might better stay home. You are like a pebble thrown into water; you become wet on the surface, but are never part of the water."

You will find that, politically correct or not, some countries seem to have a decided preference for younger people, and especially those unencumbered with spouse or family. Of course, that does not mean that if you don't fit that category you should not apply, but it may be more difficult. While that may seem strange, it is not our country, and they make the rules.

You may find that the pay is lower than you expect, but is the housing free? Is there a food allowance? Is the pay in Canadian or U.S. dollars? Consider the savings you will realize with the much lower income tax levels in many off-shore areas! Every dollar you save on income tax equals up to two dollars in additional

"I don't know what your destiny will be, but one thing I know. The only ones among you who will be really happy are those who have sought and found how to serve."
—*Albert Schweitzer*

"There is nothing either good or bad but thinking makes it so."
—*Shakespeare*

"Why are we in such desperate haste to succeed, and in such desperate enterprises? If a man does not keep pace with his companions, perhaps it is because he hears a different drummer. Let him step to the music which he hears, however measured or far away."

—*Henry David Thoreau*

income, depending upon your personal bracket!

Remember, as well, that as a "foreigner" you may have to earn the trust of both your neighbours and local authorities. Many North American tourists do not create the most favourable impression in the minds of their hosts. No one likes to have their customs and traditions described as "quaint" or "primitive." If you are diplomatic, and accustomed to keeping your opinions to yourself (responding to their questions about their land and customs in either a positive or a non-committal fashion), you will find yourself more readily accepted.

Before you go anywhere, check some Usenet groups on the internet to get real people's experiences; listen to those who have gone there! This is also a great place to find out the "hot hiring hits" for application and how/where to apply. Some embassies will also provide information about teaching opportunities in their country.

If you would like to teach children associated with a Canadian Embassy in a foreign country, contact the Canadian Department of External Affairs.

If you adhere to their beliefs and lifestyle, there are often teaching opportunities in church missions. The children of the medical missionaries, for example, need education. The pay is usually poor, but it's a way to experience a foreign country and have somewhere to live.

International schools look for good teachers. They offer excellent pay and an opportunity to work in some really exotic locations. These are private schools established to educate the children of (usually rich) expatriates working in a Third-World country. They usually operate in the English language and, while many follow American programs, quite a few follow, believe it or not, the Ontario curriculum! The pay and living conditions tend to be very good. If you are looking for just a little more refined or cosmopolitan adventure, while still living in an exotic location, check out this opportunity!

There are other less exotic opportunities which arise; you just need to follow the trends and get on while the opportunity you like is there. For example, in November of 1996, there was a major hiring-spree in California, and in January of 1997, there was an extraordinary shortage of teachers in the British Isles, as a result, apparently, of changing early-retirement opportunities there which created a sudden shortage of teachers. For these shifting opportunities, keep current with what's on the internet, maintain your contacts with other under-employed teachers, and another good resource is the Student Employment Centre at a Faculty of Education. They sometimes have exceptional leads.

Other Opportunities to Put Your Teaching Skills to Work

Completely outside of "education," as we normally think of it, is the idea of running a small business. When you think of it, though, your inter-personal and teaching skills are what will determine your success. In business you are teaching customers to need and want your product or service. You may well find that your emotional and financial rewards through this by far exceed what you would have received in the traditional teaching environment.

The training you received, your ability to inculcate by precept and example, and your ease with people can be a real benefit in running a "small business." One very unexpected area in which some teachers found their skills have put them in very good stead is in the field of network marketing. You might want to be careful to talk to teachers and others you know who have been in that particular field for a few years before getting involved, however. I know some former teachers who have done incredibly well financially, but remember that it takes a lot more,

"I've been rich and I've been poor. Believe me, rich is better."
—*Mae West*

consistent, hard, work and commitment than the "opportunity meetings" tend to suggest!

If you have a law degree, and know a foreign language, you might be able to get a job in "off-shore commerce," where your ability to explain concepts to others will be valued. If you are an I.T. whiz and there are no major concerns with your abilities or background, as mentioned earlier in this book you will probably already have a job, but you might want to consider something like an information systems specialist. If your background is accounting, your teaching skills can be a significant advantage in some jobs.

How about working for the Canadian National Institute for the Blind (with additional training), or the Canadian Mental Health Association (if you have a background in psychology), or the Addiction Research Foundation (with a background in psychology or sociology), or the Public Health Unit (if you have a degree in life sciences)? The trick is to let the ideas flow—this whole thing requires several paradigm shifts!

Personality-Types and Career Selection

Something you might find useful is a Myers-Briggs Personality Type analysis. This might help you to identify other, related, areas of employment where your character type pre-disposes you to success. This is considered a reliable and very valid test. You can have this assessment done by some psychologists. There are also some very good books about it on the self-help market. The best one, in my opinion, is *Please Understand Me*, by David Keirsey and Marilyn Bates (Del Mar: Prometheus Nemesis, 1984). It contains a self-assessment format and gives very extensive descriptions and insights into the sixteen character and temperament types. For a more theoretical background, see *Gifts Differing* by Isabel Briggs Myers and Peter B. Myers. A very practical and applicable book on the topic of relating career to "type" is *Do What You Are*, by Paul D. Tieger In this one, he focuses in on each of the types (you would do better to know yours beforehand—he's not as clear on this as Keirsey & Bates) and discusses some very creative directions in which you could go and succeed.

Summary

Teachers tend to be intelligent and, by definition, one measure of intelligence involves "adaptability." If you weren't in the top quarter of the population in intelligence you would not have come this far, so don't hesitate to show what you've got! Any of the above may be good for your particular personality and skills set, and each would, in the final analysis, look good on a résumé!

And remember: no matter what you do, serendipity is often more useful than perspicacity and can always later be claimed to be the latter. Your applied intelligence, if mixed with persistence, will make you survive and thrive.

Congratulations! You now know how to get onto the "inside track" or, if you prefer, onto "another track." You can do it!

"When one door closes another door opens; but we so often look so long and so regretfully upon the closed door that we do not see the ones which open for us."
—*Alexander Graham Bell*

"Honest criticism is hard to take, especially from a relative, a friend, an acquaintance or a stranger."
—*Franklin P. Jones*

APPENDIX 13

HOMEWORK IDEAS FOR KINDERGARTEN PUPILS

"The spirit and sense so easily grow dead to the impressions of the beautiful and the perfect that one ought every day to hear a little song, read a good poem, see a good picture and, if it were possible, speak a few reasonable words."

—Johann Wolfgang von Goethe

The following may be of use to you in preparing answers to questions about "homework in the early school years," for either during an interview, or when you have been teaching a while. It may even be a handy start on a newsletter! It is modified and expanded from an article by Dr. Beverly Dexter of Honolulu.

HOMEWORK!!!

Parents of kindergarten and grade one children frequently ask teachers for "homework," expecting that they will receive "extra" assignments similar to that being taught and done in class. Then, when this work isn't done—though it was not even going to be assigned if it hadn't been specifically requested—a struggle develops between child and teacher or child and family or family and teacher. The parents also often become upset if it isn't corrected immediately. The result is frustration on the part of pupil, parent and teacher, and "homework" develops a negative flavour right at the beginning of a child's educational career!

Is there a better way? Perhaps we should consider that—especially for the young child—homework which increases the understanding of early concepts and skills can be work which is (or could be) done in the home as part of the regular family routines! These learning opportunities and activities can reinforce the skills and concepts which the school is teaching and can be more real-world-oriented. The following are, also, activities which the child may be performing life-long, and which have the added benefit of developing an attitude of "mutual support in the family"—an important concept in its own right.

DUTIES/CHORES	RELATED SKILLS/CONCEPTS/ATTITUDES
1. Sorting laundry: putting groups of sorted clothes in the washer, dryer, dresser drawers, closets	1. Likenesses, differences, organization, self-sufficiency, repetition of routine
2. Setting the table	2. Sequencing, organization, pattern repetition, responsibility.
3. Planning meals or snacks for themselves or whole family	3. Sequencing, organization, problem solving, supply and demand, measurement, decision-making
4. Scheduling special jobs on certain days and doing other jobs to be ready: emptying wastebaskets the night before taking out garbage, laundry collection before wash-day	4. Responsibility, organization, sequencing, planning, time management
5. Tracing, colouring, cutting, pasting, using staplers and other simple tools	5. Fine motor skill development, sequencing
6. Doing daily chores (making bed, putting dirty clothes in hamper, vacuuming)	6. Responsibility, budgeting time, setting priorities
7. Dressing self, tying laces, buttoning, opening and closing zippers	7. Fine motor control, self-reliance, decision-making
8. Setting aside and organizing recyclables	8. Sorting, problem-solving, sensitivity to environmental issues, increase in awareness of relationships in nature
9. Choosing TV shows from among pre-approved ones	9. Decision making, setting priorities, development of cultural and spiritual values, media-literacy

DUTIES/CHORES	RELATED SKILLS/CONCEPTS/ATTITUDES
10. Retelling sequence of events and main ideas from selected stories or shows.	10. Sequencing, finding the main idea, attention span, para-phrasing
11. Conveying messages from one family member to another	11. Memory, auditory processing, reliability and responsibility
12. Computer games	12. Fine-motor development, attention span, problem-solving, analyzing
13. Internet surfing	13. Forward and backward chaining, general knowledge, decision making, keyboarding, research, recording main idea, information processing.
14. Following simple directions or requests such as: "please close the door"	14. Social co-operation, auditory processing
15. Reading signs and print on grocery bags, etc.	15. Reading, literacy skills
16. Banking with savings account	16. Money management, understanding of banking process, writing (deposit slips), math
17. Making a "TV Guide" of favourite programs	17. Decision-making, analyzing, synthesizing, evaluating, writing/keyboarding
18. Making a calendar of jobs, broken down into days, weeks, months, and associating days with specific jobs, events	18. Sequencing, association, organization, setting priorities
19. Keeping a diary, journal, or log	19. Language, composition, handwriting/keyboarding, organization
20. Letter writing to pen pals, grandparents, relatives or friends who have moved, also "Thank You" notes (can begin with a picture and adult transcribes "note")	20. Language, writing, organization, manners, appropriate expression of appreciation
21. Checking the newspaper for sales or bargains when planning meals or shopping trips	21. Decision-making, organization, budgeting, conservation of resources, money management
22. Reading cartoons or books to younger siblings.	22. Reading, sequencing, interpretation
23. Summarizing sports events—live, on TV, or in newspapers, magazines	23. Sequencing, organization, comprehension, less/more
24. Examining maps and checking weather reports in other geographic areas, where friends live or in connection with travel plans	24. Map reading, comprehension, natural sciences
25. Packing own suitcase for a trip	25. Predicting, setting priorities, estimation, sequencing, self-reliance
26. Taking imaginary trips (transportation? clothing? cost? sights? weather? when? route? why go there?)	26. Organization, decision-making, time, geography, social issues, general knowledge, analysis, synthesis, evaluation.
27. Making a "travelogue" from newspapers, magazines, photographs	27. Organization, decision-making, societal awareness
28. Making a scrapbook related to a hobby, theme, sport or putting cartoon strip frames in sequence	28. Decision-making, on task behaviour, organization, fine-motor co-ordination
29. Putting together a booklet of food groups (likes and dislikes, food for special meals or parties)	29. Organization, decision-making, fine-motor co-ordination, evaluating
30. Playing card games, keeping score	30. Attention span, math facts, following rules, decision-making
31. Playing board games (check reading level required and rule explanations)	31. Attention span, decision-making, reading comprehension, strategy planning, problem-solving
32. Going for walks or rides and looking for specific categories of objects, such as birds, flowers, house numbers	32. Memory, organization, generalization, differentiating, physical development, observation, categorization

DUTIES/CHORES	RELATED SKILLS/CONCEPTS/ATTITUDES
33. Preparing a shopping list in order of store layout (based on earlier visit to make notes or drawings of general locations of merchandise)	33. Organization, sequencing, analyzing, synthesizing
34. Making a map or drawing of shopping mall, school, or neighbourhood	34. Organization, spatial awareness, problem-solving decision-making, fine-motor co-ordination, map skills
35. Keeping a file of "cents-off" coupons (alphabetize, figure out savings, keep money saved)	35. Sequencing, math facts, decision-making, reading, percentages, money management, budgeting, research/dictionary skills
36. Keeping track of allowance or money earned from odd jobs	36. Money management, writing, budgeting, decision-making, math, analysis, evaluation
37. Reading newspaper columns, magazine articles, or books on barter, budgeting and refunding	37. Reading comprehension, media literacy, social issues, budgeting, money management
38. Comparing prices of similar or same articles in different stores while shopping	38. Organization, decision-making, math facts, analysis, evaluation
39. Making a list of which stores carry certain articles that are frequently purchased	39. Organization, sorting, combining, handwriting
40. Obtaining a street map from Chamber of Commerce, and plotting colour-coded routes to school, shopping areas, other places frequently visited	40. Map reading, fine-motor co-ordination, geometry, measurement
41. Planning a pretend shopping spree with a set amount of money to spend	41. Decision-making, math facts, analysis, evaluation
42. Visiting library, with younger sibling (help select books, read to sibling)	42. Responsibility, decision-making, reading
43. Marking calendar with special holidays, birthdays	43. Sequencing, handwriting
44. Putting dishes and cutlery away after washing	44. Likeness, difference, sorting, organization
45. Cleaning mirrors, sweeping floor	45. Perseverance, thoroughness, intrinsic reward
46. Keeping a scrap-book of family or school events and memorabilia	46. Responsibility, history, decision-making, organization, priority-setting, fine-motor skills

Adapted from work by Beverly L Dexter, formerly with the Faculty of Education, Lynchburg College.

APPENDIX 14

WORKING WITH AN EDUCATION ASSISTANT / CLASSROOM ASSISTANT

Educational Assistants or Classroom Assistants are not parent or community volunteers, but trained para-professionals, hired to work in a classroom, with and under the direct supervision of a teacher. Their work will likely be predominantly with one or more exceptional pupils, in a classroom where there are several exceptional needs, or where there is an "overload" situation. ("Overloads" tend to occur especially in rural schools, for early grades, where there are too many pupils for one class, but not enough for two, and it is too far to transport the young children to the next nearest school—then an E.A. is hired to assist the teacher.) This section is based on my working with E.A.s while I was a teacher and, since then, my dealing with many of them in both my role as a principal and while teaching in the certification program for E.A.s at college.

Working with an E.A. can be an great opportunity for change and professional growth in your career, or something less, depending largely upon you, the teacher. Like teachers as a group, most E.A.s are caring, dedicated and skilled. Also like teachers, they have feelings. As in any other human relationship, that is the area most likely to cause grief, but it can also be the source of greatest satisfaction. (I know of two teachers who have been very close friends for many years, who got to know each other when one was an E.A. in the other's class.)

So, if you have been assigned to a room where there will be an E.A., what do you do? There are quite a few Dos and Don'ts, but the first "don't" is, don't be overwhelmed, including by this list!

First, and foremost, much of what will make the relationship a positive one is simple, old-fashioned respect. The document which the N.W.T. used to give to teachers who came from the south, to advise and help them to work effectively with the aboriginal "Teacher's Assistants" who were assigned to the classrooms to help the pupils and the teacher adapt to each others' cultures, included a very interesting bit of advice: "Make up for their lower pay and perceived lower status with a LOT of respect and courtesy." Ignoring, for the present, the fact that respect and courtesy do not buy groceries, it still doesn't hurt to remember that we all like to be treated with dignity.

The role of the E.A. is not the same as that of the teacher. Professionally, your job description and level of accountability are different. In fact, many Assistants have chosen not to become teachers just because they don't want the additional aggravation and stress that come with the higher pay and higher accountability. In some ways they are similar to a student-teacher, except that while some of them do look ahead to going on to earn a teaching license, many of them don't and are quite satisfied with the role of being an excellent E.A.

Remember, though, that just as a teacher has a different role and different pay and different responsibilities than a principal, and still most teachers want to be included and treated professionally and kept informed, so do most E.A.s. It's a matter of consideration and courtesy.

The second issue is roles clarification. What do you expect? What level of initiative do you expect them to exercise? What is their training/background? This may well be a determining factor in your decision. What do they see as their role? Ask them! How much will you micro-manage? Don't be afraid to ask their advice:

"You can observe a lot by just watching."
—*Yogi Berra*

"Nobody ever listened himself
out of a job."
—*Calvin Coolidge*

they may know a whole lot more about g-tube feeding or other medical procedures than you do. Don't be afraid to take advantage of their talents. Are they particularly artistic? Would they like to do some (or all?) of the bulletin boards? That could free you up to do some other things. Do they have a lot of computer experience? If you discuss with them the objectives of the activity, could they help you by using their experience and knowledge to select appropriate programs for your pupils? Everyone wants to be needed and important—tap into their aptitude.

You will need to take the lead in working out with them an understanding around your expectations, both of them and of the classroom. While you will probably want to be open to their suggestions, and ask in advance something like "What would you most like to do in your job here this year?", you also need them to know your priorities. What are the rules of your classroom? How do you want them involved in enforcing them? At what point do you want them to intervene in an emerging situation (for example, off-task behaviour in a pupil who is not their primary responsibility)? How do you want them to deal with parents who "drop in" and want to ask questions? Don't make the assistant have to read your mind. Discuss these things openly with them. There will be two adults in the classroom this year. Teamwork and communication will be absolutely vital.

You also need to communicate to them your own personal foibles. Are you a "neat freak," or would you appreciate it if they "sort of straighten up the shelves now and again?" Do you like to chat about pupils' progress after they get on the bus, or do you need five minutes of "down time" to recharge your batteries? Do you have a particular concern about how parents are approached about their child's behaviour?

If there is a concern about their performance, or worse yet, they have done something that you believe undermines you or the employer, you need to address it early in the relationship. Don't let it continue until there is a crisis, and don't allow yourself to fall into the trap of passive-aggressive behaviour. Expecting the E.A. to read your mind and guess what the concern is would only poison the atmosphere of the classroom without really communicating the nature of the problem and how to correct it.

If the problem persists, you will have to take it up the line to the vice-principal and/or principal, but before that happens you need to go through the intervening levels of intervention. And, all of those therapists aren't always wrong: it's surprising how often the situation will be corrected through simple, clear, direct, respectful communication. And if that doesn't solve the problem, you won't waste energy wishing "If only I had…"

What is their job description? Have they been given one? If so, what is it? Especially if you are fairly new to your career, you don't want to contravene policy, or get into a grievance with their union or yours. How much responsibility do they want? How much can you legally give them? Discuss it, but be consistent: if they cannot assume professional responsibility such as working in another room without your direct supervision when they want to, don't assign them supervision duties when it is convenient for you. How do you define "teaching"? While one teacher may welcome ideas on how a lesson can be reinforced or applied with a specific group of pupils, another may see that as an intrusion into their area of responsibility. Let the E.A. know how much initiative and autonomy you want them to have. And be aware that you may find yourself more suddenly feeling being intruded upon than you might imagine. We are all quite protective of our right to run our own classroom. And that's okay as long as you are aware of it and communicate it to your Assistant.

"A community is like a ship.
Everyone ought to be prepared
to take the helm."
—*Henrik Ibsen*

Below is a list of some of the things an E.A. can do to as a team member to support you, the children and the program. Don't overload or impose on them, but don't waste human talent and paid human resources by under-utilizing them.

The third issue is inclusion. One sage pointed out that everyone wants equality, but only with those above. While none of us wants to be in the pocket of our supervisors, it is nice to be included as an equal at least in our humanness.

If they pay into the school's social fund, do they get equal benefit? Are they invited to staff events? Staff meetings? Do they get a "going-away" party when they are transferred? Their involvement in after-school meetings needs to be with the principal's support, but if they would like to be invited, you can help by being an intermediary for them. Of course, after-school events have to be optional: they are hourly employees, and when their shift is over, they have a right to leave. That's why you need to be so careful if you invite them to stay into the evening to meet with you, or to help with classroom preparation, or to come in on the weekend to discuss program. Unlike for you, these are not considered "working hours." They might want to "share" in planning with you and other additional aspects and duties of the job, but don't expect it of them.

On a similar topic, do you want them to sit in on parent interviews? For all the kids, or just the one or two they work with most directly? How do they feel about it? Have you clarified the roles each of you will play in the interview? Did you mention on the report card that they work with the child, and have a role in the child's amazing progress that year?

Is there a reason the classroom is not recognized as having two staff members? While it is important that all communication with parents go through you, or at least have your stamp of approval (you are legally responsible for the program and activities in your room) can your newsletters be signed by both you and the E.A.? Are you non-traditional enough to even have their name with yours on the door?

Duties of Classroom Assistants

Now, let's look at what is your responsibility. 1) It is your job to diagnose pupils' needs, and design—or prescribe—a program to meet the needs of each child in your classroom, regardless of their exceptionality. Of course, an E.A. can help you with this, and advise, and help locate resources, but it is ultimately your responsibility. 2) It is your duty to manage the human and material resources available to you, and to assign them in a way that will achieve optimal benefit to the classroom and school. 3) It is your mandate to assess the effectiveness of the program, to modify the program as appropriate, and to report to the parents (or pupil if the pupil is an adult) at specific times during the school year—that means, specifically, do the report cards.

Some of the areas in which Assistants can support your classroom include child care, teaching assistance, data keeping, clerical work, health care, and perhaps others, depending upon specific circumstances. (If in doubt, discuss your plan with your principal.)

Included in the category of child care can be such things as:

- lifting or positioning children into specialized equipment such as chairs, standing boards, etc.
- helping children with special needs cope on field trips or during physical education classes or at recess
- helping supervise them on the yard (in addition to the regular teacher supervisors) or at lunch-time

"To be doing good is man's most glorious task."
—*Sophocles*

- helping supervise children during rest time
- helping pupils navigate around the school (especially if they have a physical or developmental disability)
- providing direct assistance in toiletting, including changing diapers on children who are not toilet trained
- helping children with personal hygiene, including helping them wash, brush their teeth, bathe, etc., whether part of an instructional program or a result of incapabilities in self-care
- helping children in and out of outdoor clothing, including helping them develop and refine independent dressing skills (most people have no idea how similar 40 mitts can look, or how long it takes to do up 20 coat zippers)
- feeding children, or helping them with their lunches, or implementing a feeding program
- meeting children at the bus or taxi and helping them off or on

Included in the category of teaching assistance can be such things as:

- providing immediate feedback so that a pupil doesn't do a whole assignment incorrectly
- checking that pupils have completed required work before moving on to an optional or secondary activity
- keeping pupils on-task
- providing additional instructions to a child who is having difficulty following instructions, or helping them get started
- translating teacher's instructions or pupil's responses into or from Braille, Bliss or sign language
- helping a child develop or refine Braille, Bliss or sign language skills
- supervising a group activity so the teacher can work with a single child or another small group
- supervising pupils at an activity centre
- supervising other children in the class so the teacher can do observations or individual testing
- listening to children read
- supervising them while they practice music or drama activities
- helping children participate in physical education activities and complex games, and helping them learn the rules of games
- helping children use computers, scanners, micro-fiche machines
- reinforcing activities provided by a therapist or specialized teacher
- helping pupils use teaching materials
- monitoring and helping children learn to use socially acceptable behaviour
- reinforcing behavioural skills: providing immediate reward for meeting expected behaviour, and maintaining continuity of expectation when the teacher is otherwise occupied
- supervising play, and helping children learn to play co-operatively
- playing games with the children (rhyming games, guessing games, finger plays, flash card games) to reinforce skills taught in the classroom
- reinforcing school rules
- working with the children to ensure that skills are transferred to new situations

"That which is used develops, and that which is not used wastes away."
—*Hippocrates*

- helping in implementing Life Skills programs, including community activities such as bus training, locating job-placement sites, and reinforcing on-job training

Included in the category of data keeping can be such things as:

- continuous and event-recording of behaviours
- noting and recording antecedent and consequential behaviours
- tallying
- daily reporting to parents (home-school communication books), especially in the case of children whose behaviour is being closely monitored, or when children are non-verbal
- calculation of averages, totals, percentages
- marking objective assignments or tests (where subjective evaluation is not required)
- maintaining records of individual pupil progress, including marks, and keeping work-sample folders up-to-date
- attending, contributing to, and keeping record of case conferences, I.E.P meetings, Placement and Review Meetings, etc.

Included in the category of clerical work can be such things as:

- preparing materials for use by the class or individual pupils
- modifying materials for exceptional pupils
- getting materials ready for a pupil's day
- helping with displays and bulletin boards
- helping young children place their name on all their work and belongings
- getting materials and work ready to be sent home
- operating specialized equipment such as sound systems, VCR's, etc.
- doing the logistical background work to arrange field trips, etc.

Included in the category of health care can be such things as:

- maintaining proper positioning as recommended by a therapist or doctor, and monitoring skin for pressure sores or pre-necrotic conditions
- implementing daily therapy programs as prescribed by a speech-, behavioural-, occupational- or physio-therapist
- maintaining specialized equipment: chairs, braces, etc.
- fitting such equipment as braces, splints, etc. onto a child
- doing or maintaining approved intrusive procedures (for which they have been trained and are under the supervision of a health-care professional) such as catheterization, g-tube feeding, tracheostomy care, etc.
- dispensing prescribed medication within the provisions of local board policy
- documenting all health-care procedures

(Note: the above list is expanded and adapted from documentation of the former Nipissing Board of Education.)

NOTE: As you can see, a paid Assistant can be a real help in your classroom. Just make sure you both understand their role and how they will fulfil it, and keep the lines of communication open, and—trust me—you will soon wonder how you got along without their help!

APPENDIX 15

ELECTRONIC FACTORS IN THE APPLICATION PROCESS

With computers in schools, how long could it be before board offices would catch up? The Communication Age has hit educational administration, and one of the results is the vastly increased use of I.T. in teacher applicant screening and hiring policies and procedures.

I.T. in the hiring process can range from allowing applications to be faxed, to electronic screening using OCR, to scannable forms or checklists, to posting job openings on their web site, to the ATTN electronic application system, which is in process of becoming available across Canada. Remember, each of these options fits one of three categories for those who are involved in the hiring process: a new help in doing their job and a method to be embraced, a new toy to be played with and tinkered with and revised continually, or something scary, close to black magic, and to be avoided at all cost. Fortunately, most dinosaur principals, and heads of HR departments, have retired in the past two or three years, are retiring, or are living out the Peter Principle and are merely a blip of roadkill on the information highway. I.T. is now here to stay and is incorporated to varying degrees in almost all areas of Canada. Now let's look at some guidelines, some things to avoid and some things not to be missed.

Fax-related Issues

First, a little more about fax protocol than was addressed earlier in this book. Try to remember not to fax coloured paper, especially dark-coloured. It reproduces very poorly; the colour differentiation on most fax machines, both the encoder and the decoder, is significantly below that of your average photocopier, so the result is almost illegible. Not a good start. Secondly, it feeds exceedingly slowly, as each pixel in the dark background is read by the photosensors. I recently received an 18-page document from a government agency that took 23 minutes to grind its way through the fax machine—effectively preventing out-going use for the duration. (Then they followed it up with the hard copy, in the mail, on a lovely goldenrod paper.)

E-mail-related Issues

If you e-mail your application (and then only if they invite that method of transmission) be certain to use a readily available file format, or attach it in several separate formats, with the formats labelled clearly, or best—and simplest—ask them what format they want it in. Is the Board you are applying to standardized on Office 95™ or 98? Can they open a file in an inexpensive (and obscure) format like Chi-writer™? If they use WordPerfect™, you might want to translate it at your end and check for formatting difficulties—much of the formatting that you have carefully attended to can be lost in translation. That way you can correct it before you send it, instead of letting them open your WORD file on their WP software. (This is especially the case if you are using a version more than two years old, or the very latest release.)

Scanning- and OCR-related Issues

Next, let's look at scannable documents. Optical Character Recognition (OCR) programs have, like any other aspect of I.T., made stupendous advances in the past five years. They are no longer the hit and miss software they used to be, but there are a few rules that you might want to keep in mind to ensure that your C.V. is read accurately. For example, if their posting asks for someone with extensive experience in "program," be certain your documentation doesn't refer

"The real danger is not that computers will begin to think like men, but that men will begin to think like computers."
—*Sydney Harris*

238

to your experience with "programme." They may not have entered the alternate spelling into the search string, and your application would thus be rejected. Similarly, if they are looking for a "co-ordinator," you don't want to apply for the "coordinator" position. Make it easy on them, and their software and programmers—use their spelling. Like the Canadian psyche, which pop psychologists tell us is somewhere in the middle in all categories of everything, our spelling seems caught between British and American. If they are using British spelling, you might want to stick to that (colour, programme, neighbour, paediatrician, standardized, and so on). Similarly if they have moved to American spelling, you can drop the additional letters, etc. (And don't even get going on why "reign" is spelled that way!) Pick out key words in the posting, and make very sure you include exactly those words in your application. It would be neither "humourous" nor "humorous" to miss an opportunity because of this little oversight.

A few more random points to consdier to keep your application on the "inside track" as it is being electronically scanned:

- heed the advice about envelope size: folded applications tend to jam in auto-loading machines. Don't use staples, for the same reason.
- Use commonly recongized fonts: Times, Courier, Helvetica. Avoid non-standard fonts, such as scripts or decorative types, even for titles. Keep font size above 9. Also avoid underlining, italics, bolding, shadows or white-on-black. These can play havoc with an OCR program. For titles or headings, you can use all-caps.
- Avoid the temptation to get fancy with your formatting. Don't reduce line spacing, or letter spacing, or use vertical lines, boxes or columns.
- Be certain to use plain white, 8½ x 11 paper.
- Print on one side only.
- Make sure you are using a good, clear printer, proferably a laser or high-end ink-jet.

Electronic Posting and Application Services

One of the most exciting electronic developments in the whole job search/hiring process to date is the move to electronic/web-based posting and application services. This is a whole new way of doing business, and depending upon which service you use, it may be you, the applicant, or the advertising board who gets the service free. Be aware, though, that you might want to find out which one is used by the boards in your area of search. There is a slight possibility that, while the free-to-applicants service is more appealing to candidates, the free-to-boards one may be more appealing to boards.

Two of the most popular are the ATTN (**Apply to Teach Network**) and the Education Canada network. The ATTN was developed through a strategic alliance among Industry Canada's Schoolnet and a variety of other partners. An online teacher application centre, and much more, started in Ontario, but is developing, expanding and spreading Canada-wide, as you read this! Among the services it provides teacher candidates are:

- a method for relatively low cost, direct application to multiple boards and private schools
- reasonably detailed direction on filling out the data fields, and opportunity to e-mail them with specific questions. It walks you through the process to make sure your ATTN application is complete.
- very current updates on which boards are hiring and in what fields

SHORT CAN BE GOOD

"All the great things are simple, and many can be expressed in a single word: Freedom; justice; honour; duty; mercy; hope."
—*Sir Winston Churchill*

- the opportunity for you to update your package at any time, to match changing opportunity demographics
- free e-mail service, if you don't already have an account
- direct e-mail links to the boards and private schools who are hiring
- direct e-mail links from hiring principals to you
- extensive advice on how to refine your application data
- perhaps most important of all, search capabilities for both you and the boards, to facilitate matches. You can do a search on what is available, and they can do a search for teachers whose qualifications match what they are looking for. (ATTN statistics show that the advertising boards use the database search feature more frequently than they use the job postings feature.)
- a newsletter for subscribers filled with current information, and features such as a "featured Internet site of the month" relevant to teachers.

The one downside is that there is some, but relatively little, opportunity for you to express your individuality: how you are unique, and how your experience has made you so. As a database it is intrinsically somewhat non-personal.

Interested? It's web URL is <www.attn.org> and from there it is very user-friendly, including e-mail links for on-line registration and electronic payment of fee, or help, or more information. Well worth checking out!

And, yes, you will still need a complete C.V. and application package (cover letter, etc.), for two reasons. Before you make it to the short list, or before you are interviewed, it is likely that you will be required to provide one, and secondly, preparing a C.V. will be of inestimable value in helping you to organize your career path in your mind, so that you can answer interview questions cogently.

You may also consider preparing a highly condensed version of your C.V., of two pages only—as they may well ask for that, specifically—into which you will carefully incorporate 10 to 15 key words related to their search string. Sound like a lot of work? Not if you are particular about the type of teaching job you want. It's an investment in something really important—your future.

The **Education Canada Network** <www.educationcanada.com> results from a partnership among B.C.-based Columbus Communications, the Ontario Public Supervisory Officials Association and the Canadian Association of School Administrators. Like the ATTN, it started in Ontario, but its spread across Canada has been rapid. It offers most of the benefits of the ATTN, above, as well as the opportunity for teachers to post, edit, renew or delete their C.V. from their site *at no charge!* (Boards using the service pay a fee.) It, too, is very well designed and user-friendly, and guides the user through its workings in both official languages. You can browse or do a specific search based upon specific areas of each province and territory, or other criteria. It is definitely worth a look, and one more benefit to being I.T. literate! Remember, though, the comment on this site that "résumés in the ECN are only a brief outline of your qualifications and background. Should you be contacted by an employer, you may well be ask[ed] to provide more information as required by that particular employer." Again, a full résumé is in order.

"We must always change, renew, rejuvenate ourselves; otherwise we harden."
—*Johann Wolfgang von Goethe*

Technology is speeding, and in some ways simplifying, the process, but it is not replacing the process. Being aware of the I.T. trend, however, and using it to your best advantage will be a decided asset to you in getting hired to the exact job you want, whether you are just starting your career as a teacher, are experienced and want a move within Canada, are looking to move to Canada, or are a Canadian teacher who has gone off-shore during the years of teacher surplus, and have decided that now is the time you want to come back home. Whoever you are, welcome to electronic application and communication!

APPENDIX 16

A FEW WEB SITES OF INTEREST TO TEACHERS

With the exponential growth of the Internet, it is impossible to keep track of the education-related sites, but below are a few that might be interesting and may get you interested in browsing to broaden and deepen your information and idea base.

Be aware, too, that there are companies that, for a fee, will provide you with web URLs that might interest you, but a good search engine will often do almost as well. You might also ask if getting a list of several hundred new sites a month will result in you having to, essentially, do a search among the recommended sites. Speaking of search engines, Alta vista <www.altavista.digital.com> is my personal favourite. Because of the actual method it uses to conduct a search (scanning the whole site, and its capability with Boolean methodology) it seems to work best for me. You may find another, such as Yahoo, that is more aligned with how your brain works. The intention of this little appendix is only to encourage teachers who have never done so to try accessing the Internet to get school-related sites.

- <www.askanexpert.com/> will give you a list of experts in very interesting and varied fields to "interview" on-line.
- <www.ajkids.com> otherwise known as "Ask Jeeves," is a search engine especially for kids.
- <www.clo.com/~canadainfo> provides a wealth of information about Canada.
- <www.cmec.ca> will take you to the Council of Ministers of Education, Canada. This is the group that brings together the education ministers from across Canada to discuss issues of mutual concern. The site contains press releases, links, and other useful stuff.
- <www.ctf.fce.ca> takes you to the Canadian Teachers' Federation. Useful for union-related background information.
- <http://curry.edschool.virginia.edu/go/frog/menu.html> will prevent you from having to bring frogs into class to disect!
- <www.ed.gov/databases/ERIC_Digests/index/> takes you to the ERIC Digest of educational research.
- <www.eduplace.com/ss/history/index/html> gets you the Houghton Mifflin History Update pages.
- <www.en.eun.org> is the European schoolnet equivalent.
- <freeweb.pdq.net/head-strong> will take you to interesting do-it-at-home science experiments and demonstrations. All safe, but exciting for the Primary-aged child.
- <www.geocities.com/Athens/Oracle/8314/currgrid.htm> will bring you good curriculum tracking templates for K-8 Ontario curriculum, if you happen to be in that province.
- <www.historychannel.com> is a good site, and if you like the "what happened in history on this date" sort of thing, go to <www.historychannel.com/tdih/tdih.html>.

"The organization capable of continuous renewal is interested in what it is going to become; and not what it has been."
—*John W. Gardner*

- <www.letsfindout.com> provides a good spot for children to start searching, and has information interesting enough to whet their appetite on everything from dinosaurs to dragonflies.
- <www.oise.utoronot.ca/~mpress/eduweb.html> will get you a site called "Canadian Education on the Web" with a lot of good links.
- <www.pdkintl.org/kappan/kappan/htm> is the site for Phi Delta Kappa. Worth a look for teachers who are thinking about being a school leader.
- <www.schoolnet.ca> is a site educators owe it to themselves to check out. This is the absolute "mother-lode." Great links. A teacher-oriented search engine (by grade, subject, key words, etc.). A Canadian focus, with international information as well. A "one-stop-shopping" site!
- <www.startribune.com/stonline/html/special/homework> is a site on which volunteers will help students with their searching. Just leave a message or question, and you can get help with that project!
- <http://tommy.jsc.nasa.gov/~woodfill/SPACEED/SEHHTML/she.html> will get you the same sort of "calendar" on space-related events, as well as other good resources.

"Never give up. Never, never give up."
—*The seven words spoken by Winston Churchill when invited to speak about the most important lesson he had learned in his long life. He then sat down.*

Check out other web sites of interest to teachers at:
www.thompsonbooks.com/insidetrack

APPENDIX 17

READING PRACTICE

Teachers of children in the early grades frequently have difficulty convincing parents that reading at home is important. If you think a letter like this might help, why not incorporate it into one of your own?

DEVELOPING READING SKILLS AT HOME

Dear Parents:

You may be one of the many parents who ask teachers what they can do to help their child learn to read or to be a more fluent reader. Reading is an extremely complex process. That most of us actually master it is a bit of a wonder. Fortunately, however, in all but a few cases, it is very simple to help children improve reading, although it does take time and commitment.

What is taught in school fits into one of two categories: skills and concepts. (Some will justifiably argue that we also teach attitudes, but as attitudes are taught through skills and/or concepts, and can be measured only through performance demonstrating acquisition of a skill or concept, I'm sticking to the two, for now.) Concepts are taught through use of examples and non-examples: this is a table, while that is not; this is an example of erosion by water, while that is not; this is an acceptable response to a particular situation, while that is not; etc., etc. (and then we discuss why and why not and how to differentiate and generalize within the categories).

Skills, however, are taught through practice. While it is true that there are concepts involved in learning to read, fluid and fluent reading is accomplished only through practice. Reading is a skill.

So, what can families do to ensure the successful achievement of this skill? What would you do if you wanted your child to acquire the skills necessary to be a good hockey player? To use silly examples to illustrate, would you have them skate only once a week, and only for fifteen minutes, or would you encourage them to skate every day? Would you try to provide a little rink so they could wander out to it any time they wanted to? Would you provide them with good books and magazines on hockey to stimulate their interest? Would you take them to hockey games? Play with them? Let them see you skate so they know you care about it and value good skating, and enjoy it? Have them practise? Of course you would.

Would you encourage them to actually skate and play hockey, or to just play video-hockey? (After all, they will maintain that it's all hockey, isn't it?) Do you believe that watching a monitor will help a child improve a skill? Of course not. Because they can watch TV well, will they be able to read well? Of course not. But both involve language, don't they? Yes, but so does swearing, and that doesn't help develop reading skills either.

Obviously, the best way to help them improve reading is to have them practise reading. A whole lot. Have them read to you. Read to them. (This helps with motivation, but does not replace reading to themselves or to you.) Make sure there are books they find interesting around the house. As they have only a few words per page, and are intrinsically rewarding (funny), cartoon books can really help catch the interest of a "reluctant reader," especially if the TV is kept off limits for a while! And have them read more. How many hours a week does Tiger Woods spend practising? How many hours did Wayne Gretzky spend each week? And they are already really good!

I suspect that I have achieved over-kill on this, but please allow me to remind you: while it's exciting, it can be frustrating watching a child as they begin to acquire any skill. Very few keep the ball in the fairway when they start to golf, and very few can cut perfect circles the first time they lace up skates, and when a child is just learning to throw a basketball, most of the time is spent chasing the ball (which managed to miss the whole backboard!). Just so, it can be a slow, painful time listening to your child read, but it will be worth it. (And an extremely important spin-off benefit will be the development of the skill of prolonged focus on task and concentration.) The single most effective tool in helping a child learn to read and learn to read better is the "off" button on the TV and video-games. Practice truly does work towards perfection. And there is absolutely no substitute for it, in sports or in reading or in cooking or in any other skill.

Happy reading!

This draft letter and other resources in this book are available for downloading at
www.thompsonbooks.com/insidetrack

APPENDIX 18

THE PRINCIPAL'S SIDE OF THE ON-LINE TRACK

How can a principal use the Internet to attract the best candidates? As a first step, give very serious thought to the design of your school's site. Does it give the information you want? Will it be information they want? Is the subconscious impact as desirable as the facts that are presented? Is it interesting without allowing the technology to overwhelm?

One way to increase the number of hits is to keep your site current. A marquee of updated information about your school or board shows it is not a "one-shot and then forgotten" thing. If your site has interesting, updated links to other teaching-related sites, that alone can bring a browser back. Regularly amended information about educational changes in your province can give your site added value. If there is a direct e-mail link back to you, that can facilitate contact from those who are ready to identify themselves as a potential. Be certain to include your fax number, too, in case a candidate wants to send their C.V. that way, if they are concerned about formatting loss in program translation.

You might want to appeal to the whole person—and their family—by having a brief description of lifestyle opportunities in your area: sports teams (professional, and amateur for their kids to join), recreation areas and opportunities, or ski facilities. Is your area is right on the Trans-Canada Hiking Trail,or the Trans-Canada Snowmobile Trail, or there are excellent road- or mountain-biking routes and facilities in the area? Does your school have showers for staff who bike-commute? Are there a lot of lakes in your area? Are there places a family can roller-blade? How about a link to your local Chamber of Commerce along with a description of shopping in the area? What about cultural or educational opportunities, and a link to local facilities? Are you within half an hour of the Royal Winnipeg Ballet, or Stratford Festival, or the Tyrell Museum? Let them know! The site at my former school had an incredible amount of local information, everything from photos of our teams and tournaments to local colour and history, upcoming events, lists of trophy winners throughout the years, what was in Lost & Found, links to local award-winning local artisans, board policies on current topics of discussion, and so on. (It was over 600 pages deep, and I think the sheer magnitude of it, together with its ease of navigation, was part of the reason for its popularity.) And it was a high-use site, especially considering the early architecture of linking back then.

If you include photos, make certain they are interlaced .gif files—not .jpeg—so they load quickly, and can be quickly interrupted if they are not of interest. Some top candidates are very time-conscious people, and don't like having to "ponder" any more than principals like to have to "wallow" their way through a poorly constructed C.V. Limit the resolution to 256 colours, too, and small photos—2.5 inches wide max—load faster.

And make sure your URL is listed along with all the other data on all of your promotional print media, such as business cards, letterhead and brochures. Make certain the board's link to your school site is working. (I have had that happen to me and wondered why the hits were down.)

Remember, recruitment is a "two-way street"!

IT'S A LONG-TERM THING

If your site has a section on, or a link to, local opportunities (including those in your own school), instead of calling it "Jobs," how about referring to it as "Careers." Ambitious, top candidates don't want a job, they want a career!

INDEX